A Tropical Fish Yearns for Snow

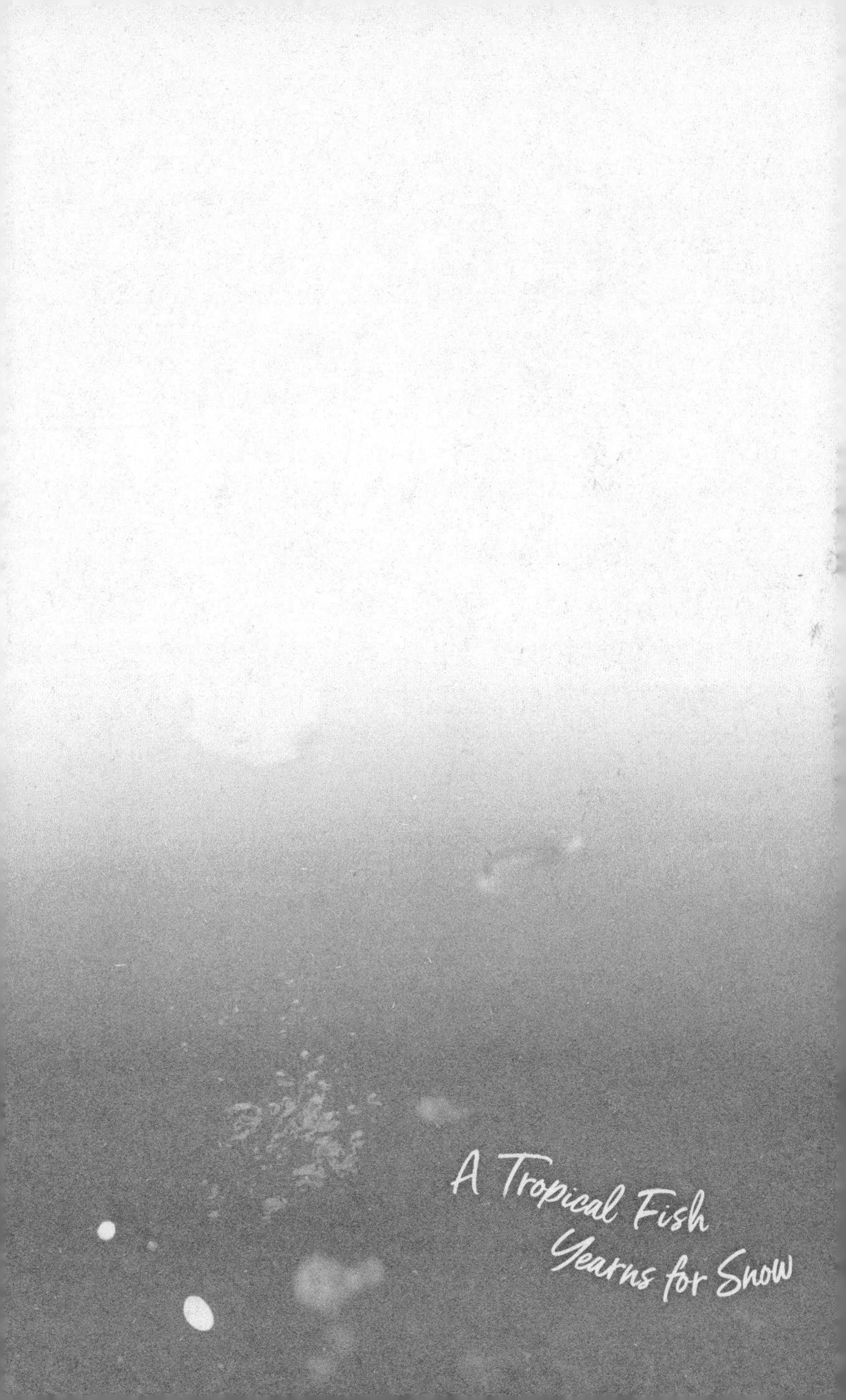
A Tropical Fish
Yearns for Snow

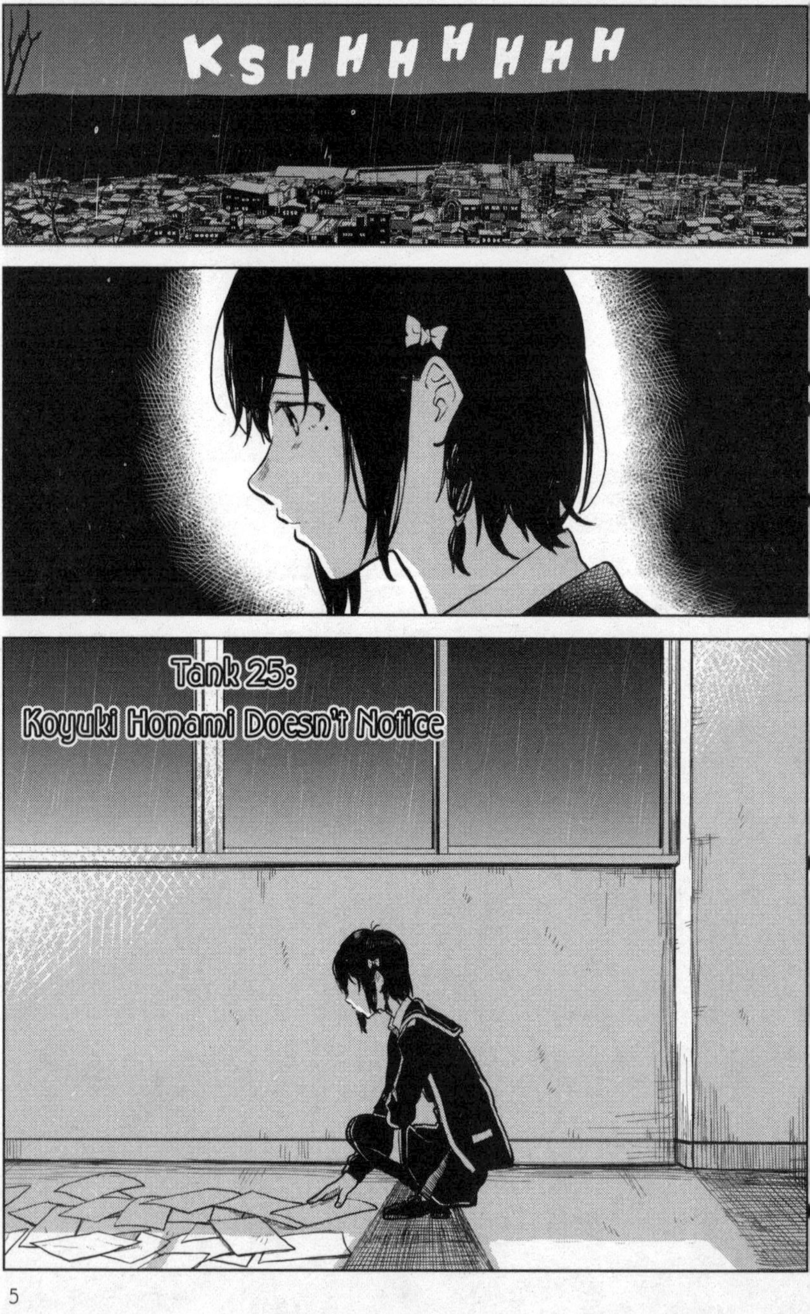
KSHHHHHHH
Tank 25:
Koyuki Honami Doesn't Notice

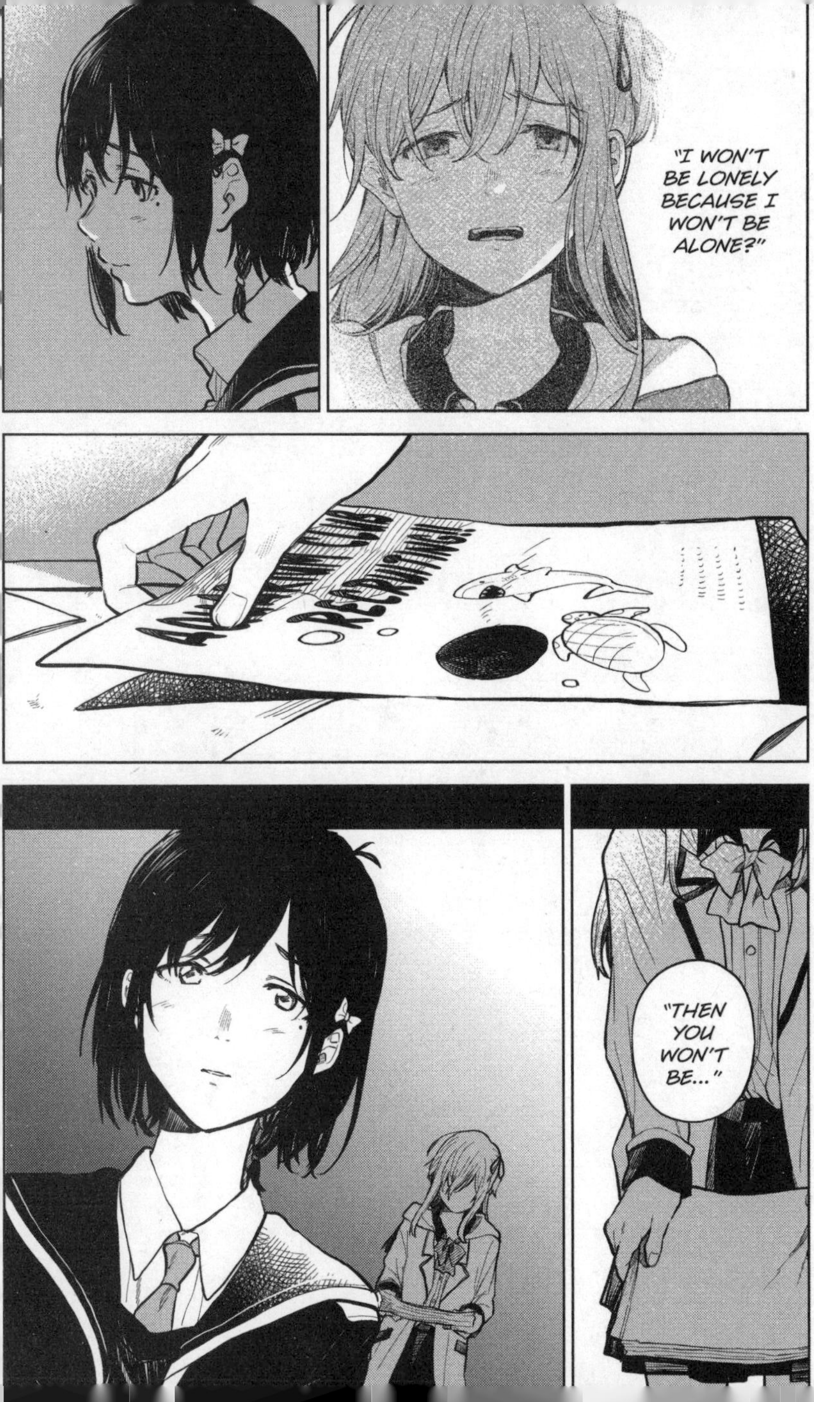
"I WON'T BE LONELY BECAUSE I WON'T BE ALONE?"
"THEN YOU WON'T BE..."

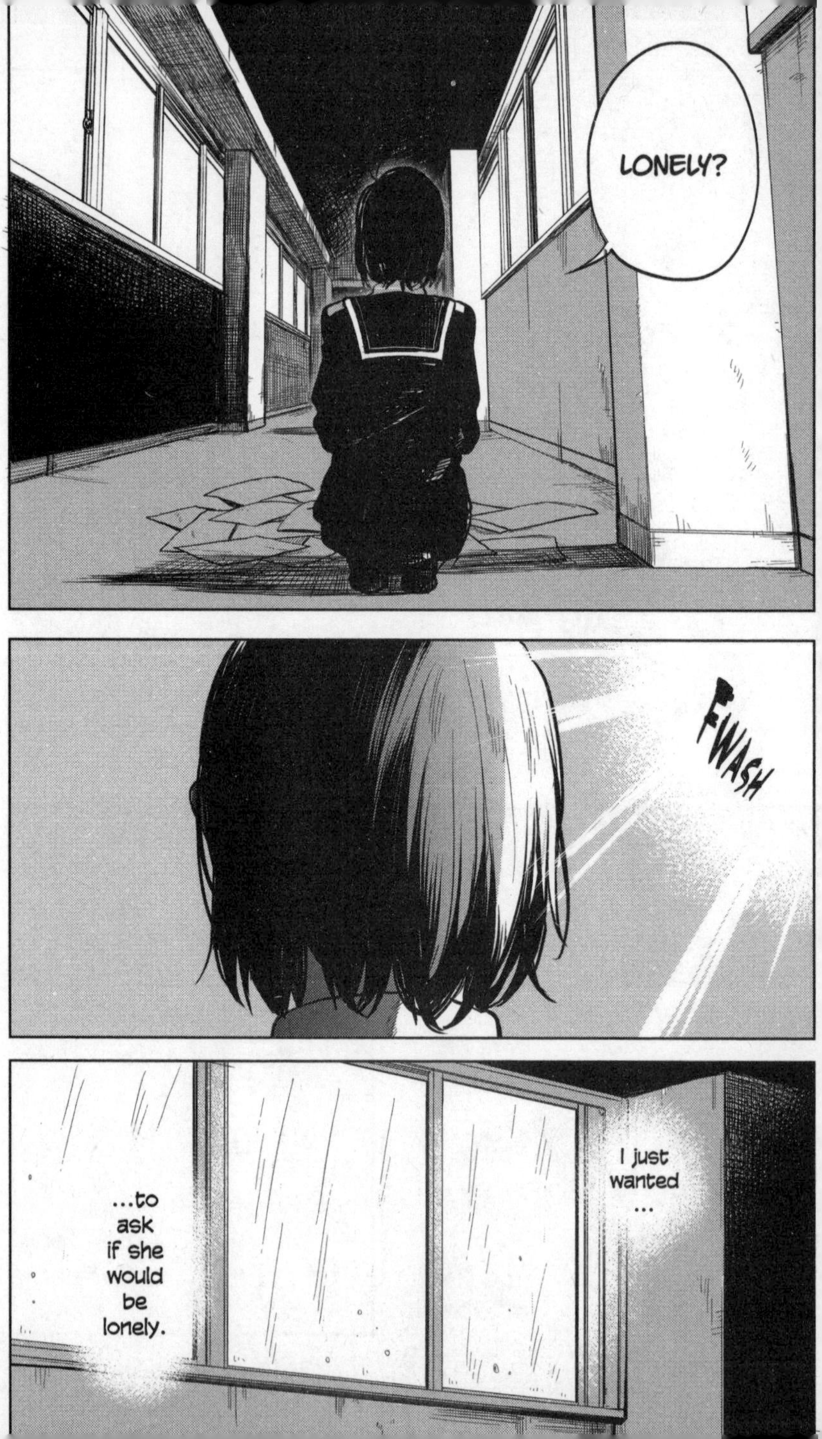
LONELY?
FWASH
I just wanted ...
...to ask if she would be lonely.

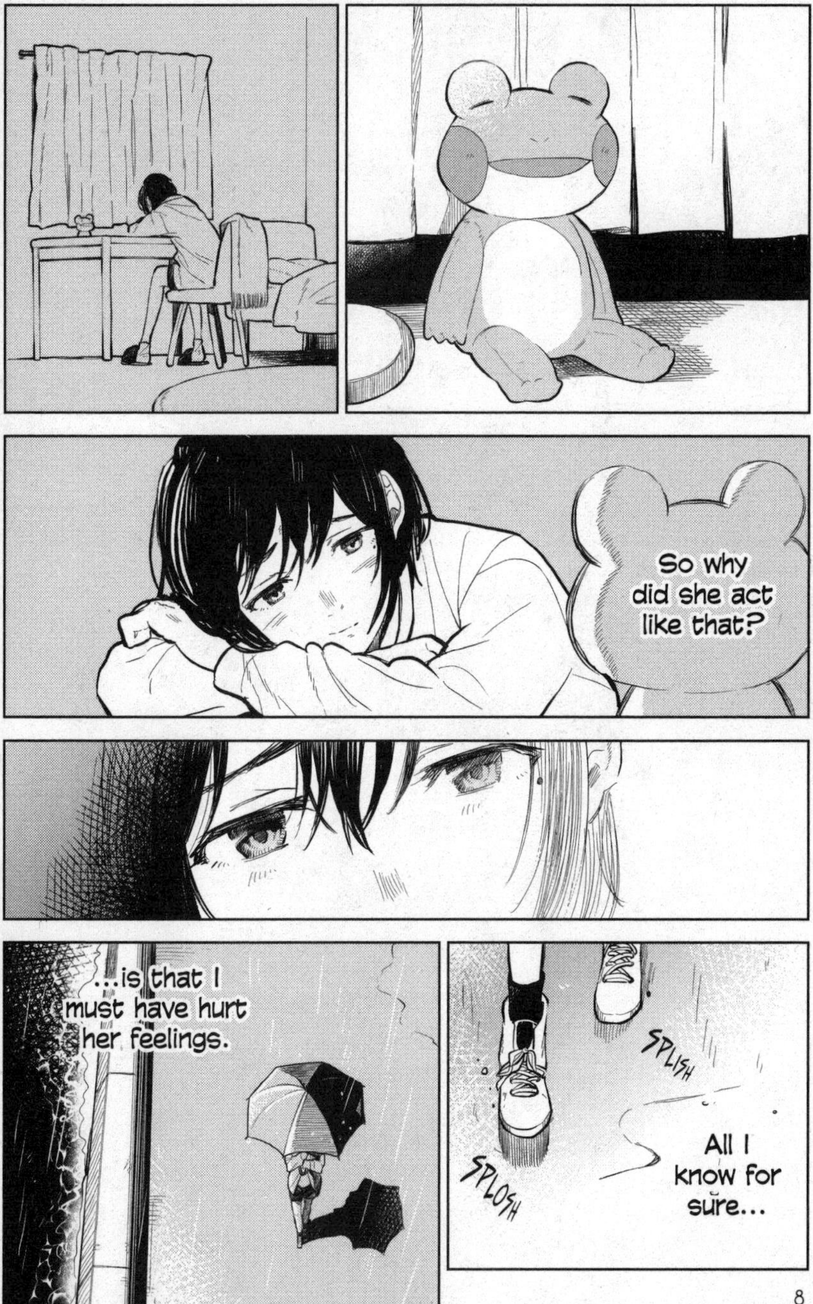

So why did she act like that?
SPLISH
All I know for sure...
SPLOSH
...is that I must have hurt her feelings.

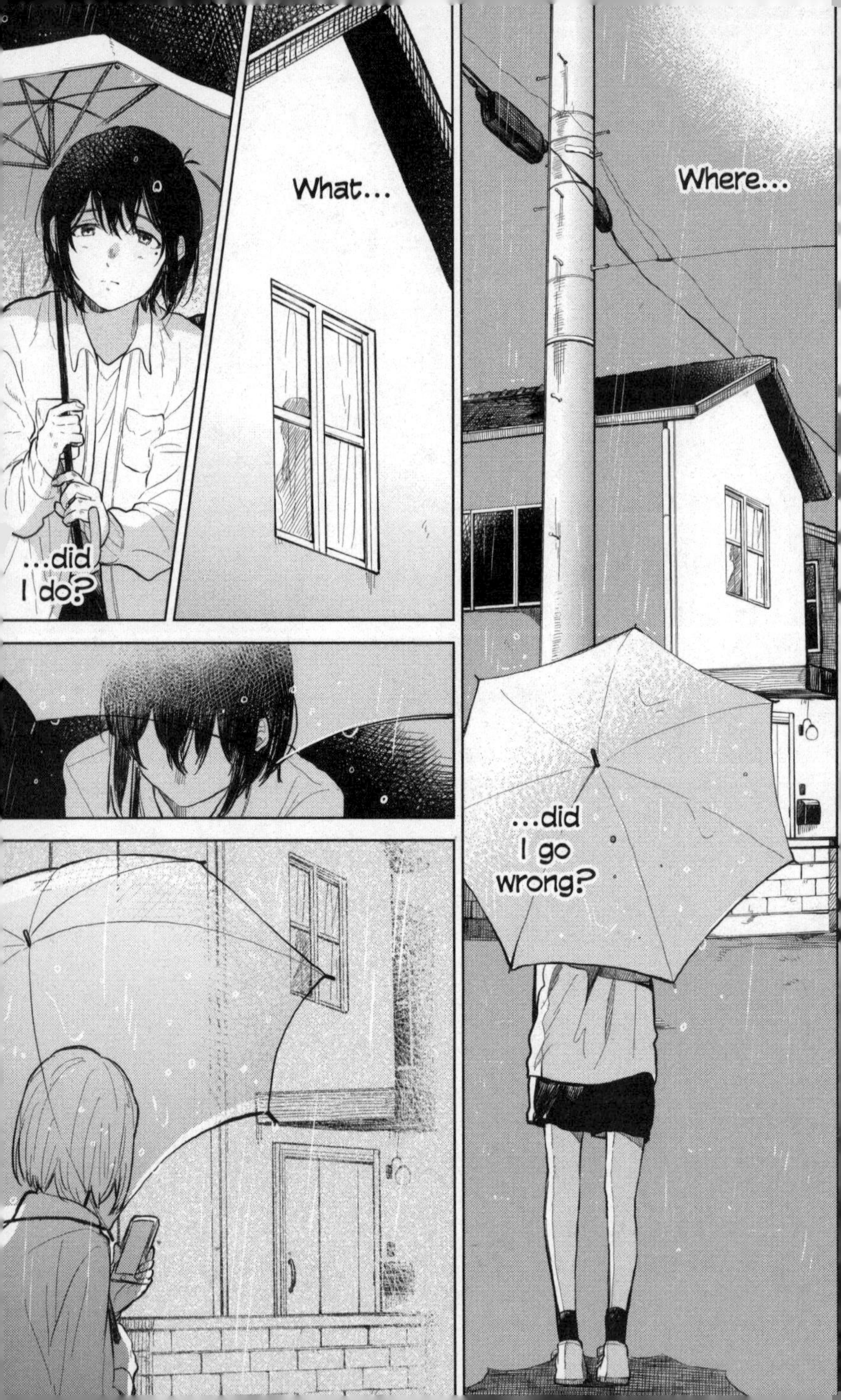
Where...
...did I go wrong?
What...
...did I do?

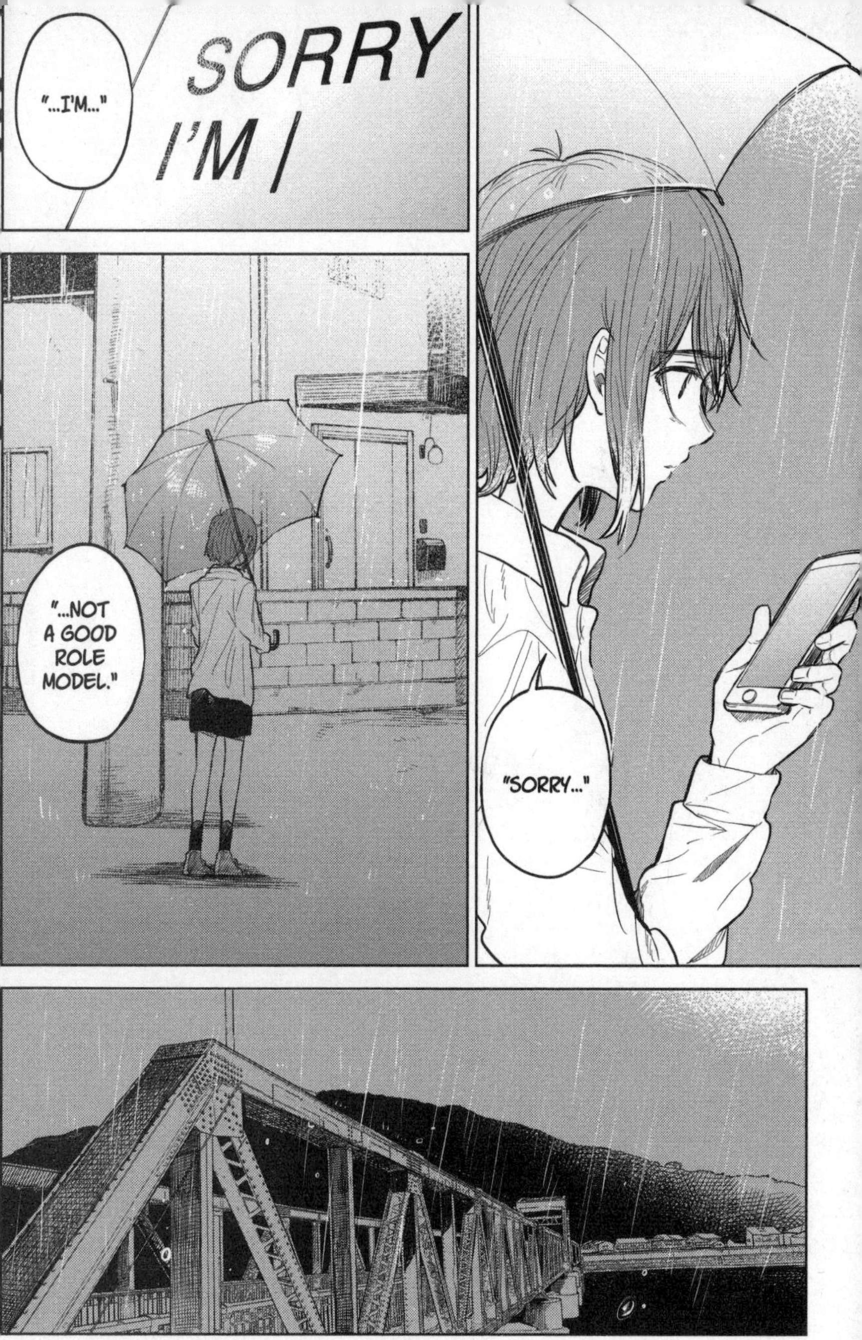
"SORRY..."
"...I'M..."
SORRY
I'M
"...NOT A GOOD ROLE MODEL."

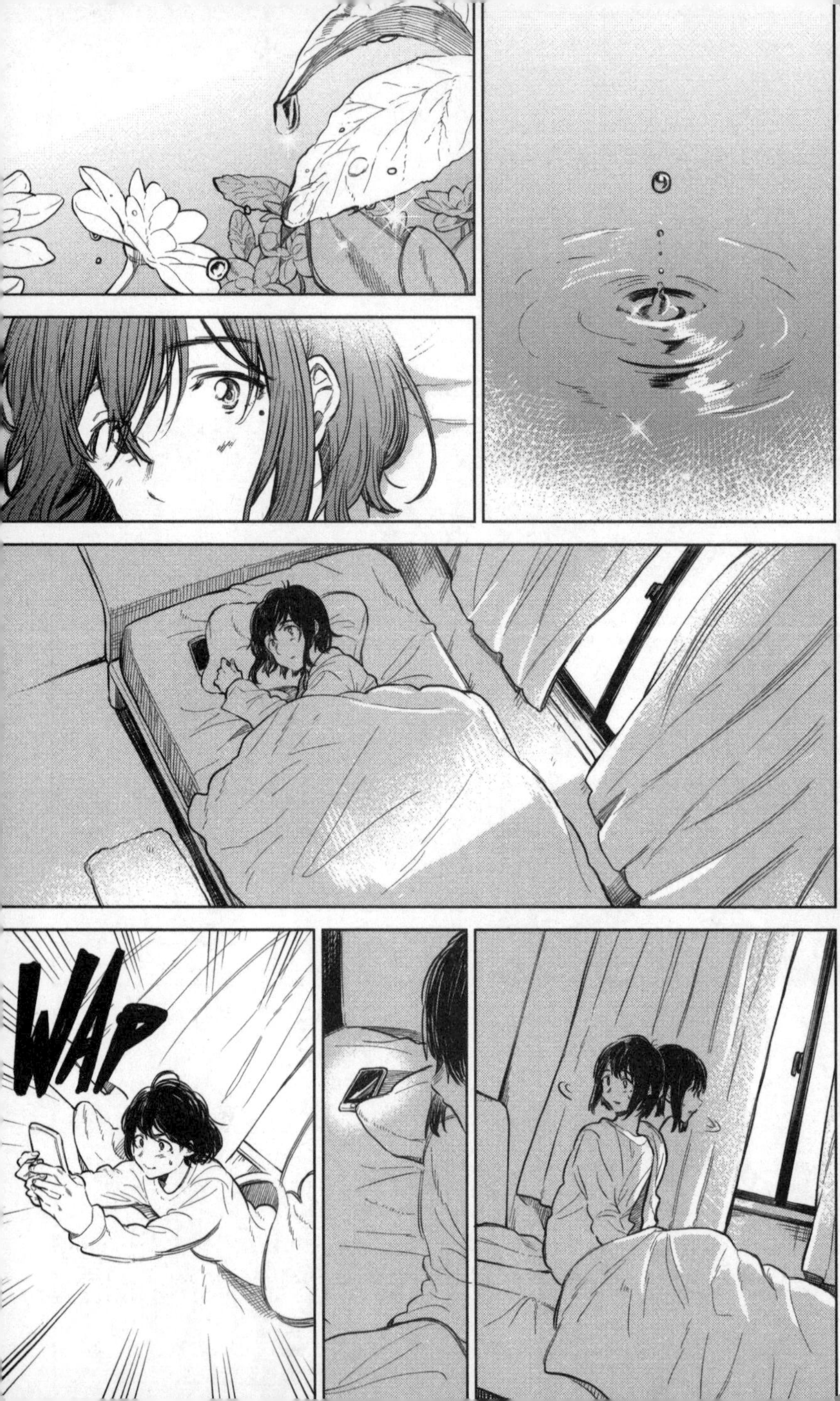
WAP

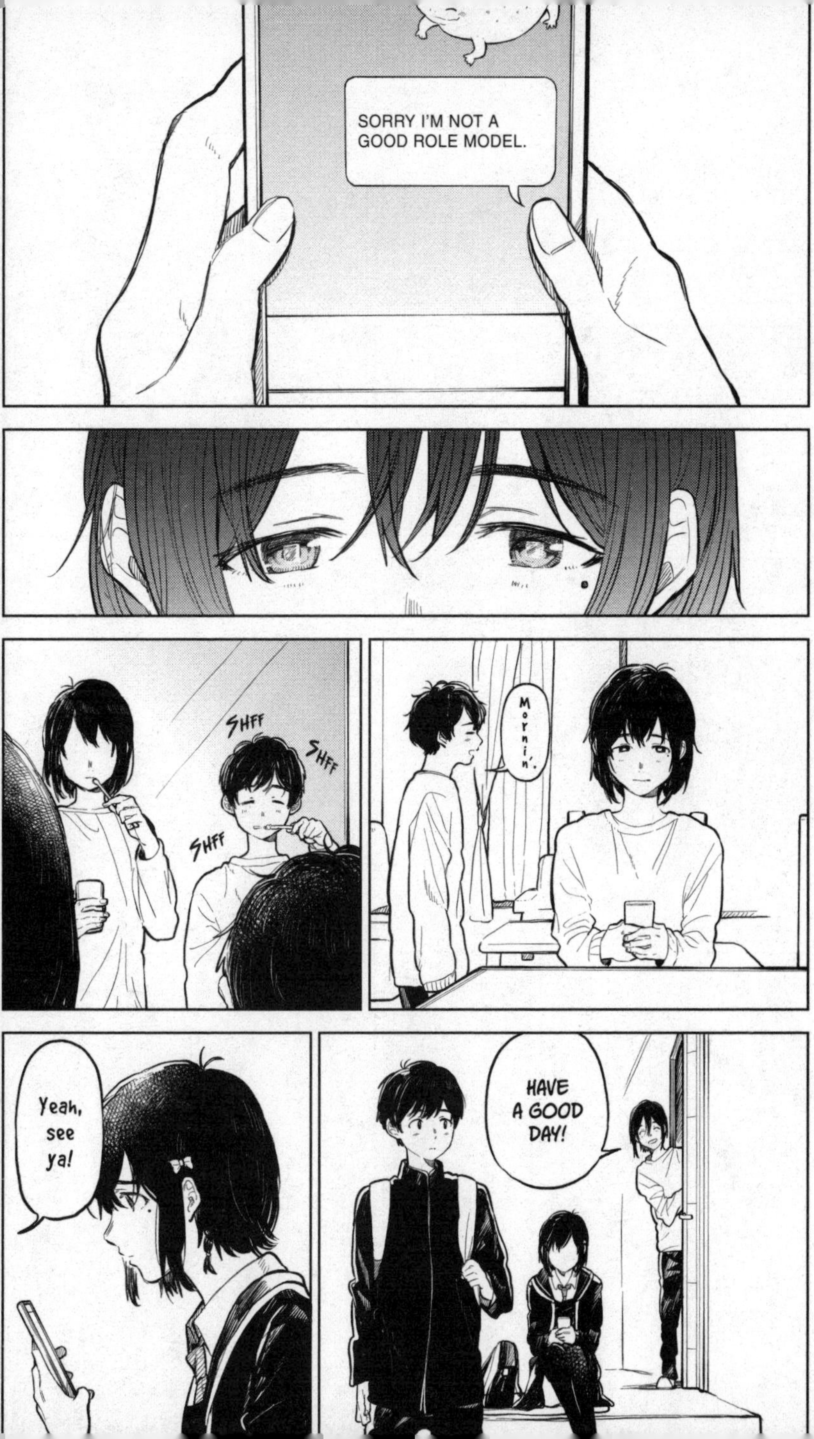
SORRY I'M NOT A GOOD ROLE MODEL.
Mornin'.
SHFF
SHFF
SHFF
HAVE A GOOD DAY!
Yeah, see ya!

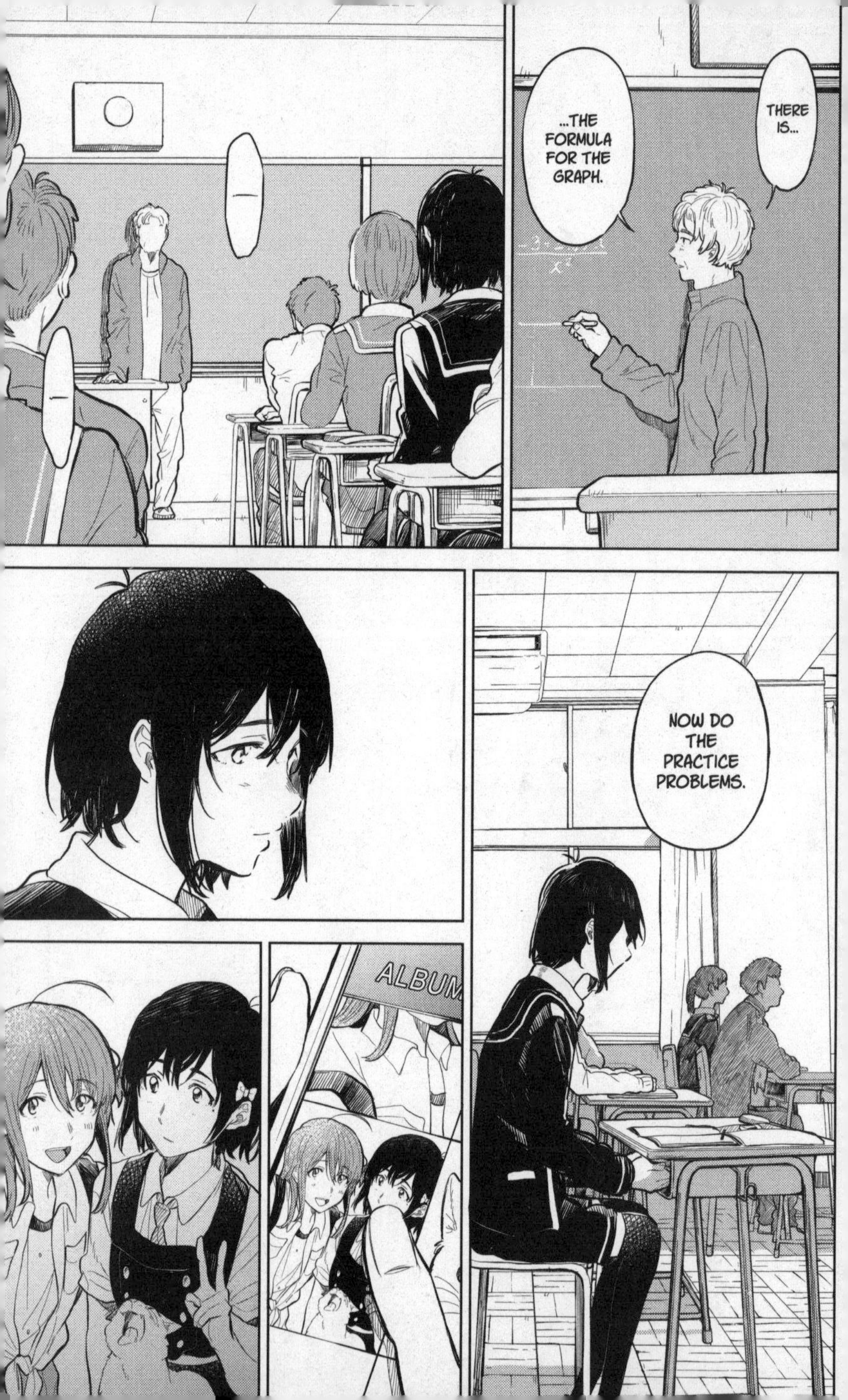
THERE IS...
...THE FORMULA FOR THE GRAPH.
—
—
NOW DO THE PRACTICE PROBLEMS.
ALBUM

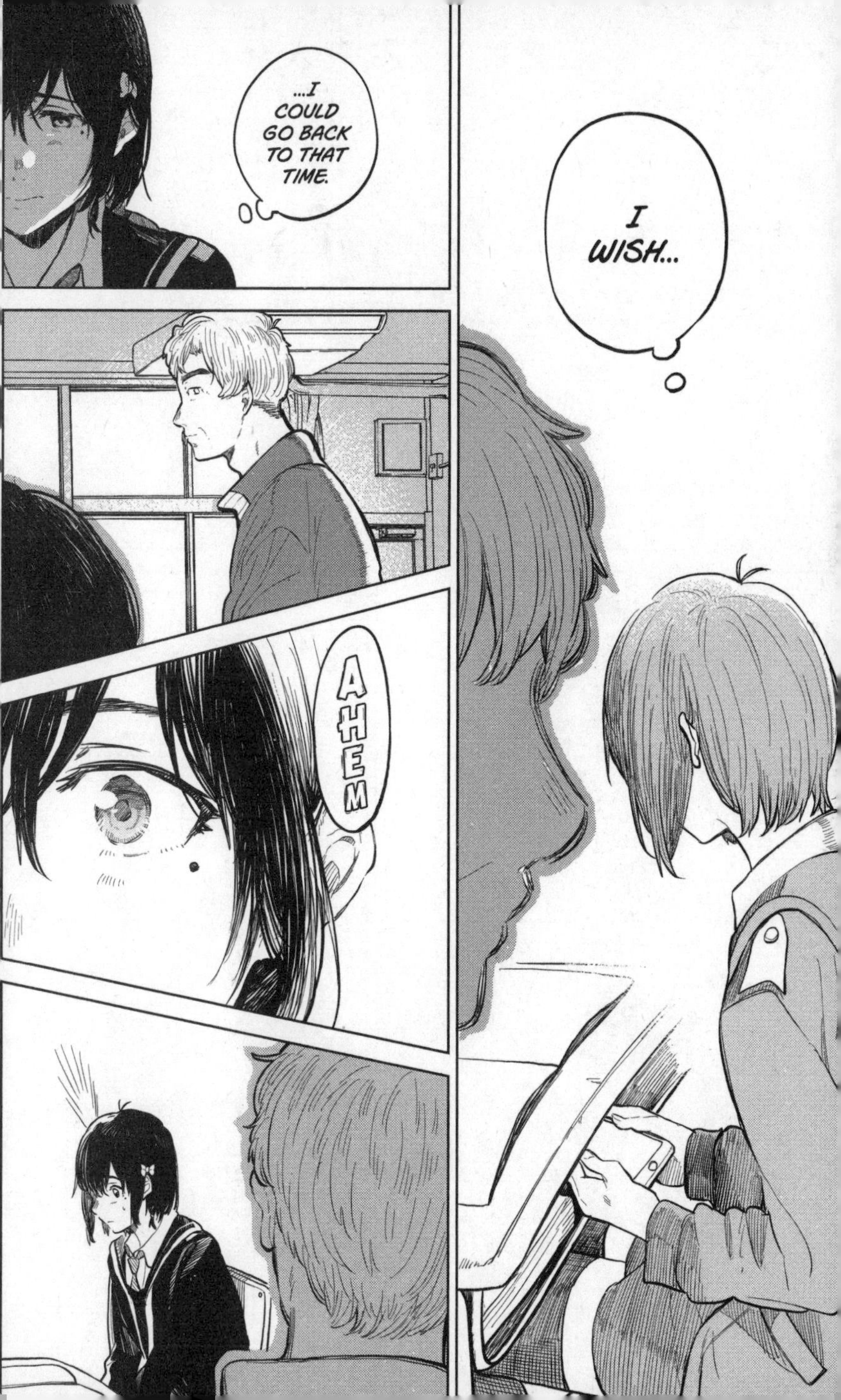
I WISH...
...I COULD GO BACK TO THAT TIME.
AHEM

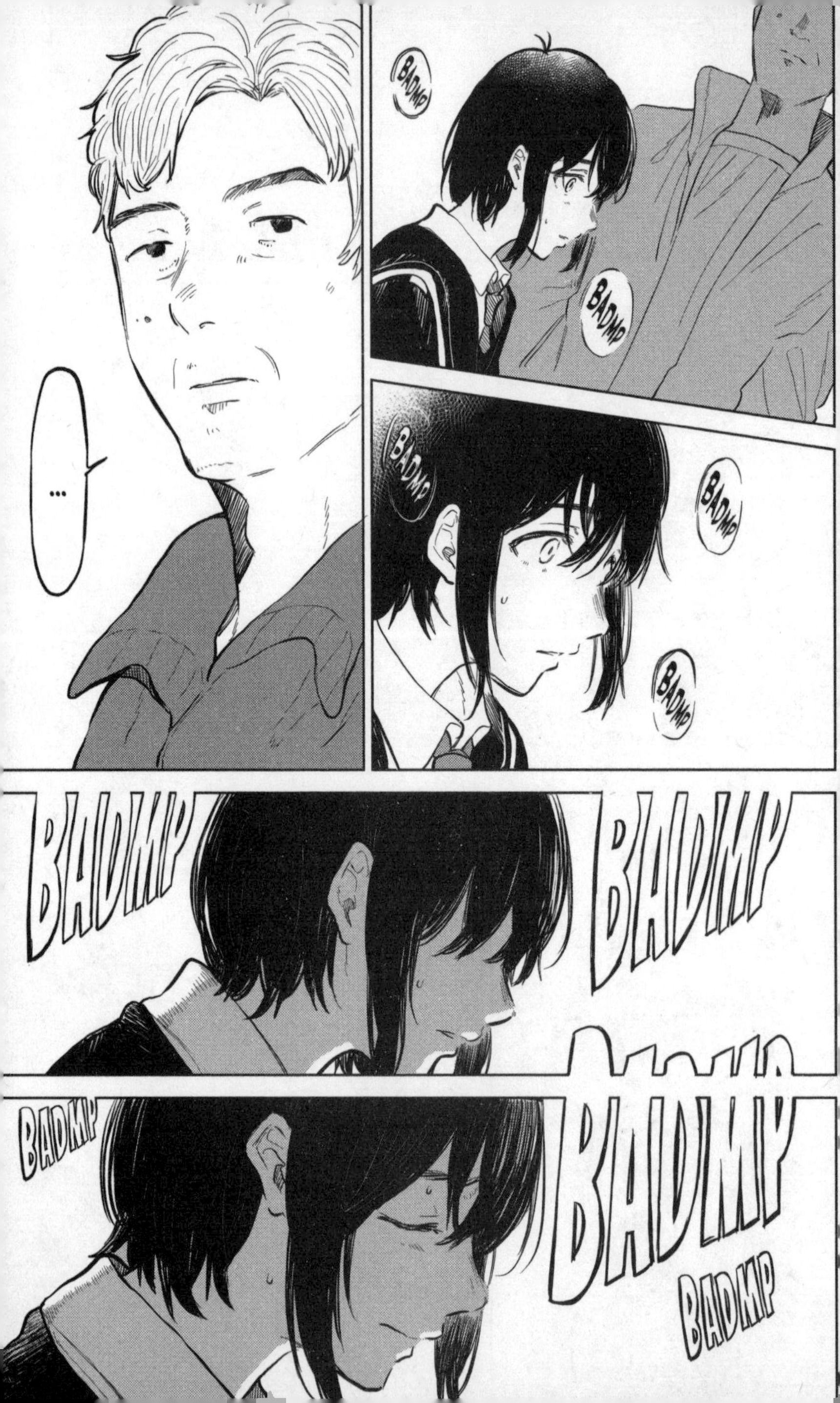

BADMP
BADMP
BADMP
BADMP
BADMP
...
BADMP
BADMP
BADMP
BADMP
BADMP

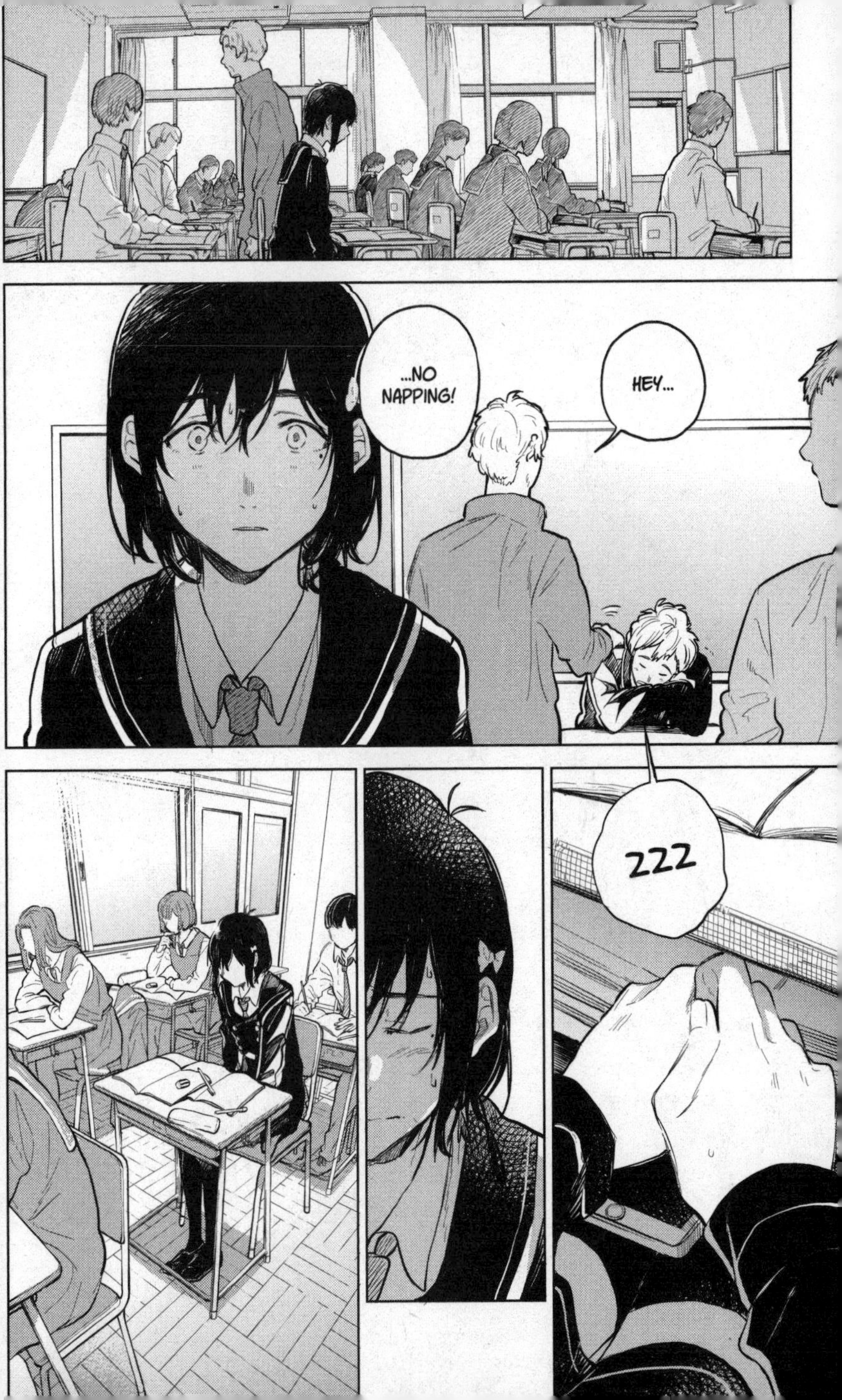
HEY...
...NO NAPPING!
ZZZ

I'm so dumb.

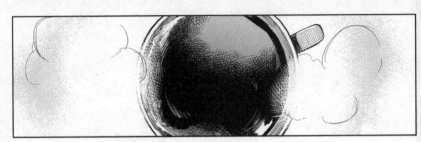

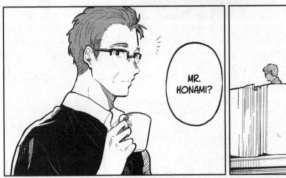

MR. HONAMI?

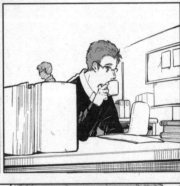

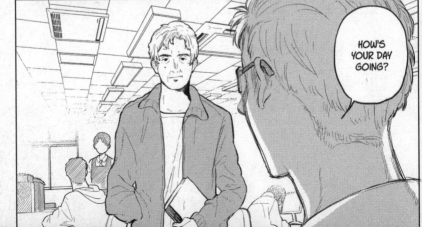

HOW'S YOUR DAY GOING?

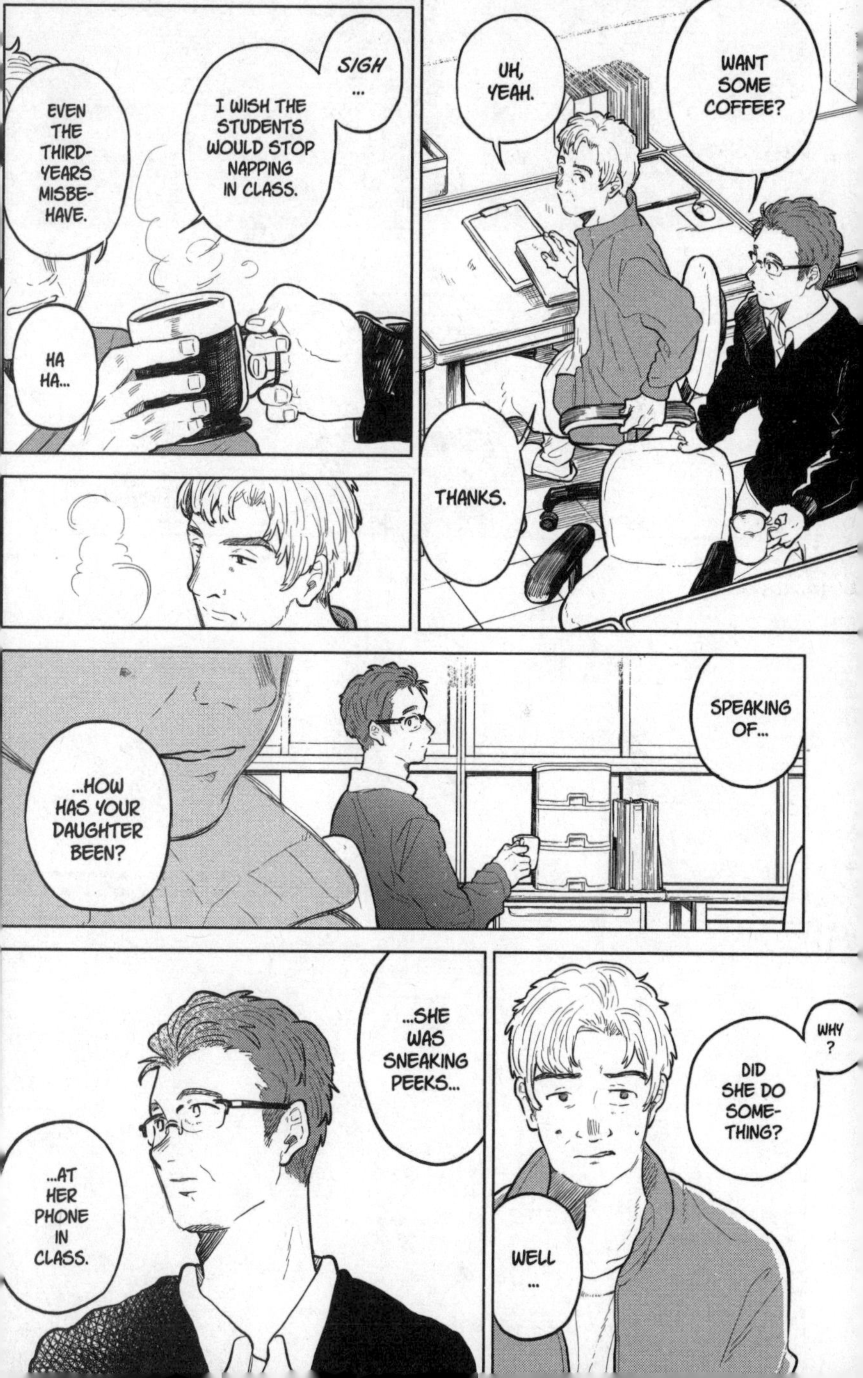
WANT SOME COFFEE?
UH, YEAH.
THANKS.
SIGH ...
I WISH THE STUDENTS WOULD STOP NAPPING IN CLASS.
EVEN THE THIRD-YEARS MISBEHAVE.
HA HA...
SPEAKING OF...
...HOW HAS YOUR DAUGHTER BEEN?
WHY?
DID SHE DO SOMETHING?
WELL ...
...SHE WAS SNEAKING PEEKS...
...AT HER PHONE IN CLASS.

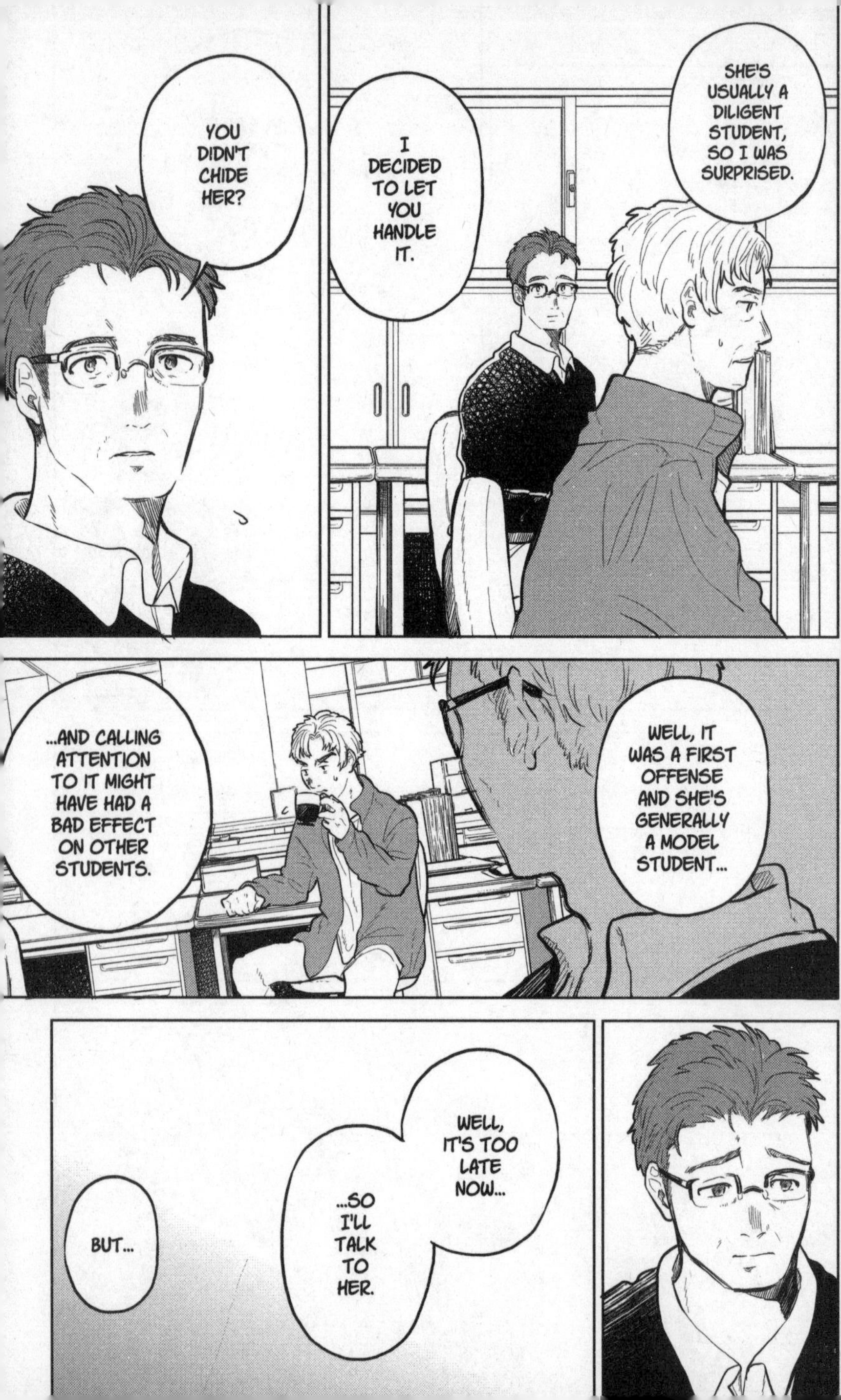
SHE'S USUALLY A DILIGENT STUDENT, SO I WAS SURPRISED.
I DECIDED TO LET YOU HANDLE IT.
YOU DIDN'T CHIDE HER?
WELL, IT WAS A FIRST OFFENSE AND SHE'S GENERALLY A MODEL STUDENT...
...AND CALLING ATTENTION TO IT MIGHT HAVE HAD A BAD EFFECT ON OTHER STUDENTS.
WELL, IT'S TOO LATE NOW... ...SO I'LL TALK TO HER.
BUT...

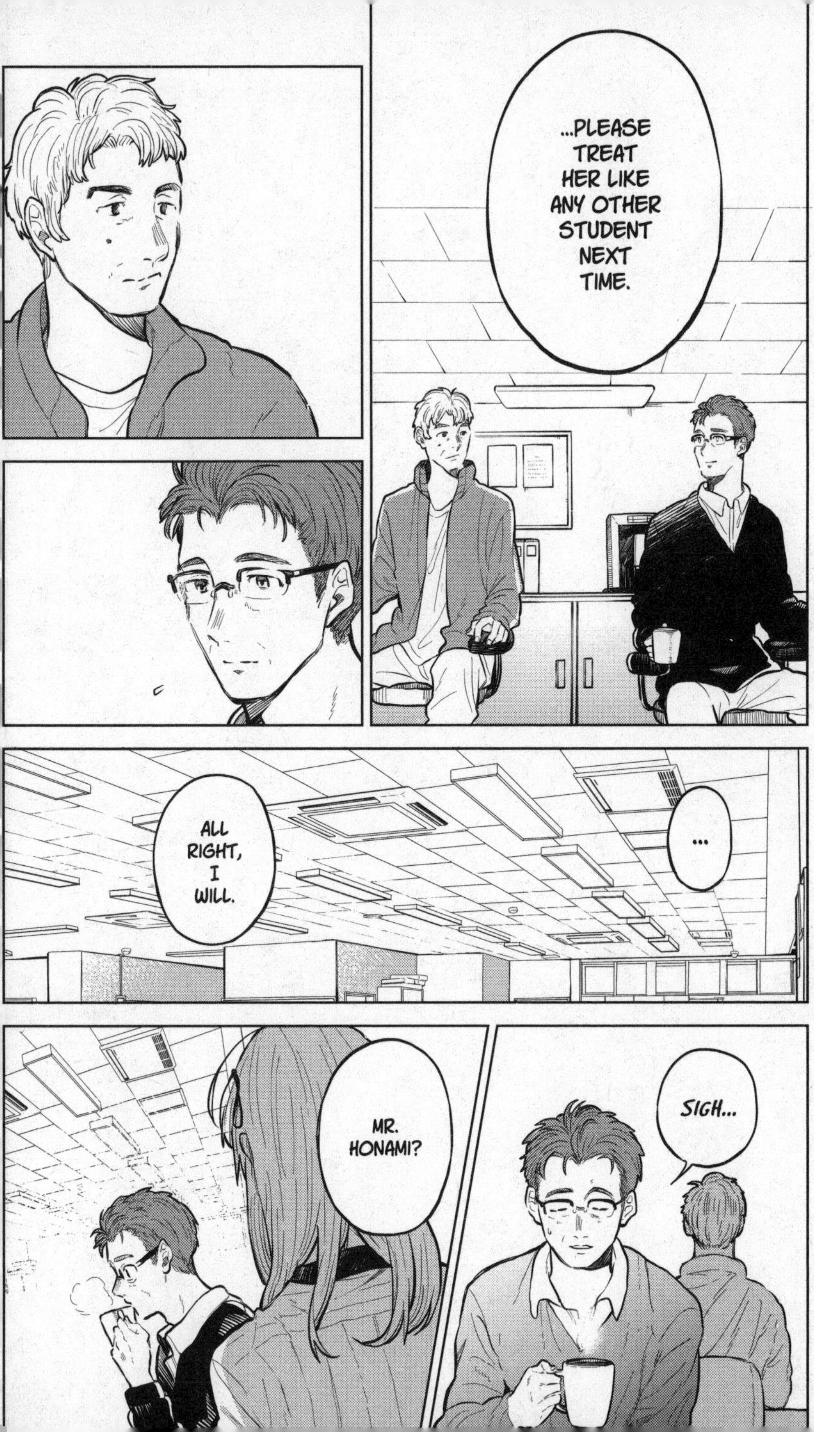
...PLEASE TREAT HER LIKE ANY OTHER STUDENT NEXT TIME.
...
ALL RIGHT, I WILL.
SIGH...
MR. HONAMI?

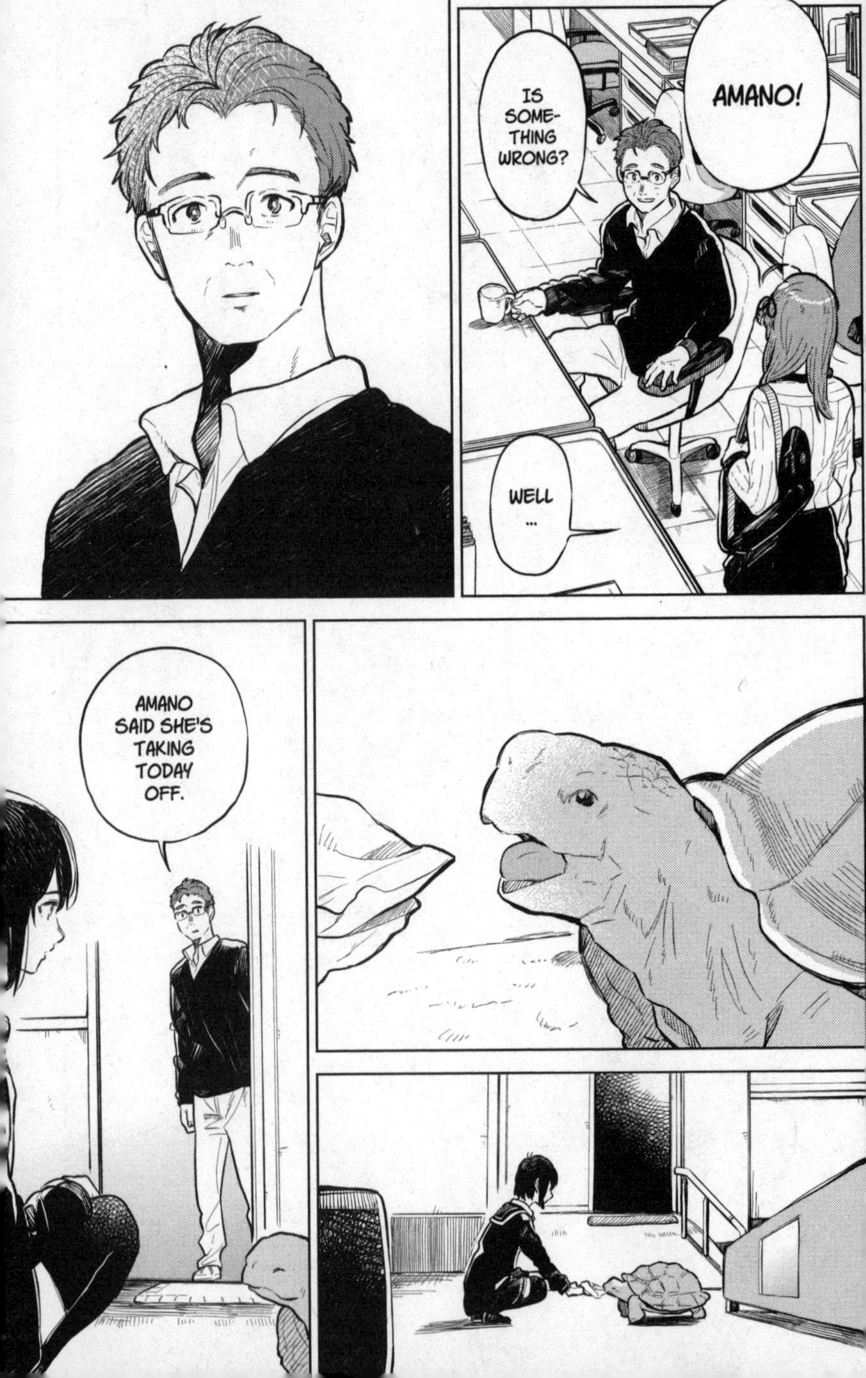
AMANO!
IS SOME-THING WRONG?
WELL ...
AMANO SAID SHE'S TAKING TODAY OFF.

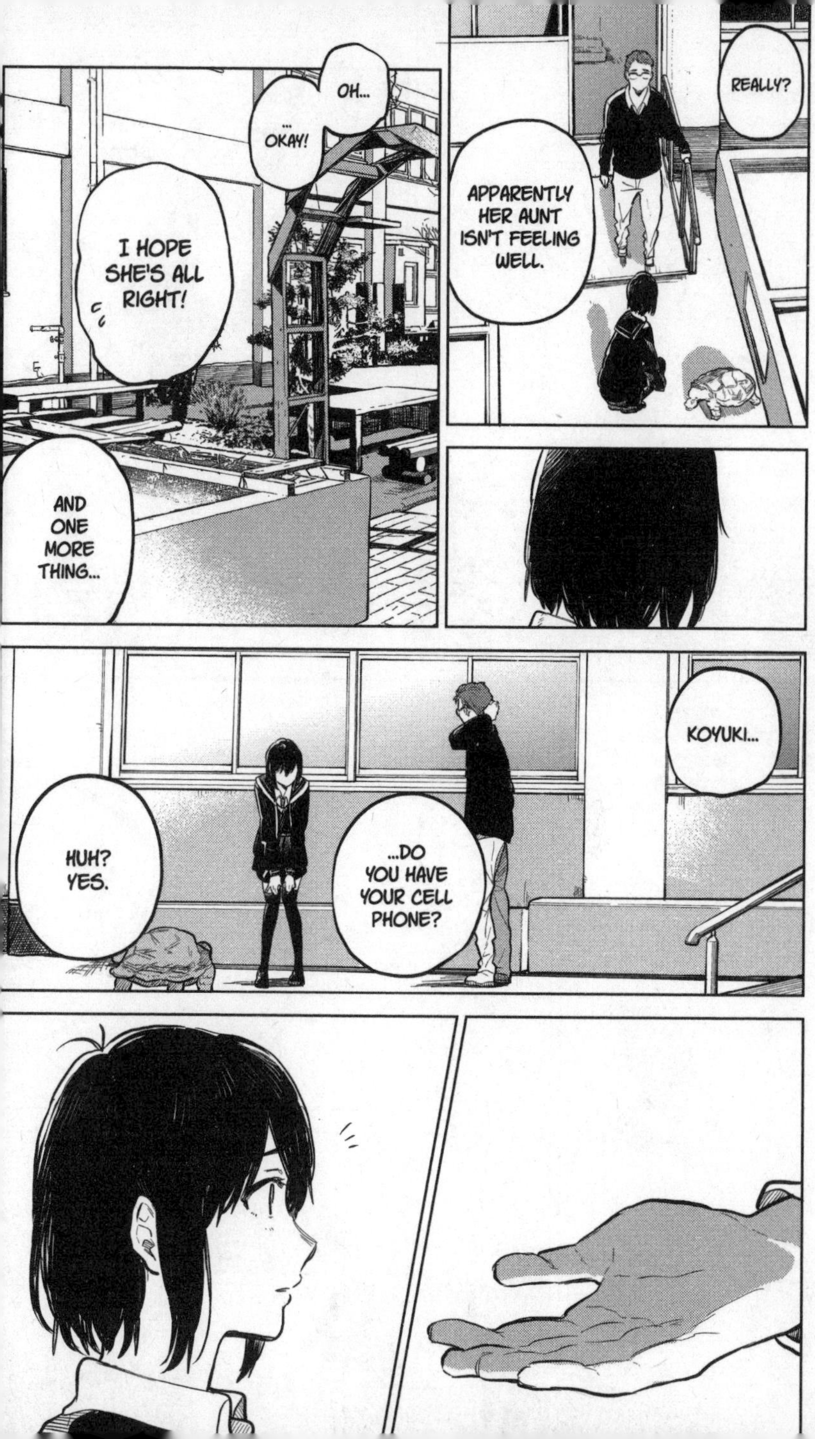
REALLY?
APPARENTLY HER AUNT ISN'T FEELING WELL.
OH... ...OKAY!
I HOPE SHE'S ALL RIGHT!
AND ONE MORE THING...
KOYUKI...
...DO YOU HAVE YOUR CELL PHONE?
HUH? YES.

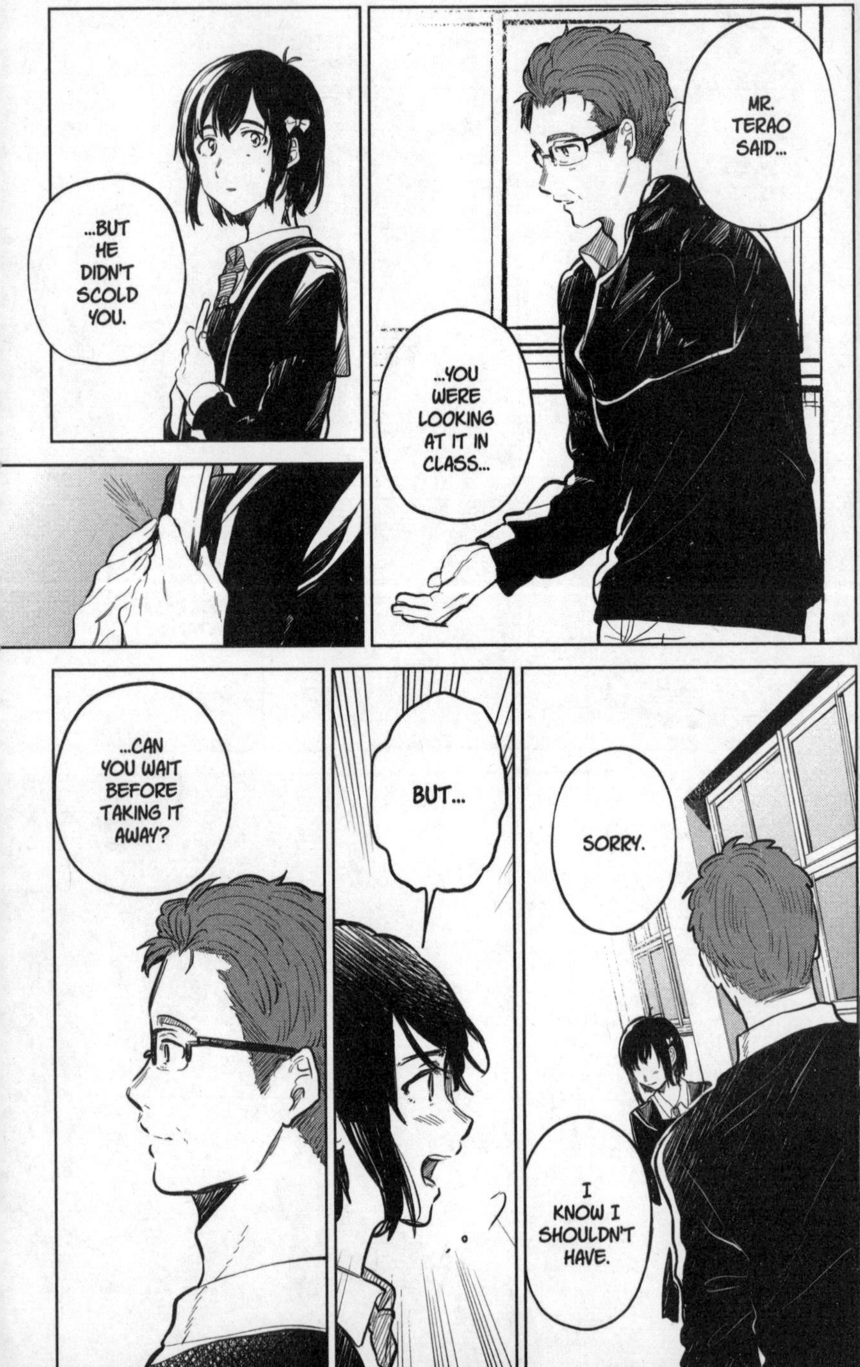
MR. TERAO SAID...
...YOU WERE LOOKING AT IT IN CLASS...
...BUT HE DIDN'T SCOLD YOU.
SORRY.
I KNOW I SHOULDN'T HAVE.
BUT...
...CAN YOU WAIT BEFORE TAKING IT AWAY?

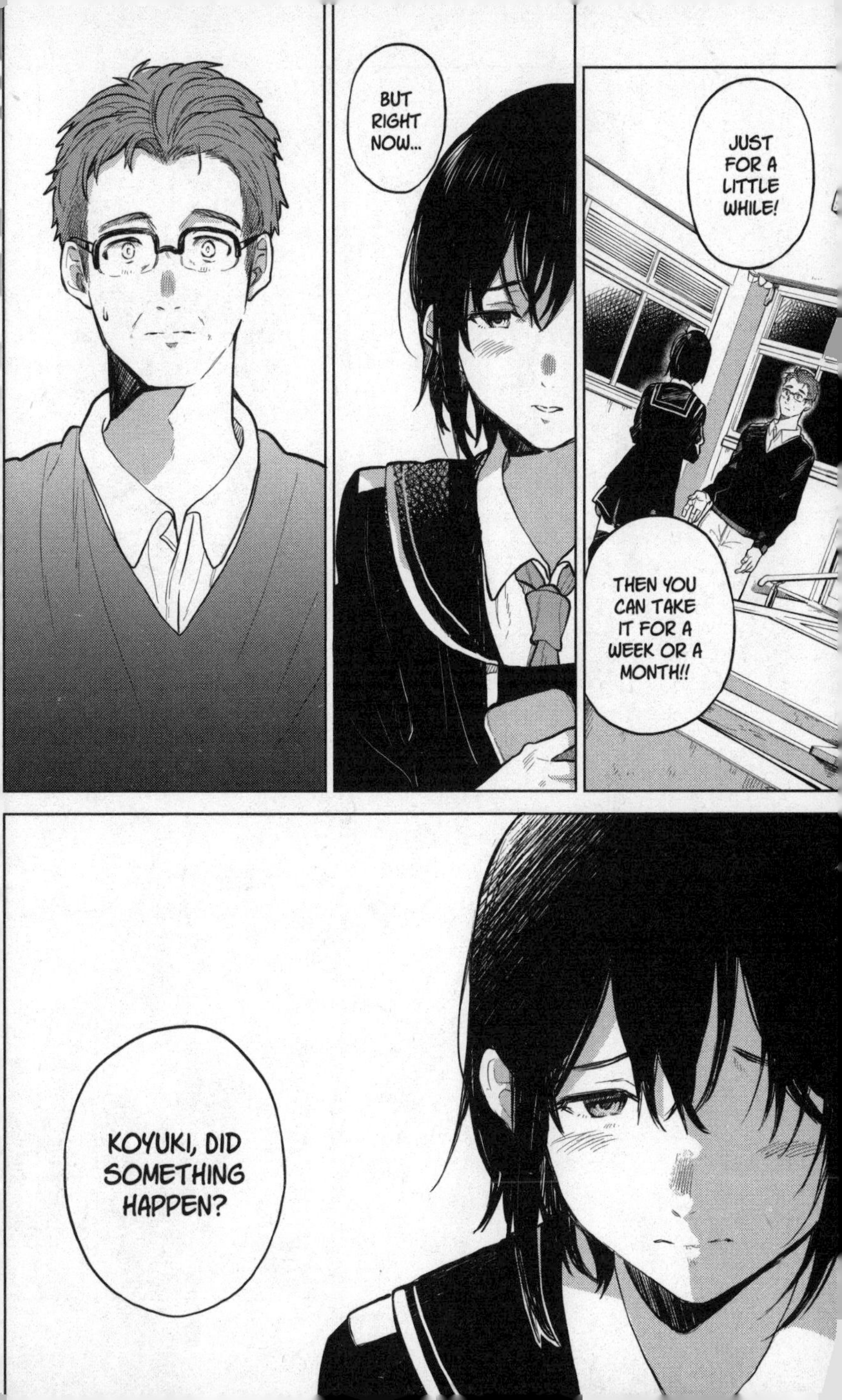
JUST FOR A LITTLE WHILE!
THEN YOU CAN TAKE IT FOR A WEEK OR A MONTH!!
BUT RIGHT NOW...
KOYUKI, DID SOMETHING HAPPEN?

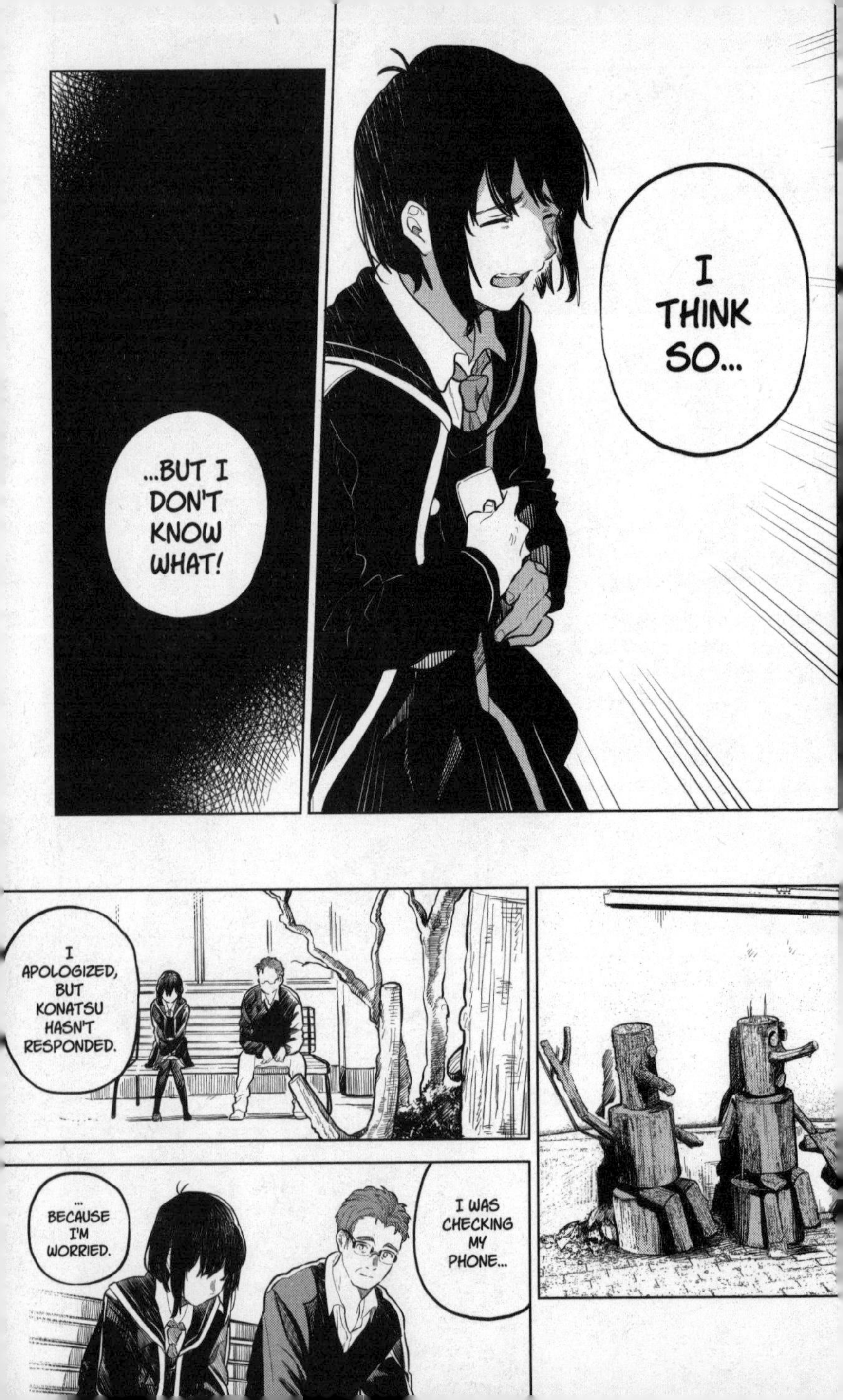
I THINK SO...
...BUT I DON'T KNOW WHAT!
I APOLOGIZED, BUT KONATSU HASN'T RESPONDED.
I WAS CHECKING MY PHONE...
...BECAUSE I'M WORRIED.

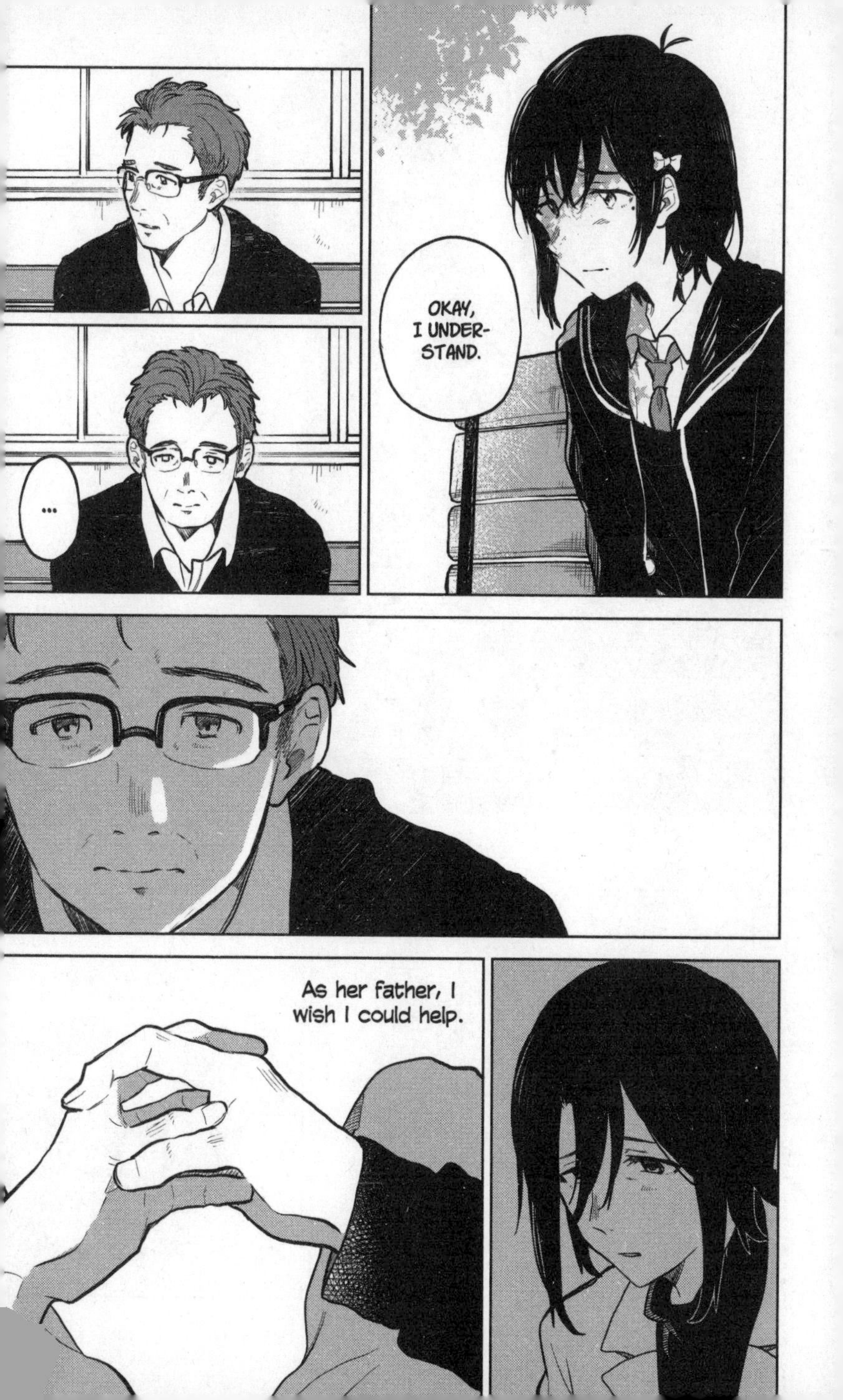
OKAY, I UNDER-STAND.
...
As her father, I wish I could help.

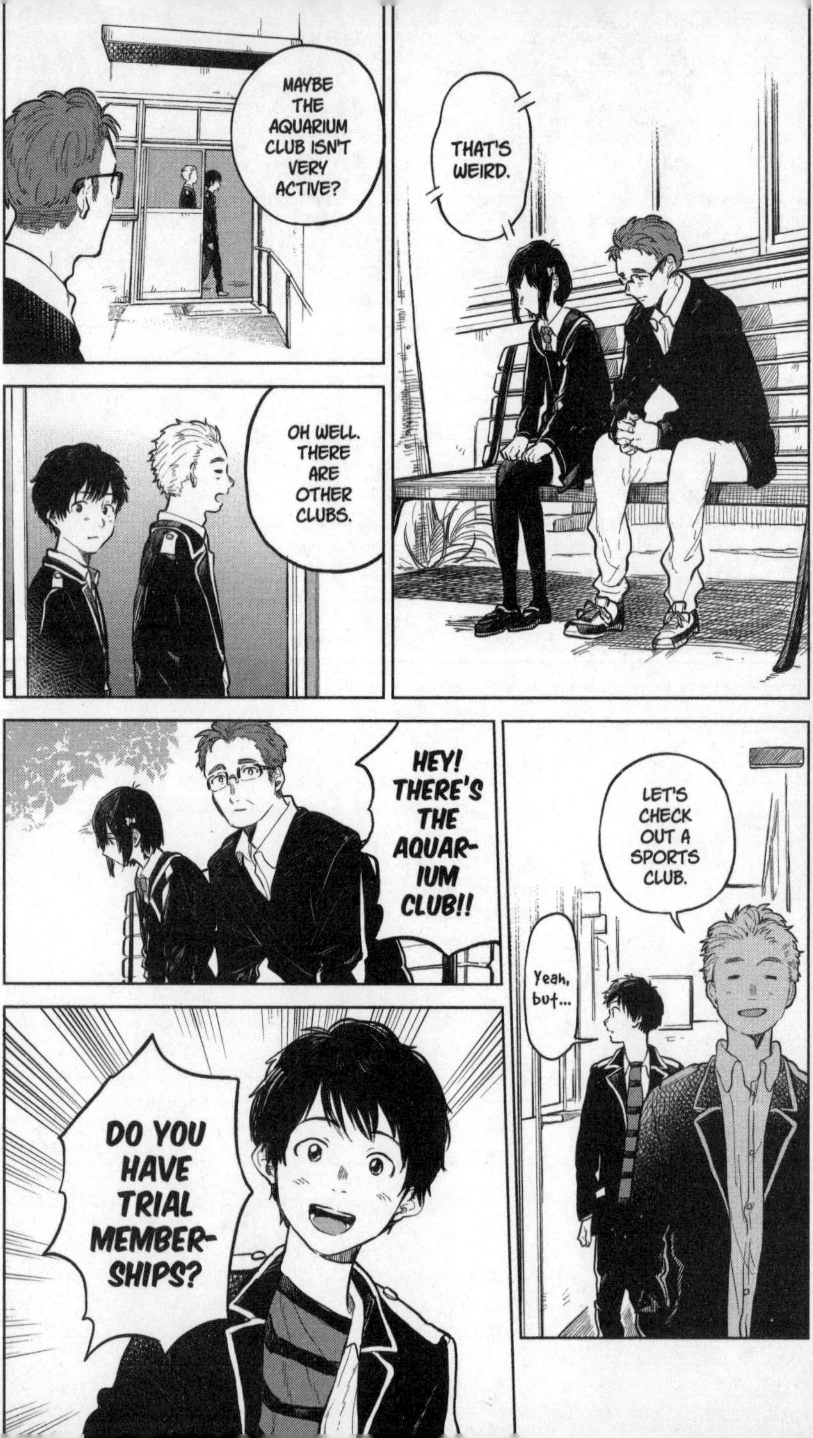
THAT'S WEIRD.
MAYBE THE AQUARIUM CLUB ISN'T VERY ACTIVE?
OH WELL. THERE ARE OTHER CLUBS.
LET'S CHECK OUT A SPORTS CLUB.
Yeah, but...
HEY! THERE'S THE AQUARIUM CLUB!!
DO YOU HAVE TRIAL MEMBERSHIPS?

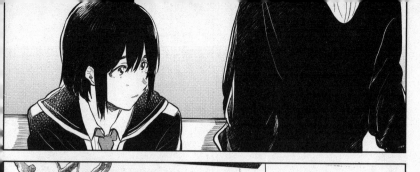

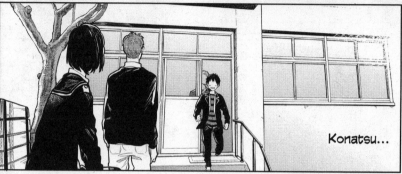

Konatsu...

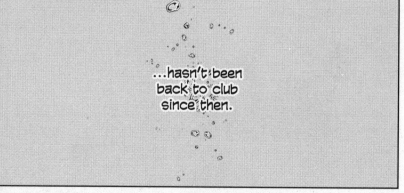

...hasn't been
back to club
since then.

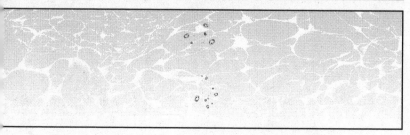

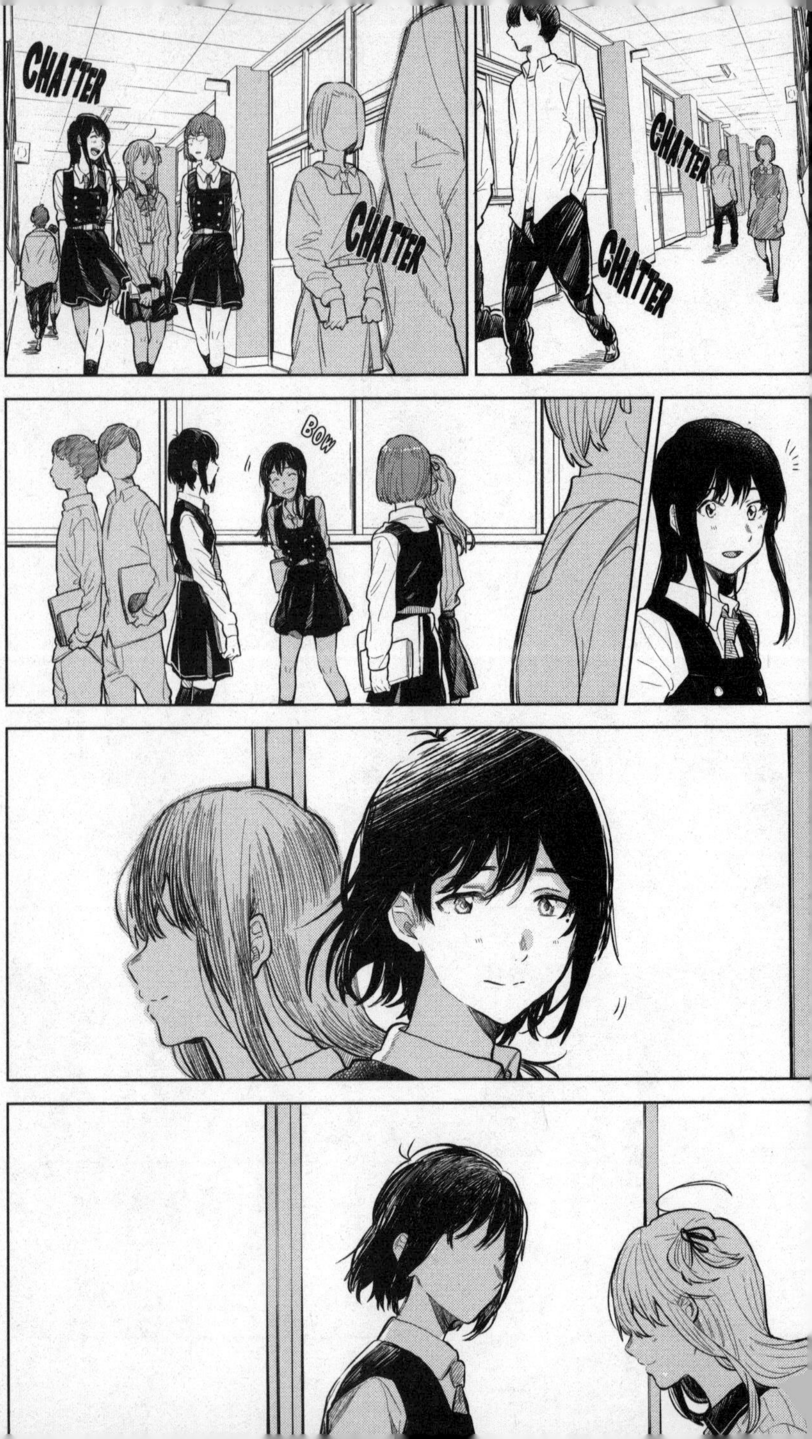
CHATTER
CHATTER
CHATTER
CHATTER
BOW

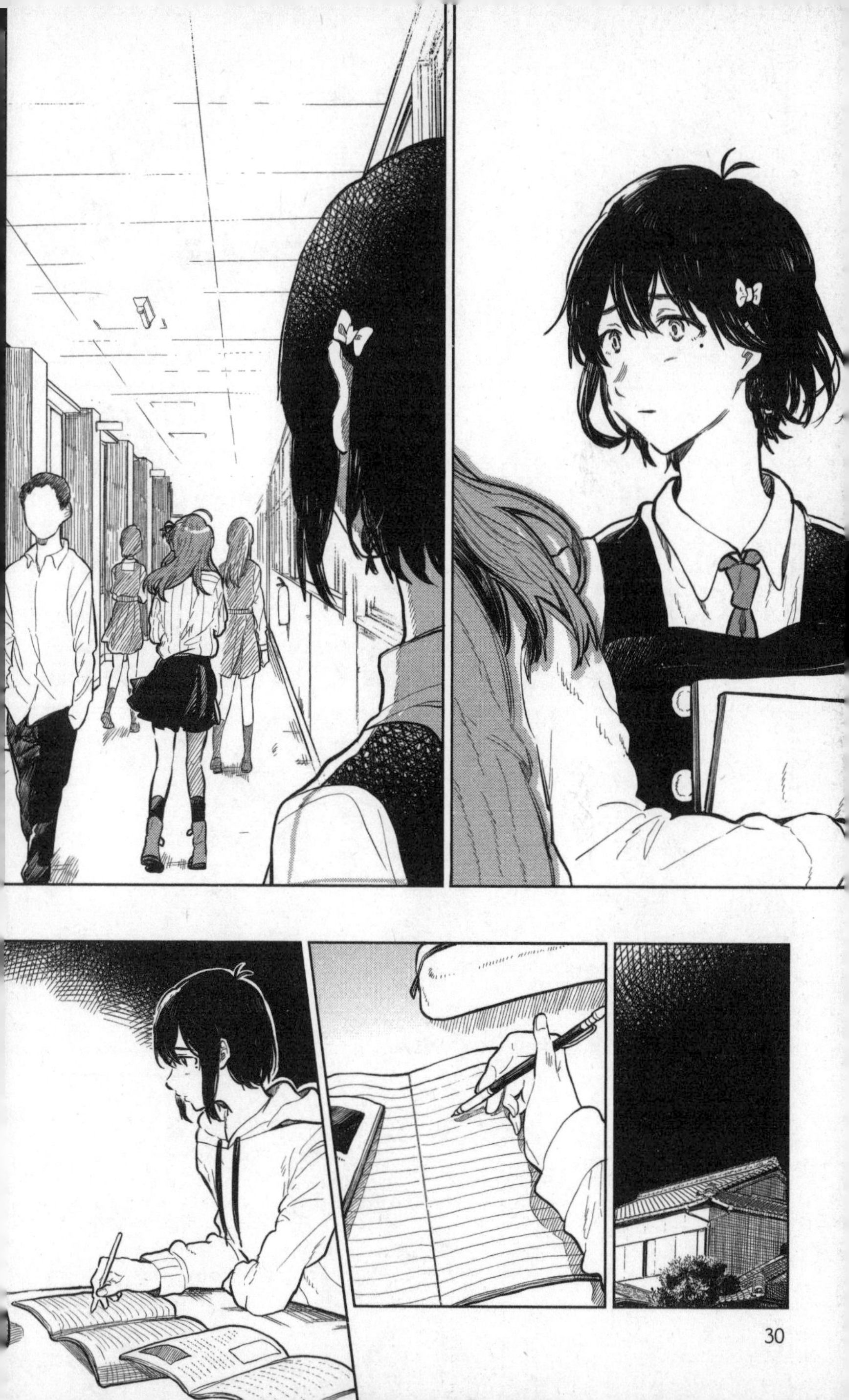

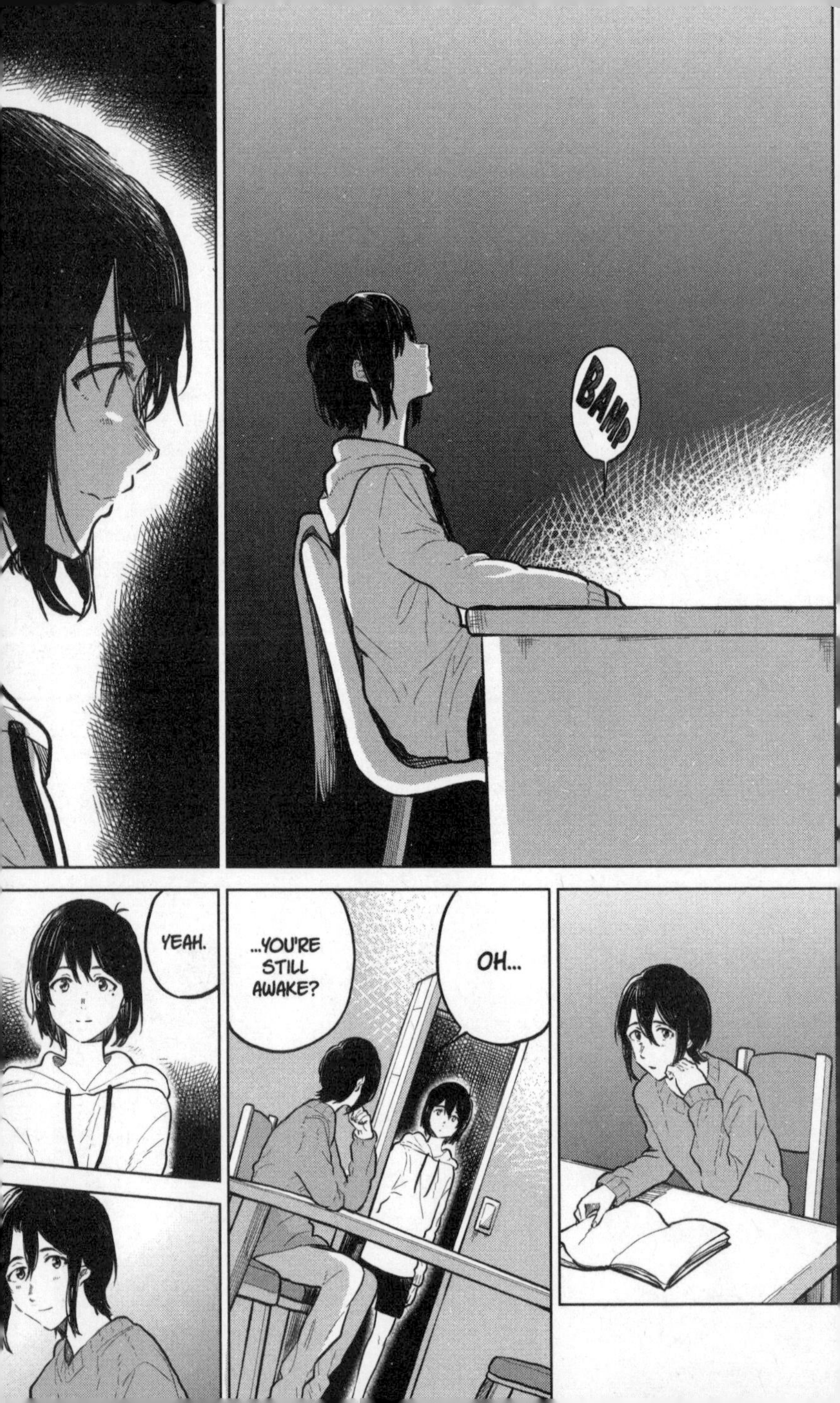
BAMP
OH...
...YOU'RE STILL AWAKE?
YEAH.

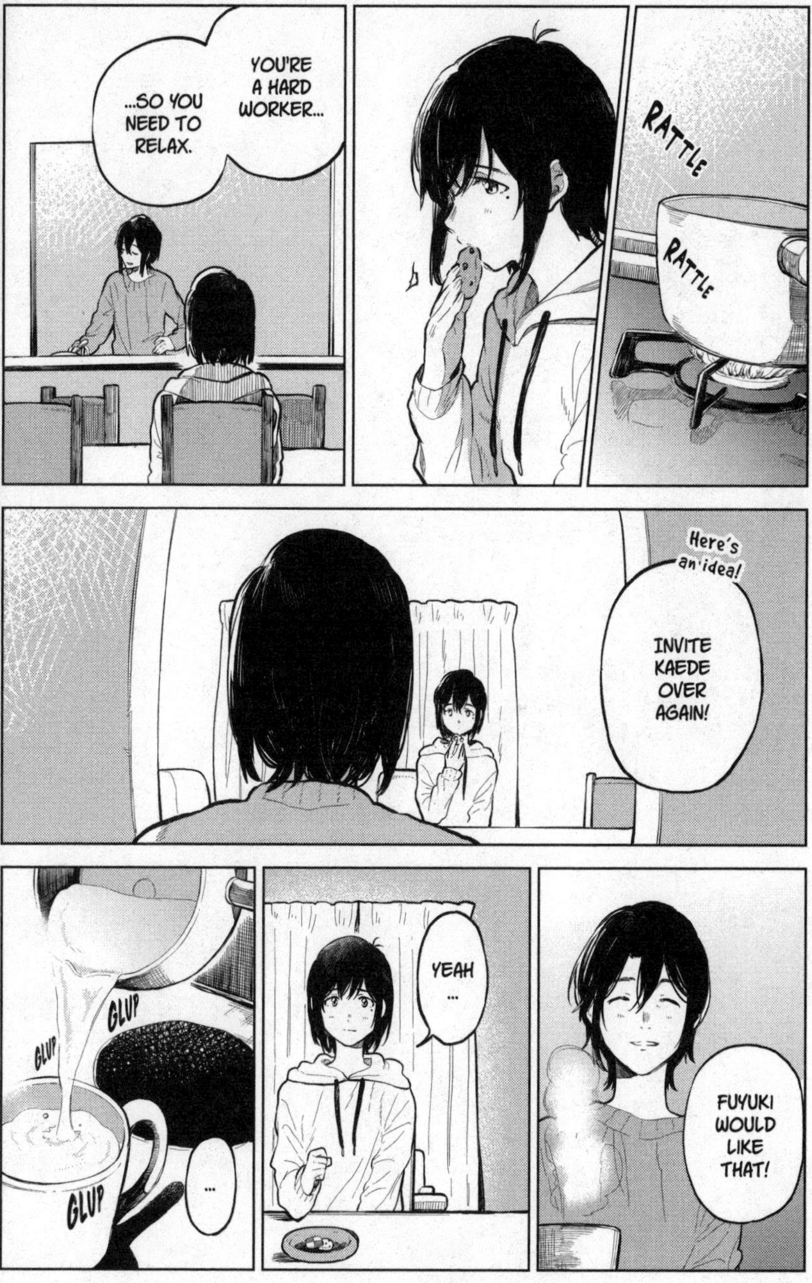
RATTLE
RATTLE
YOU'RE A HARD WORKER...
...SO YOU NEED TO RELAX.
Here's an idea!
INVITE KAEDE OVER AGAIN!
FUYUKI WOULD LIKE THAT!
YEAH ...
GLUP
GLUP
...
GLUP

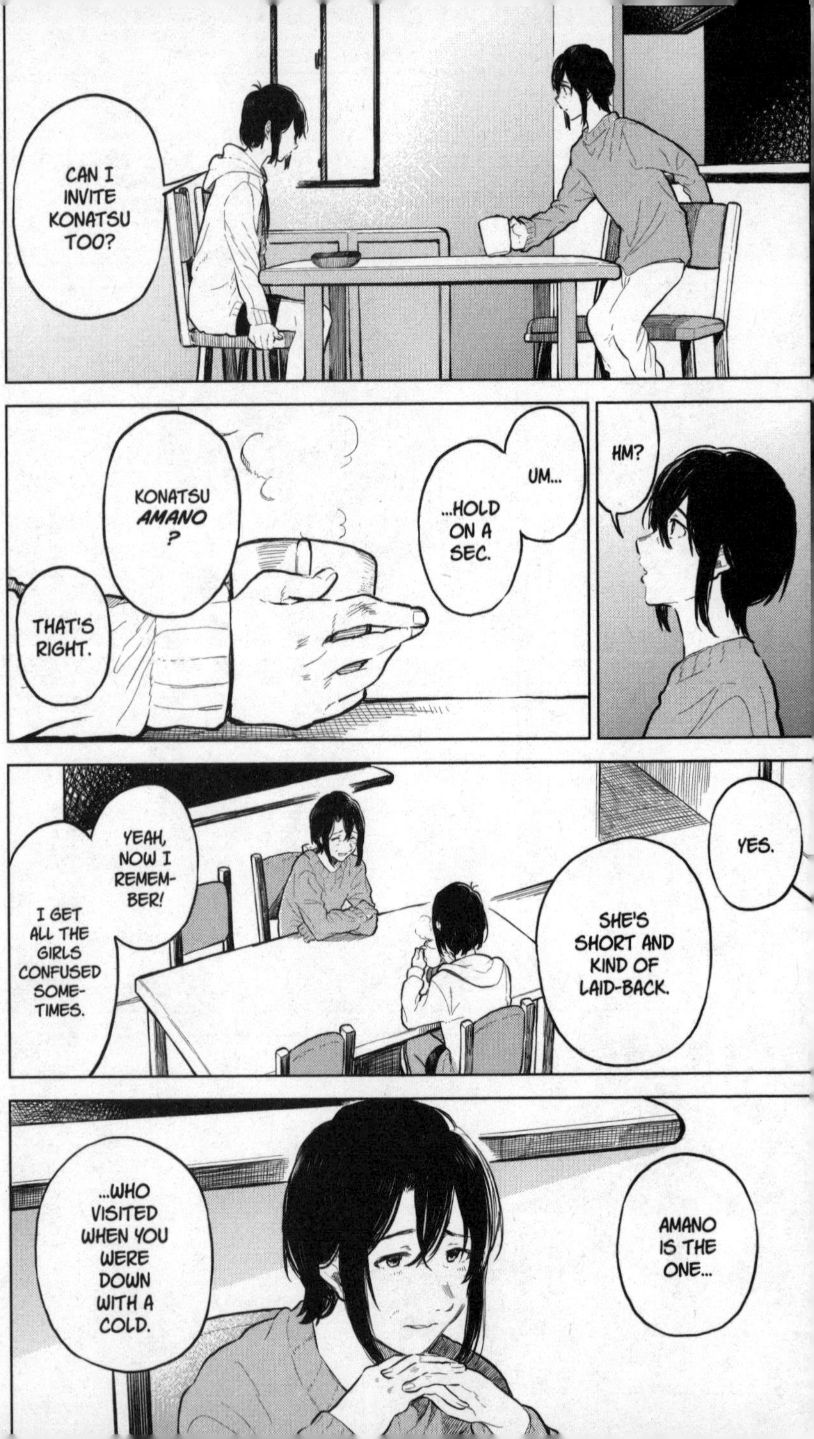
CAN I INVITE KONATSU TOO?
HM?
UM...
...HOLD ON A SEC.
KONATSU *AMANO* ?
THAT'S RIGHT.
YES.
SHE'S SHORT AND KIND OF LAID-BACK.
YEAH, NOW I REMEMBER!
I GET ALL THE GIRLS CONFUSED SOMETIMES.
AMANO IS THE ONE...
...WHO VISITED WHEN YOU WERE DOWN WITH A COLD.

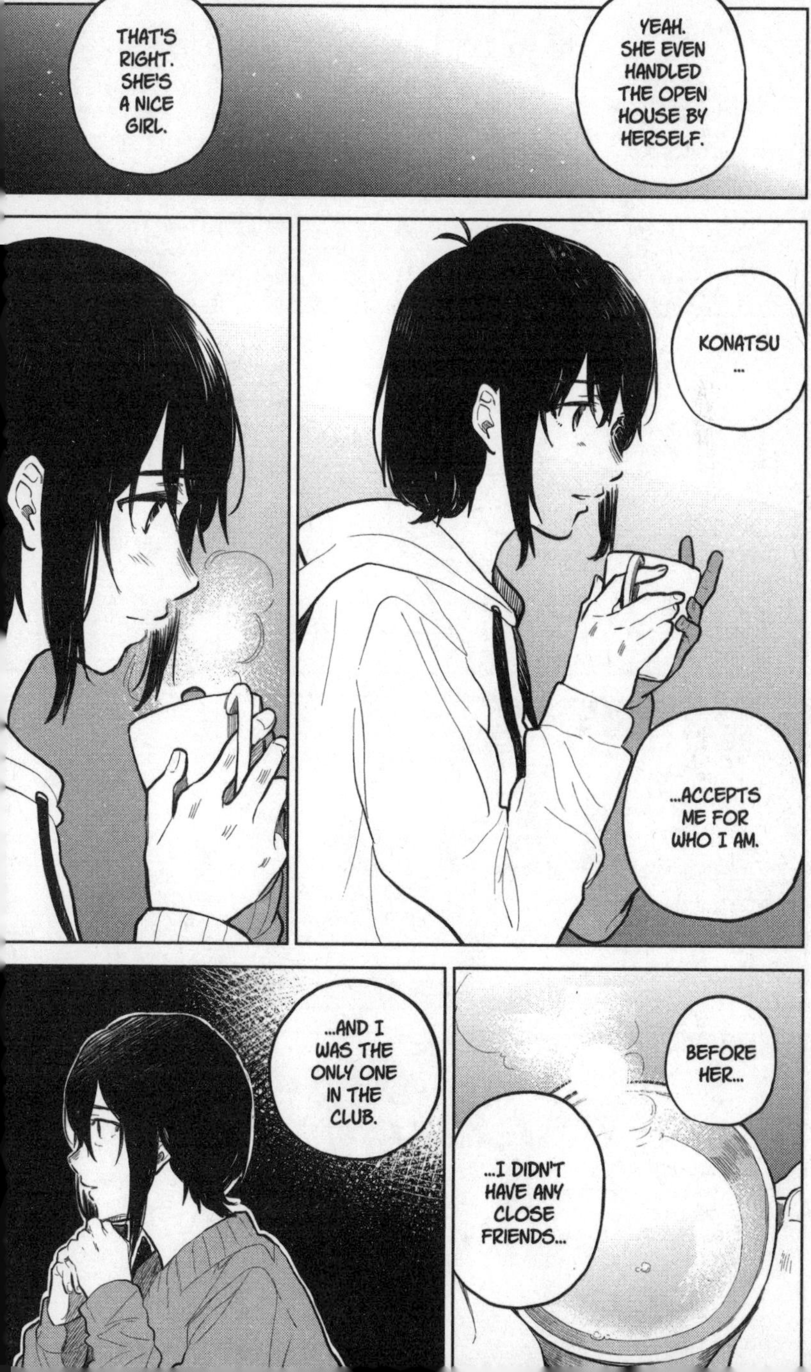
YEAH. SHE EVEN HANDLED THE OPEN HOUSE BY HERSELF.
THAT'S RIGHT. SHE'S A NICE GIRL.
KONATSU...
...ACCEPTS ME FOR WHO I AM.
BEFORE HER...
...I DIDN'T HAVE ANY CLOSE FRIENDS...
...AND I WAS THE ONLY ONE IN THE CLUB.

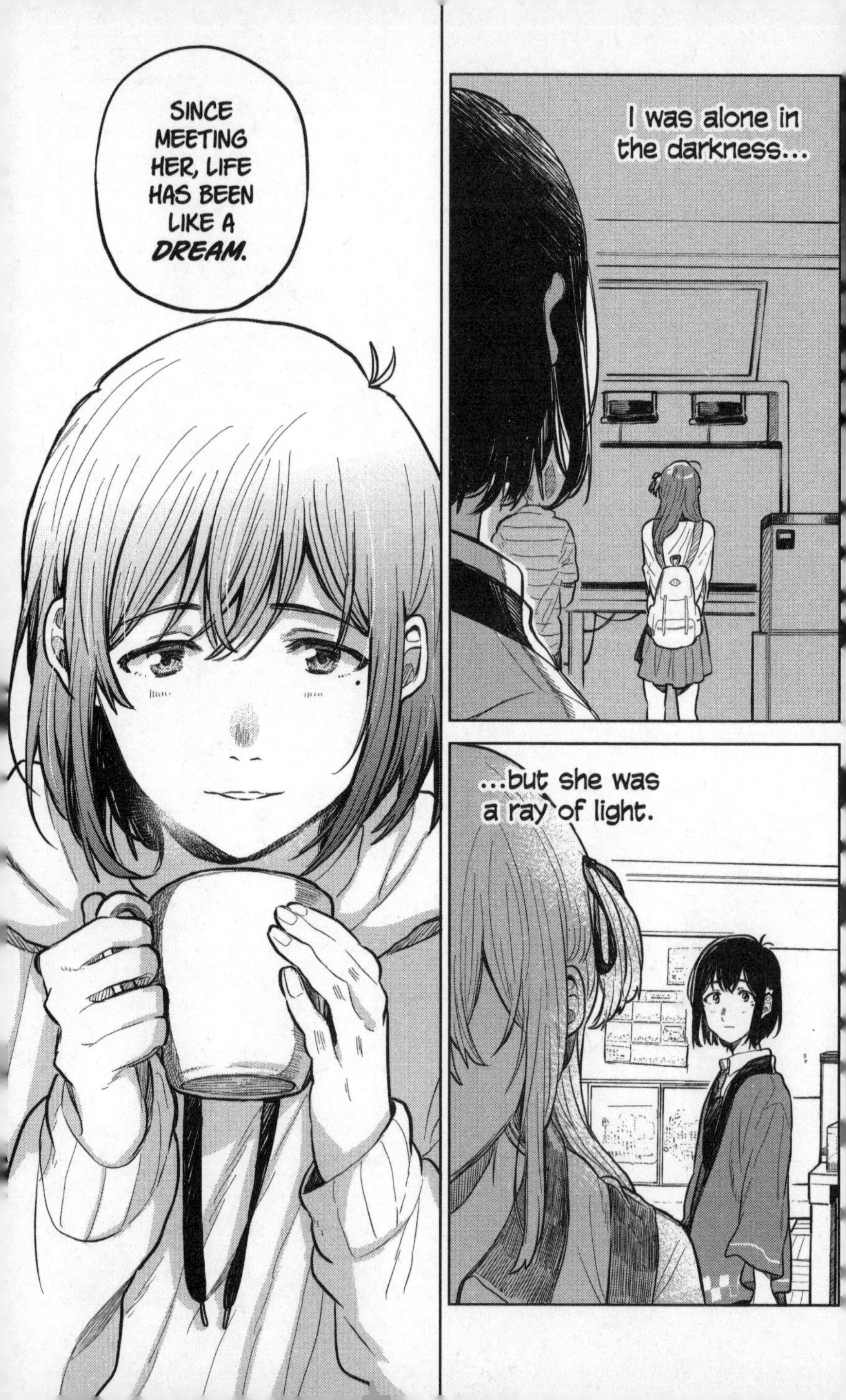
I was alone in the darkness...
...but she was a ray of light.
SINCE MEETING HER, LIFE HAS BEEN LIKE A DREAM.

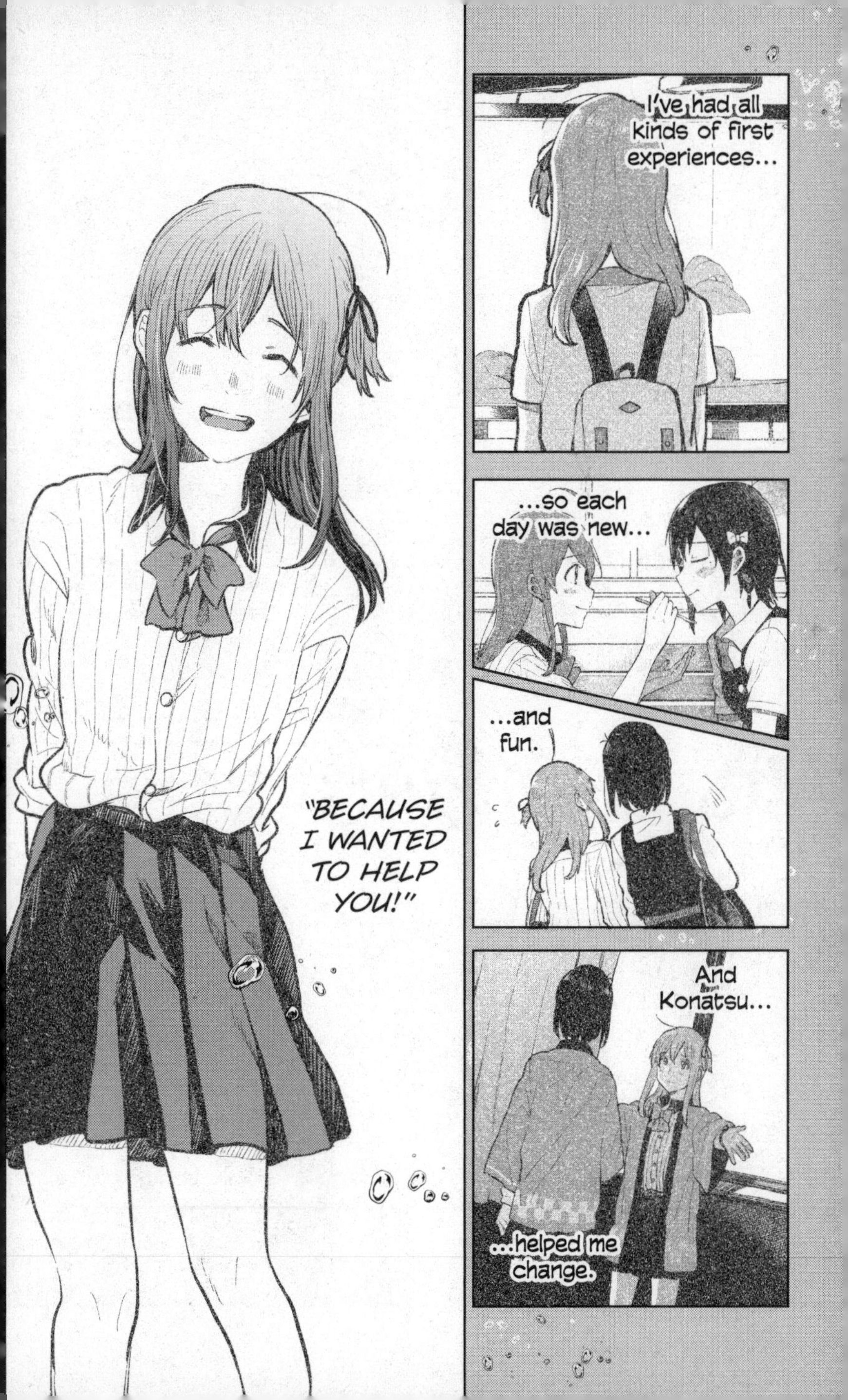
I've had all kinds of first experiences...
...so each day was new...
...and fun.
And Konatsu...
...helped me change.
"BECAUSE I WANTED TO HELP YOU!"

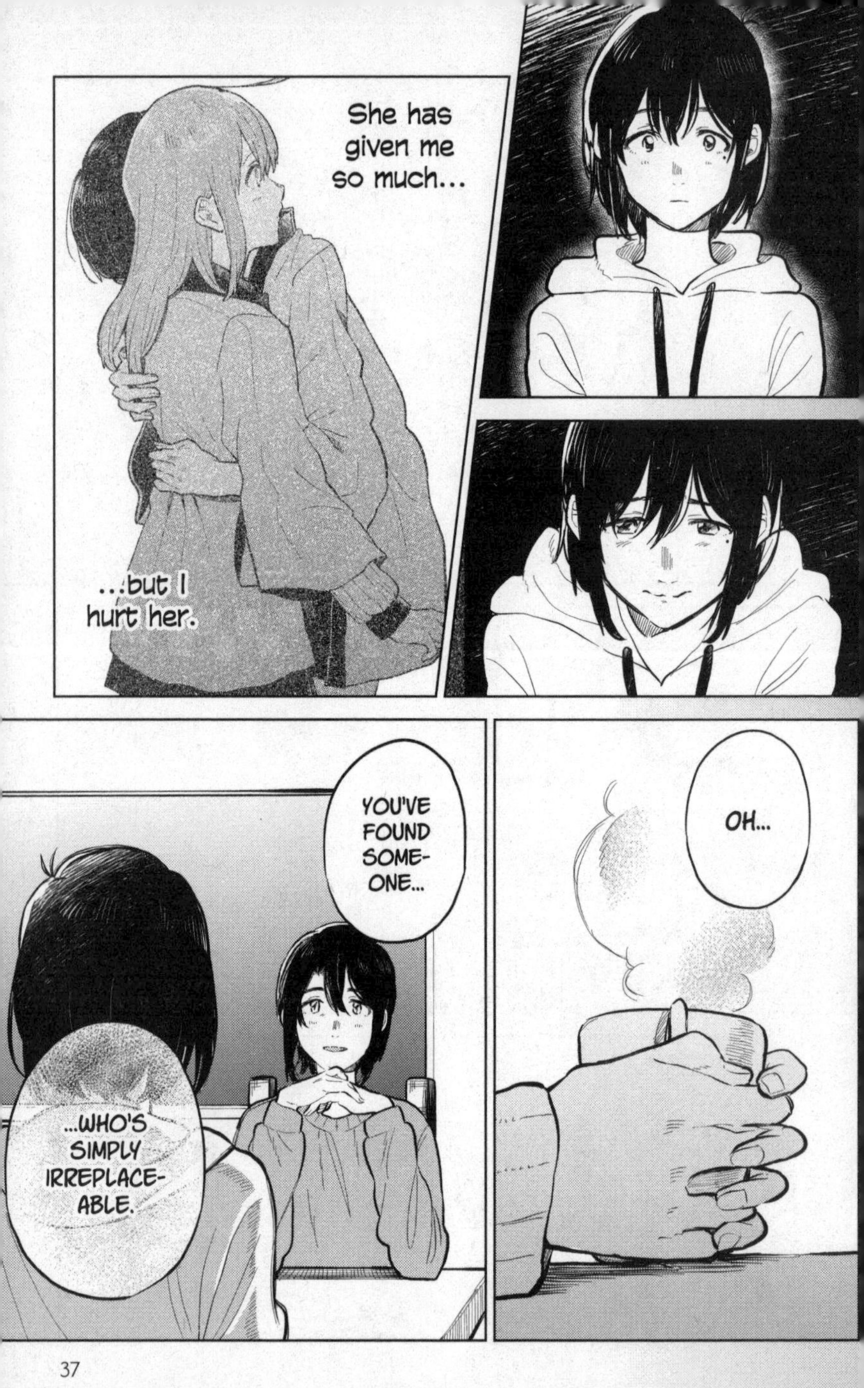
She has given me so much...
...but I hurt her.
OH...
YOU'VE FOUND SOME-ONE...
...WHO'S SIMPLY IRREPLACE-ABLE.

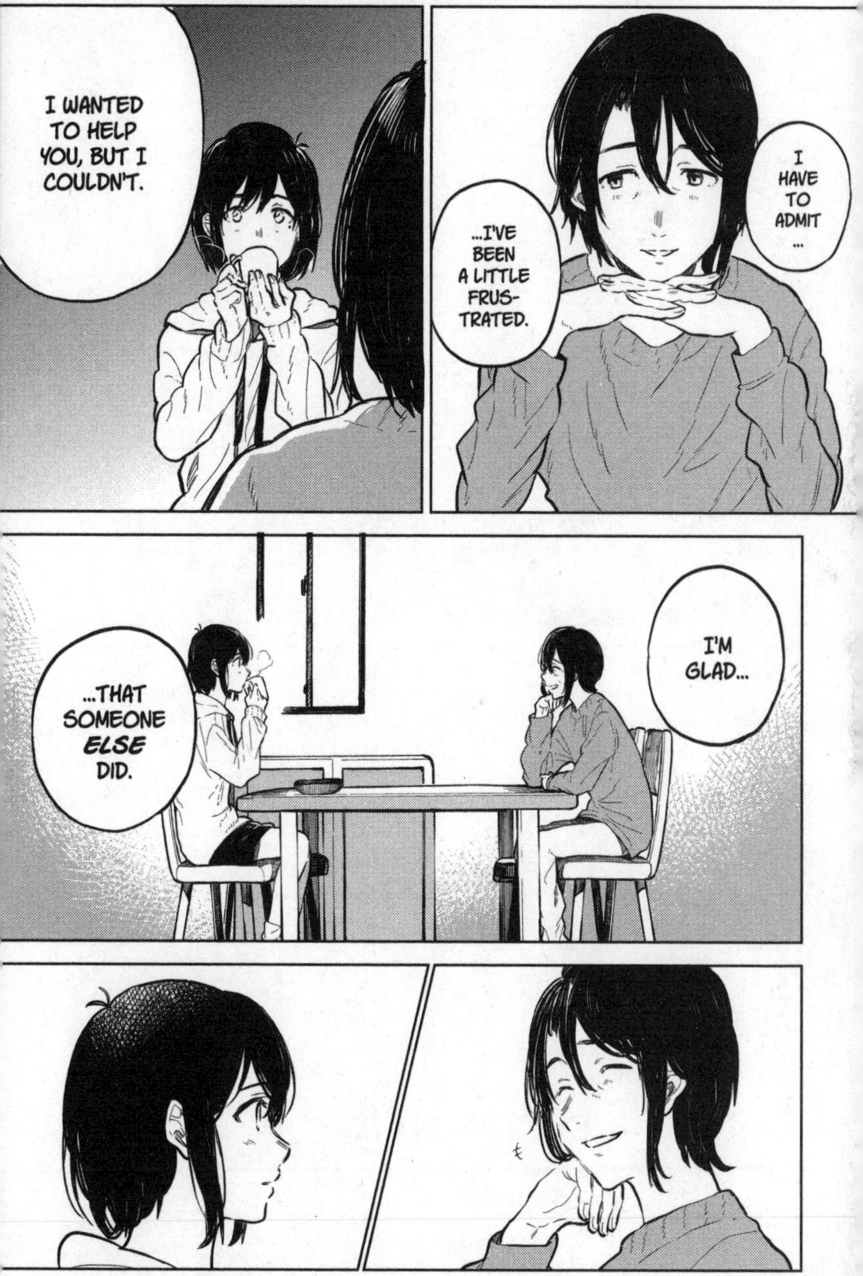
I HAVE TO ADMIT...
...I'VE BEEN A LITTLE FRUS-TRATED.
I WANTED TO HELP YOU, BUT I COULDN'T.
I'M GLAD...
...THAT SOMEONE ELSE DID.

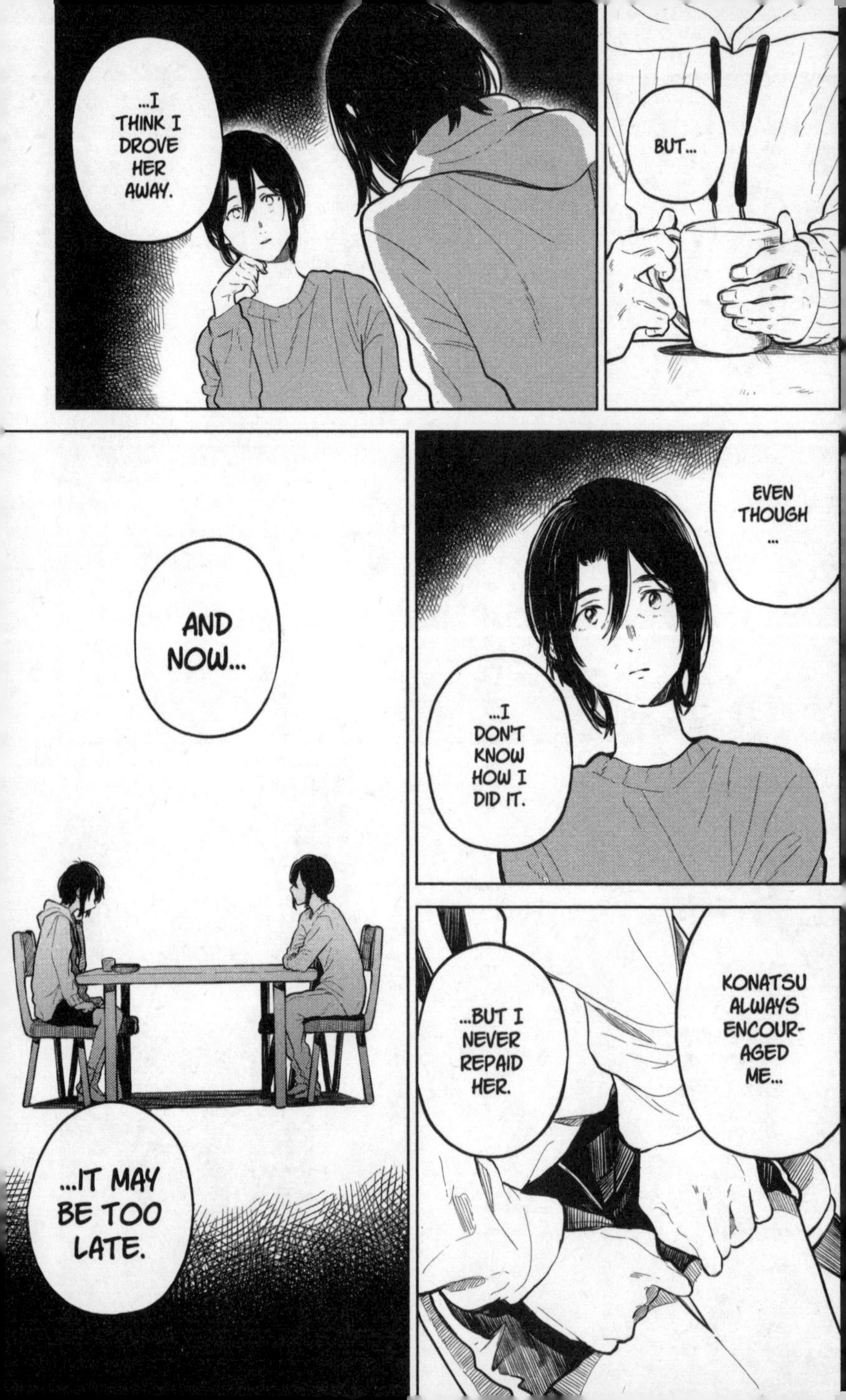
BUT...
...I THINK I DROVE HER AWAY.
EVEN THOUGH ...
...I DON'T KNOW HOW I DID IT.
KONATSU ALWAYS ENCOUR-AGED ME...
...BUT I NEVER REPAID HER.
AND NOW...
...IT MAY BE TOO LATE.

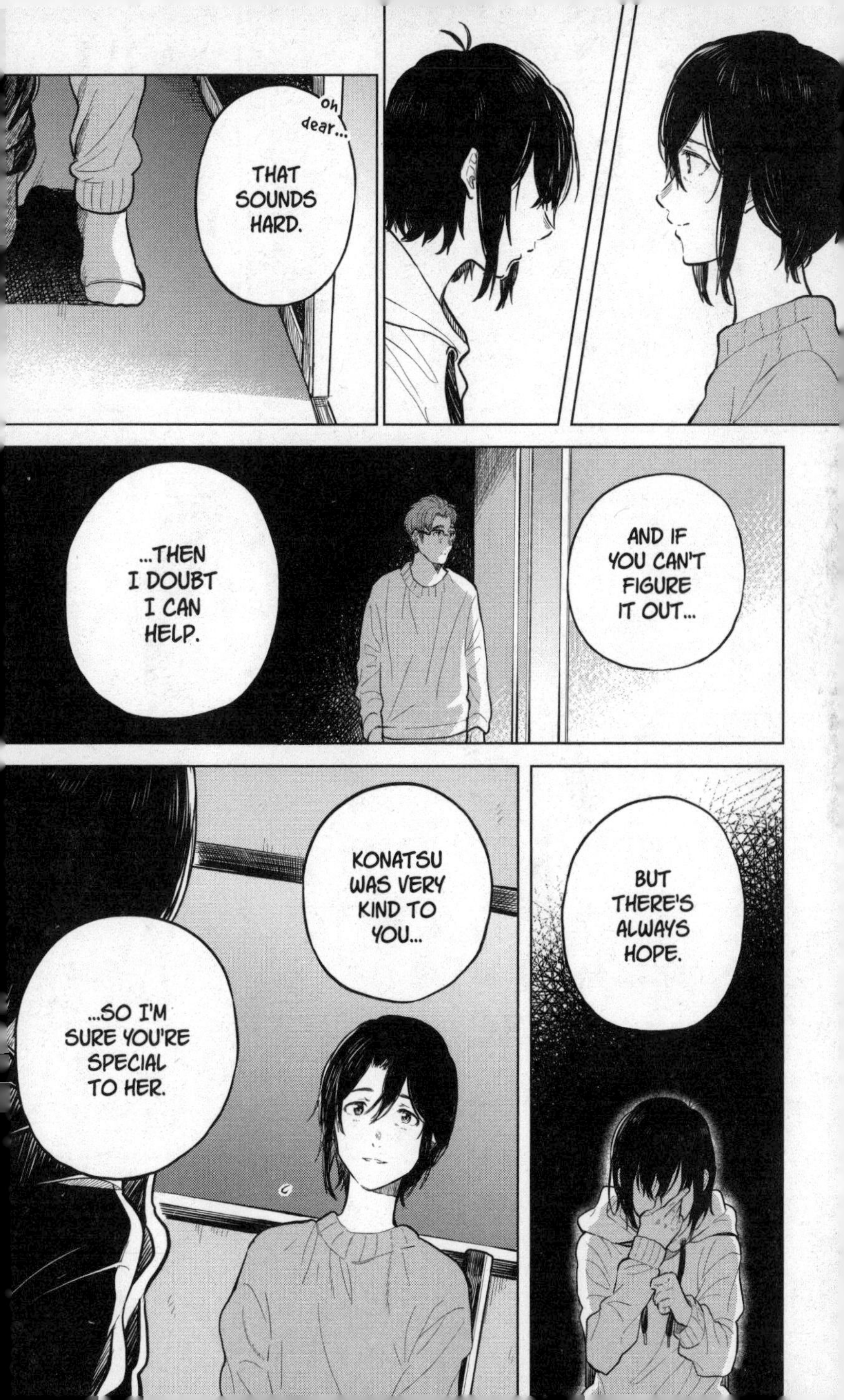
oh dear...
THAT SOUNDS HARD.
AND IF YOU CAN'T FIGURE IT OUT...
...THEN I DOUBT I CAN HELP.
BUT THERE'S ALWAYS HOPE.
KONATSU WAS VERY KIND TO YOU...
...SO I'M SURE YOU'RE SPECIAL TO HER.

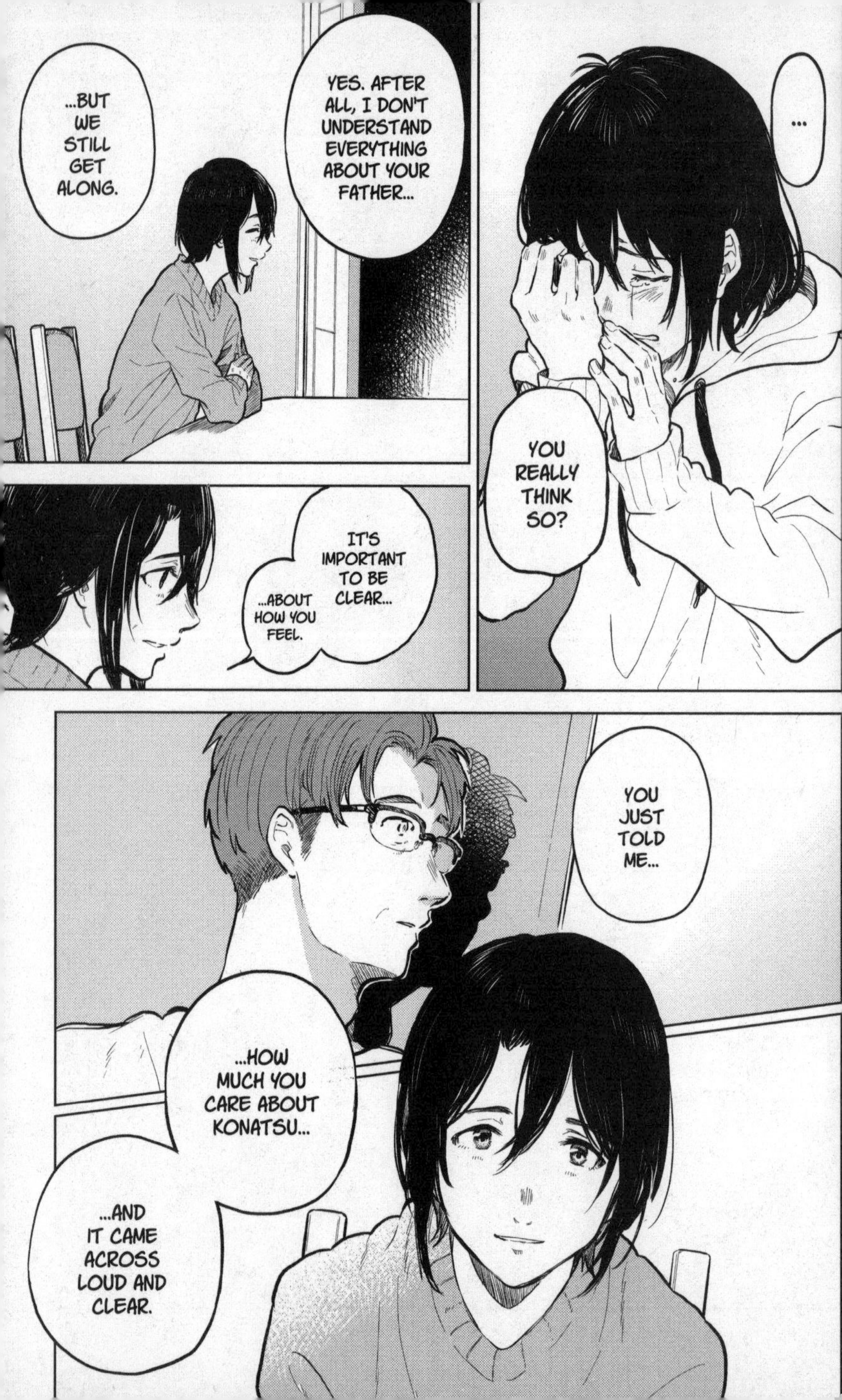
...
YOU REALLY THINK SO?
YES. AFTER ALL, I DON'T UNDERSTAND EVERYTHING ABOUT YOUR FATHER...
...BUT WE STILL GET ALONG.
IT'S IMPORTANT TO BE CLEAR...
...ABOUT HOW YOU FEEL.
YOU JUST TOLD ME...
...HOW MUCH YOU CARE ABOUT KONATSU...
...AND IT CAME ACROSS LOUD AND CLEAR.

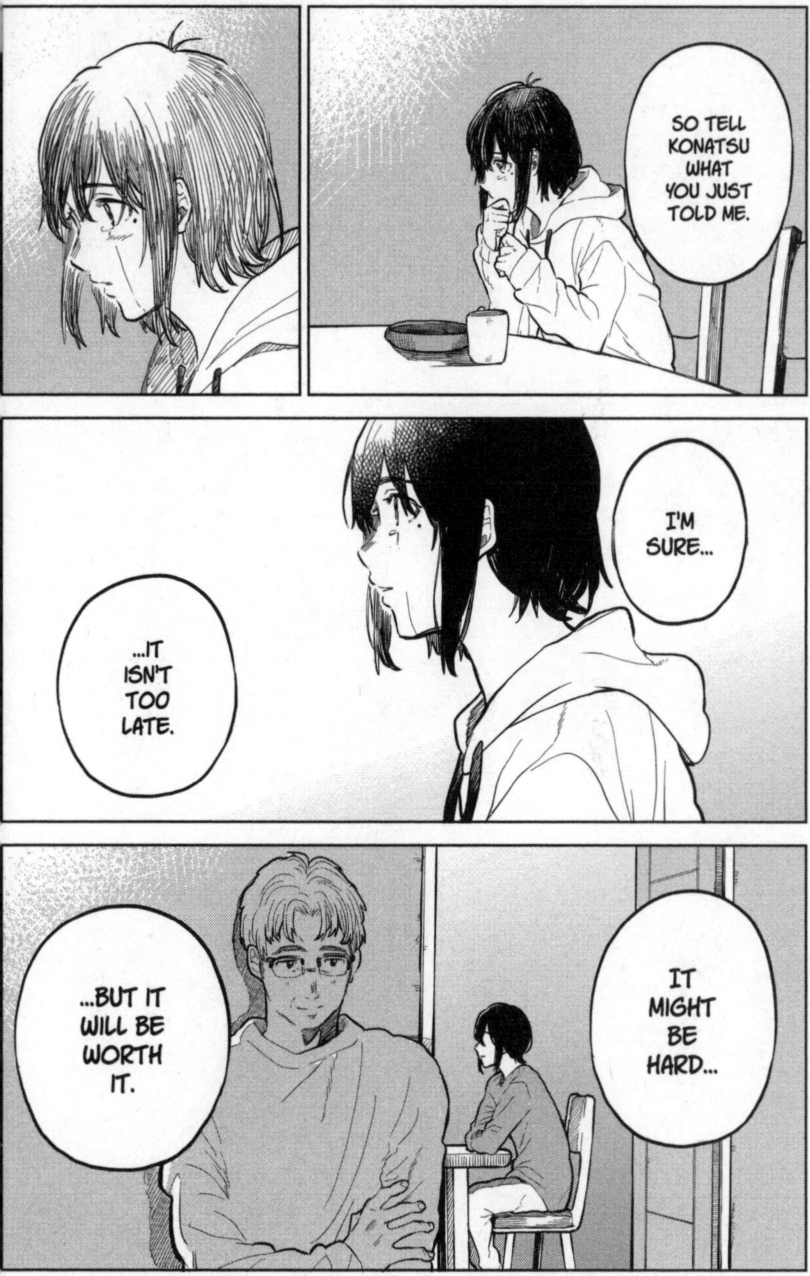
SO TELL KONATSU WHAT YOU JUST TOLD ME.
I'M SURE...
...IT ISN'T TOO LATE.
IT MIGHT BE HARD...
...BUT IT WILL BE WORTH IT.

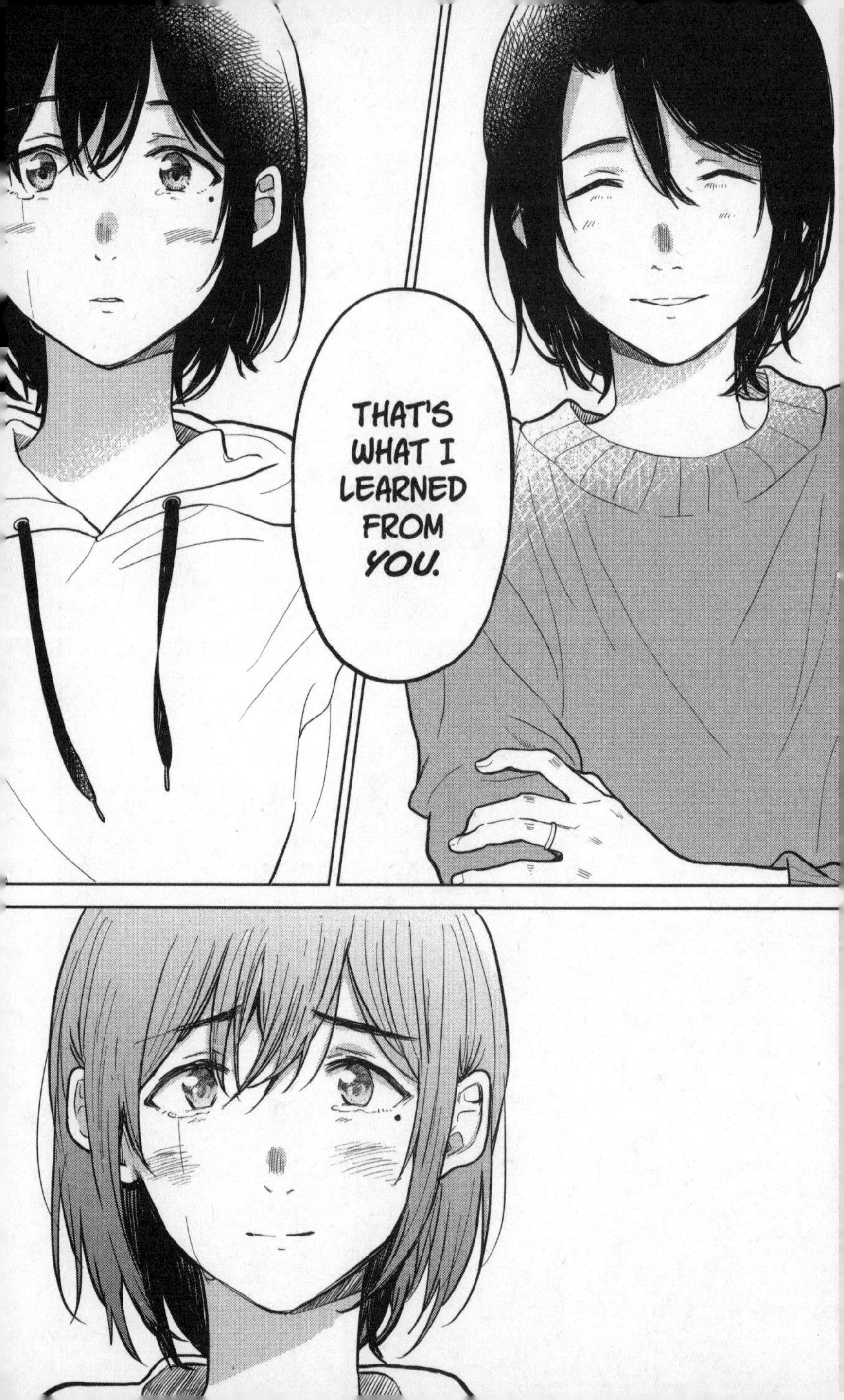
THAT'S WHAT I LEARNED FROM YOU.

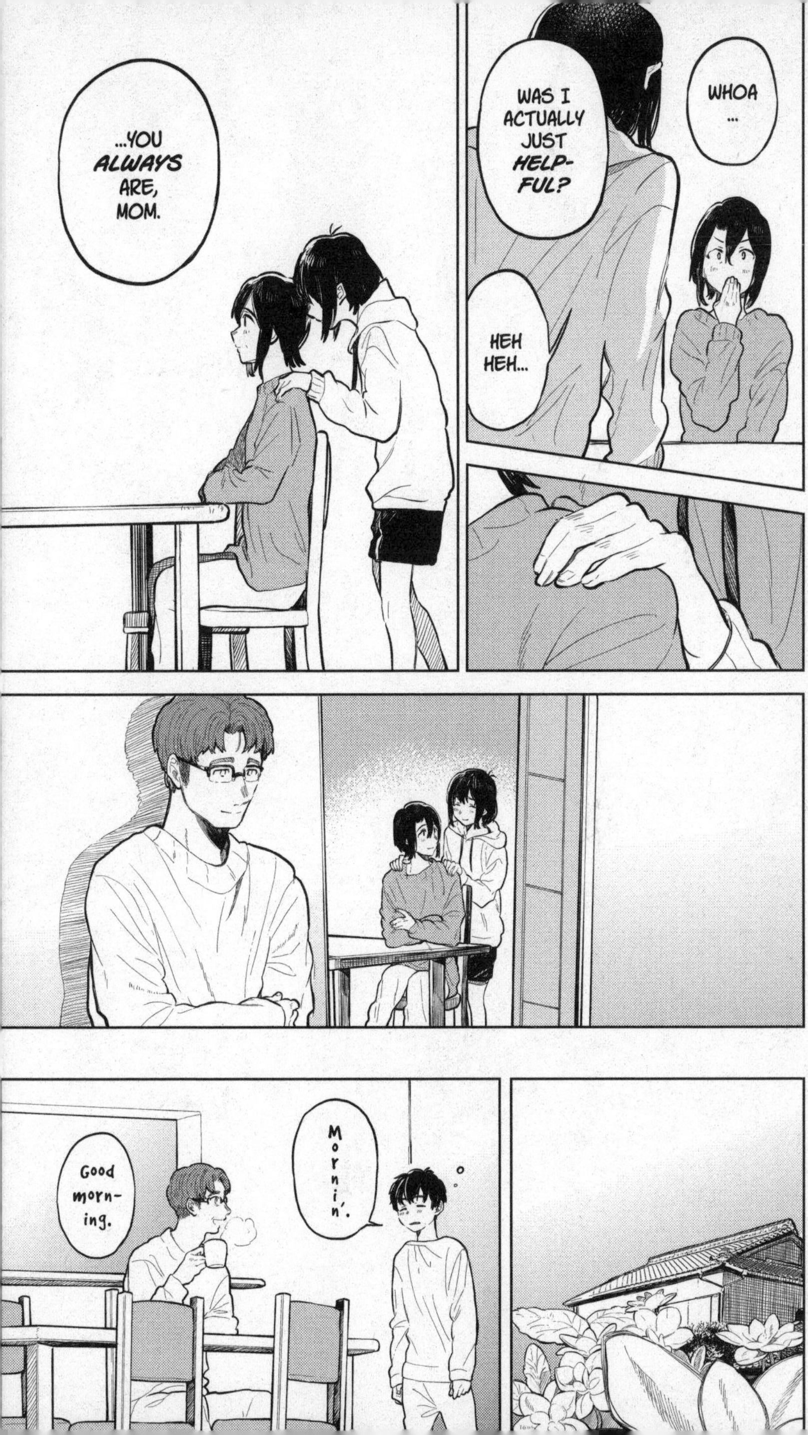
WHOA ...
WAS I ACTUALLY JUST *HELPFUL?*
HEH HEH...
...YOU *ALWAYS* ARE, MOM.
Mornin'.
Good morning.

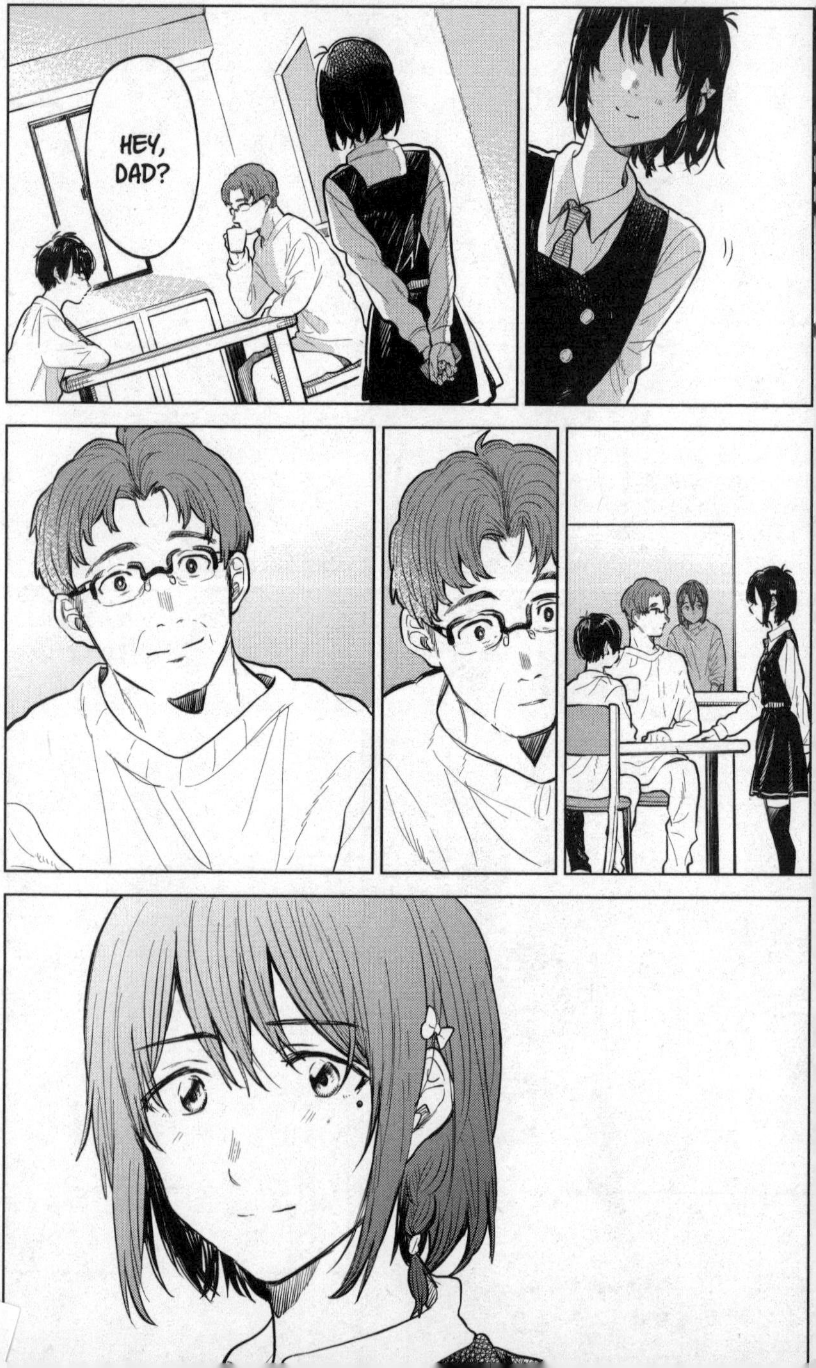
HEY, DAD?

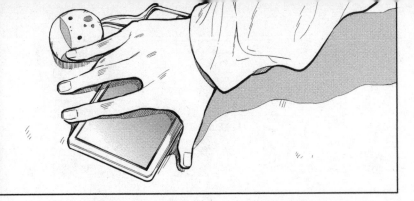

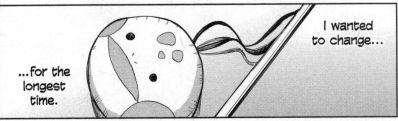

I wanted to change...
...for the longest time.
So I only thought about myself.
I couldn't pay attention to Konatsu.
And...
...I didn't even try to.

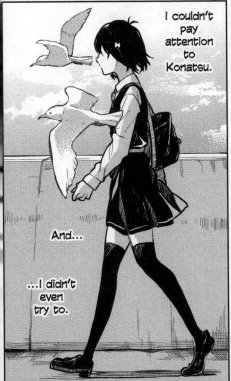

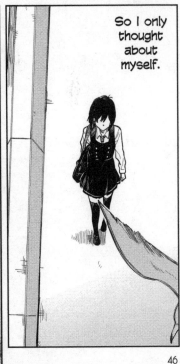

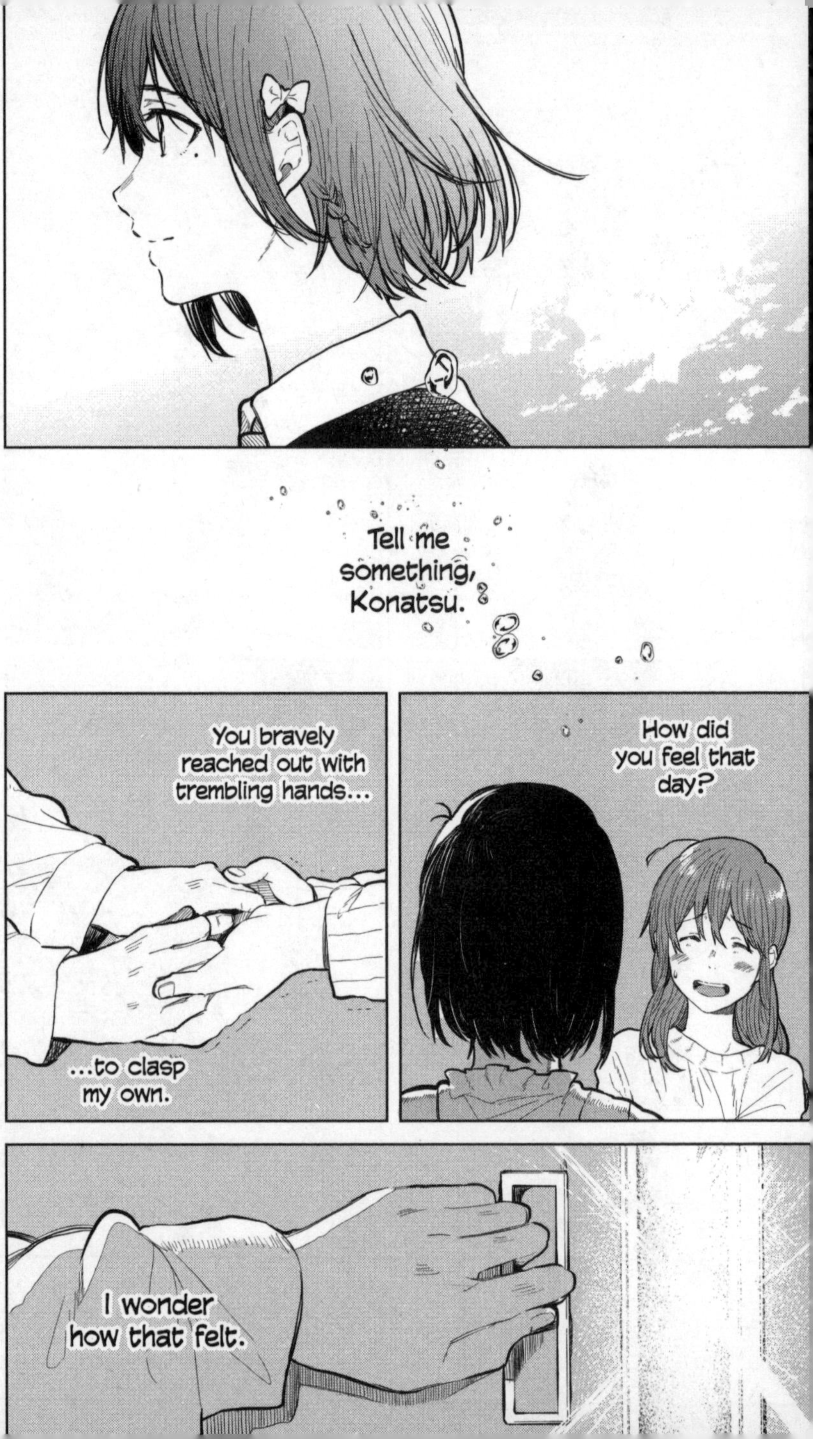
Tell me something, Konatsu.
How did you feel that day?
You bravely reached out with trembling hands...
...to clasp my own.
I wonder how that felt.

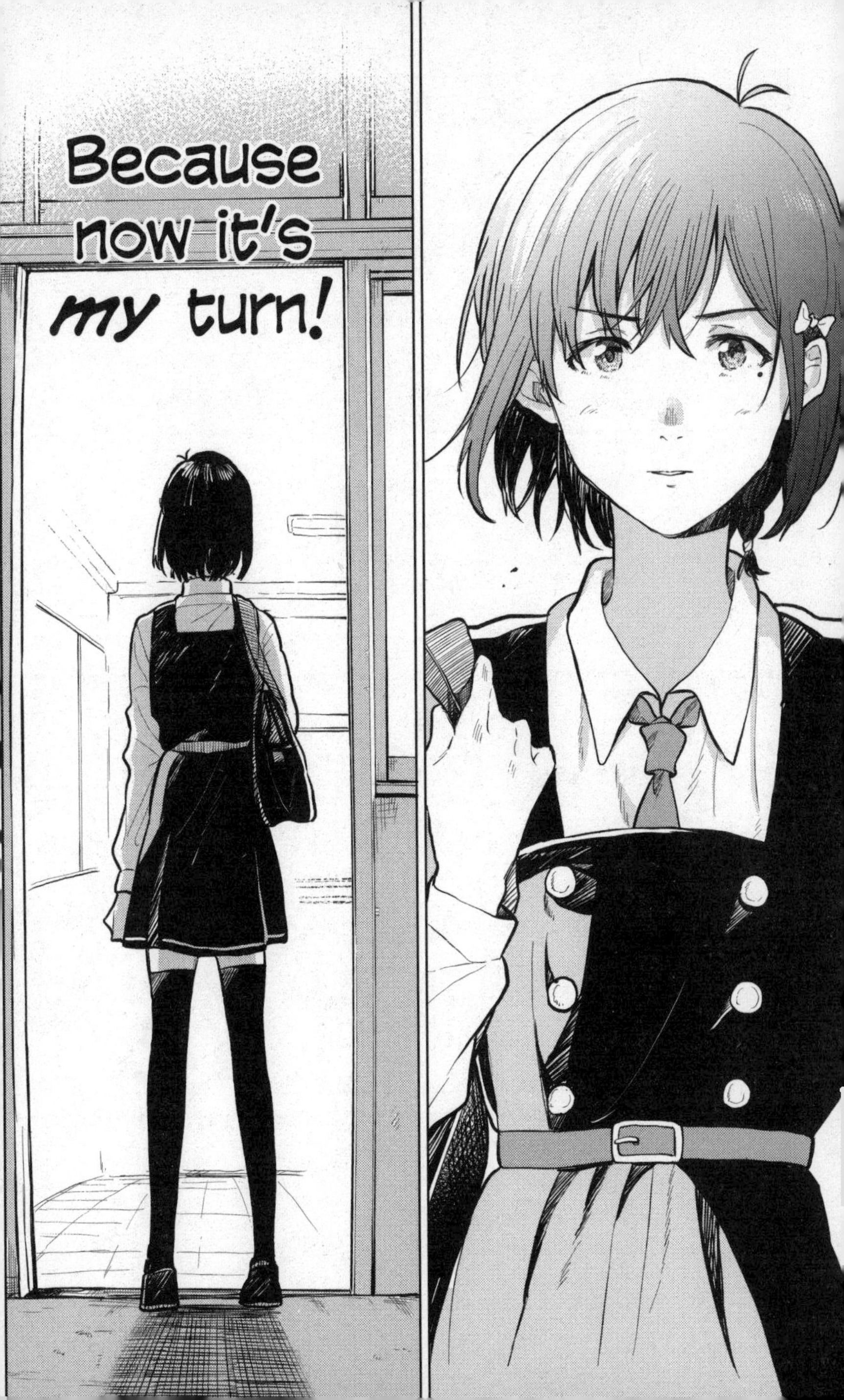
Because now it's *my* turn!

A Tropical Fish
Yearns for Snow

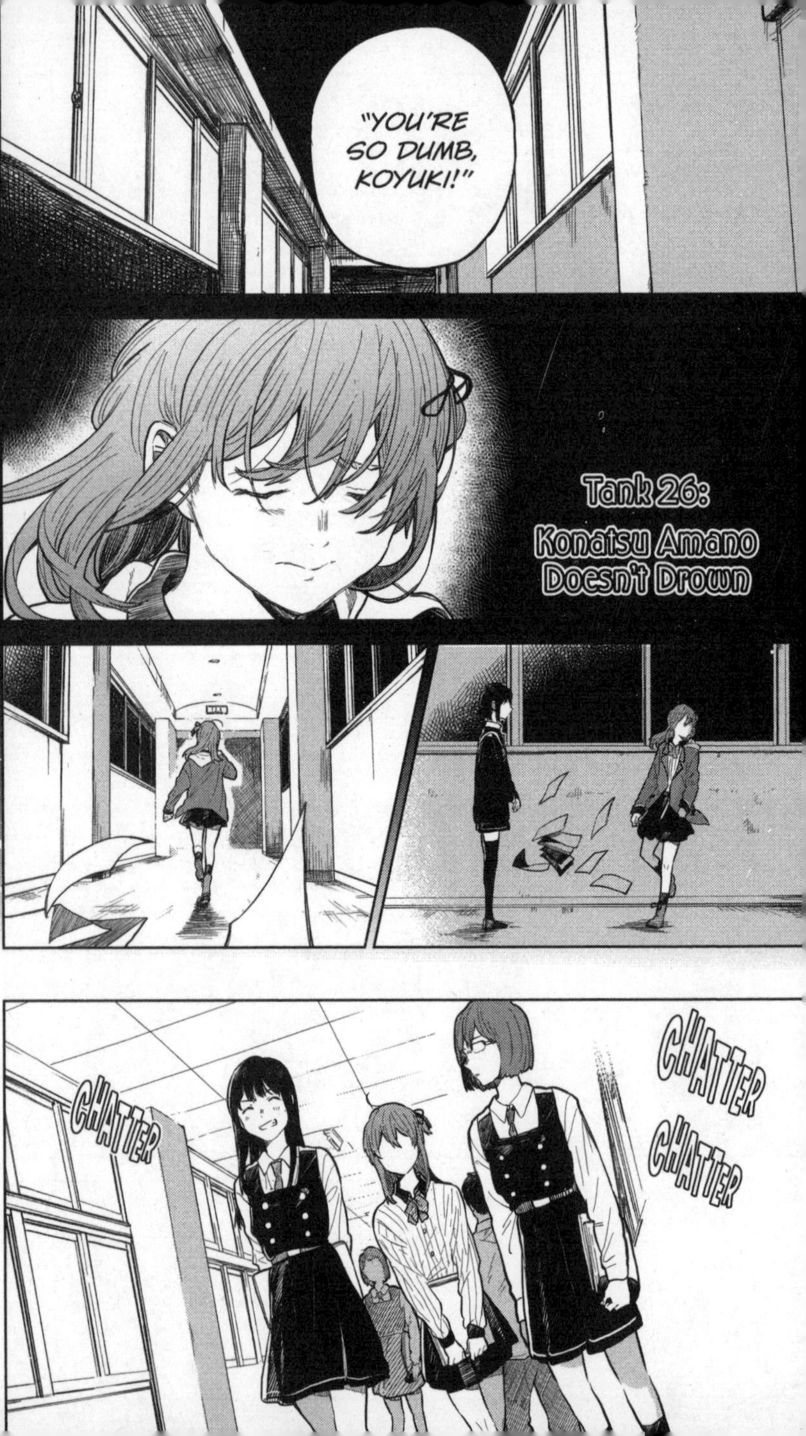
"YOU'RE SO DUMB, KOYUKI!"
Tank 26:
Konatsu Amano Doesn't Drown
CHATTER
CHATTER
CHATTER

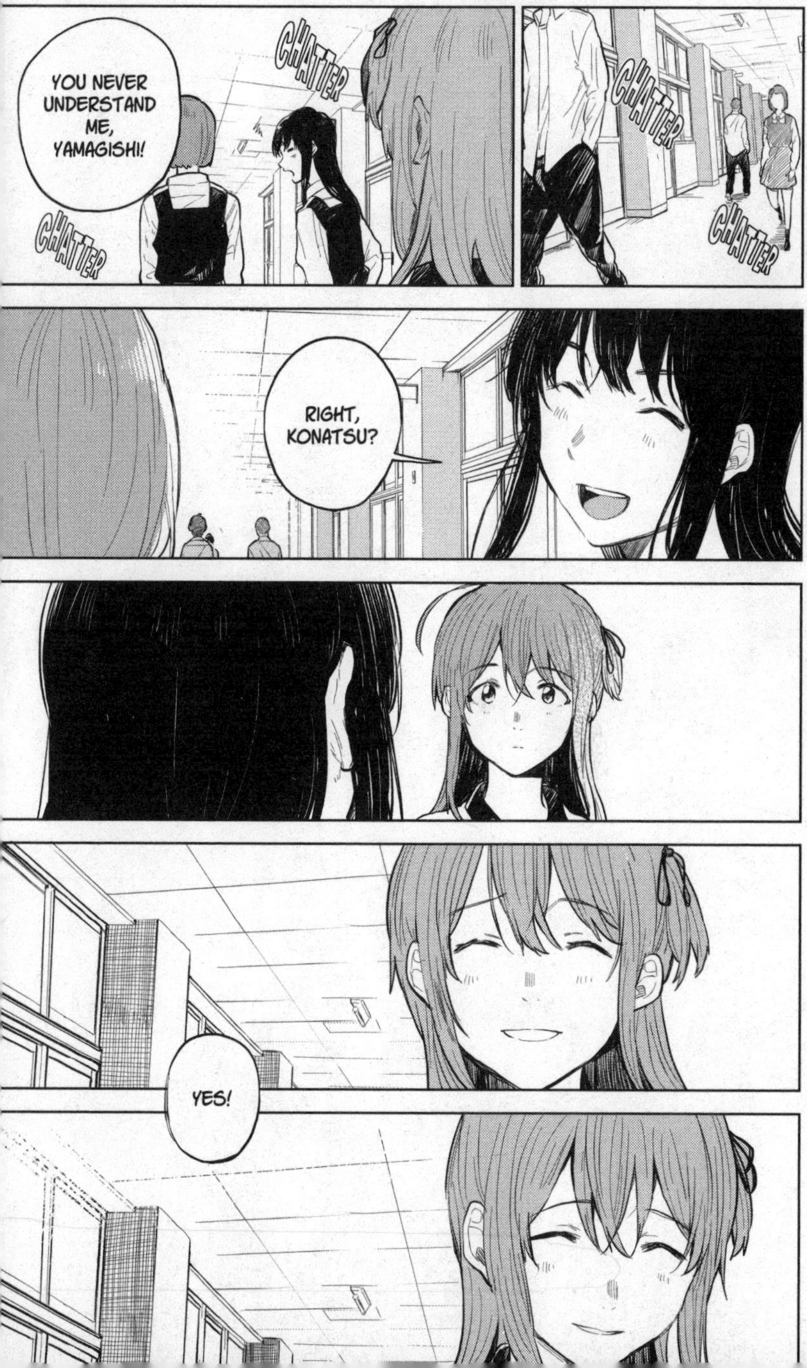
CHATTER
CHATTER
CHATTER
YOU NEVER UNDERSTAND ME, YAMAGISHI!
CHATTER
RIGHT, KONATSU?
YES!

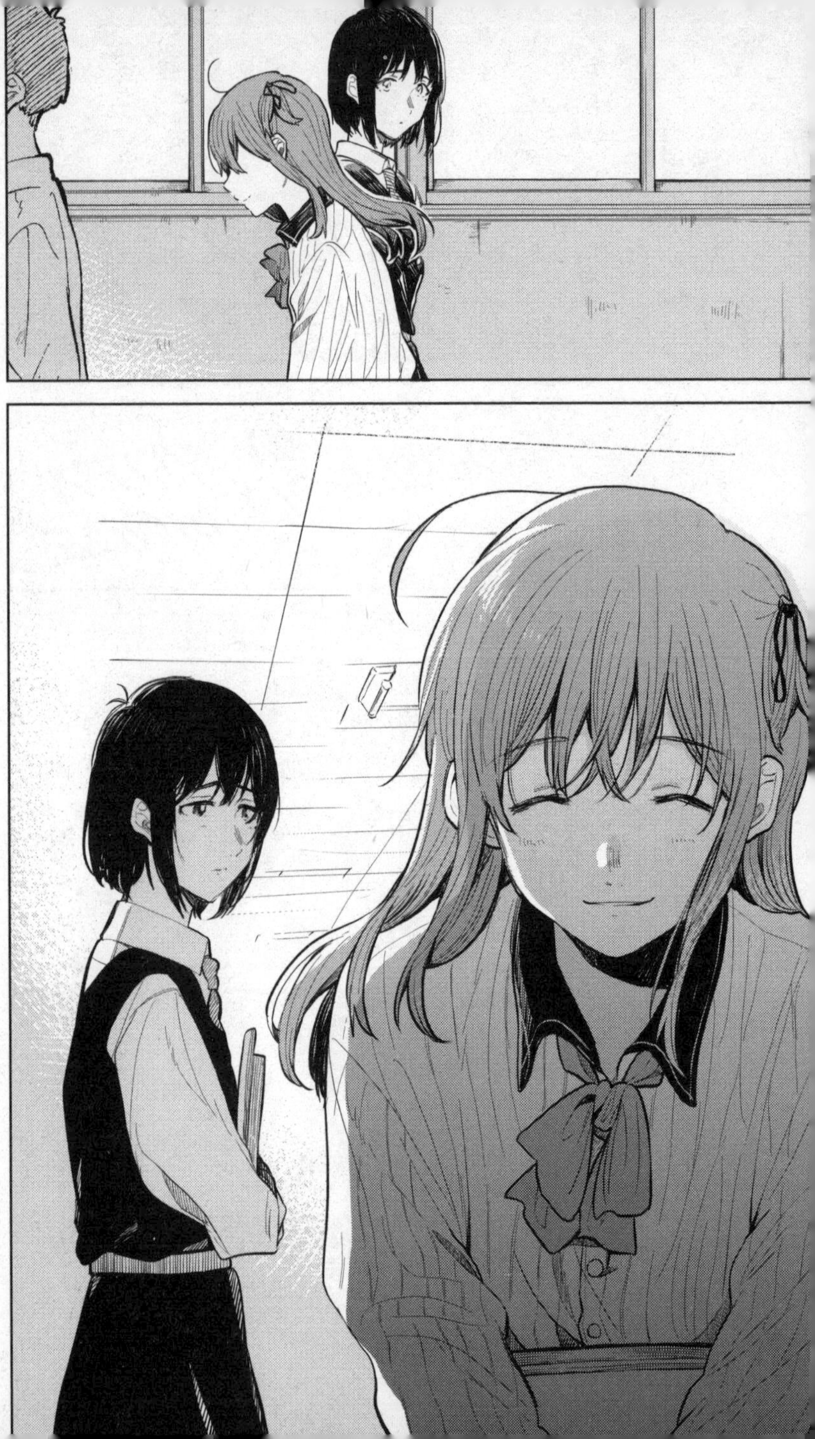

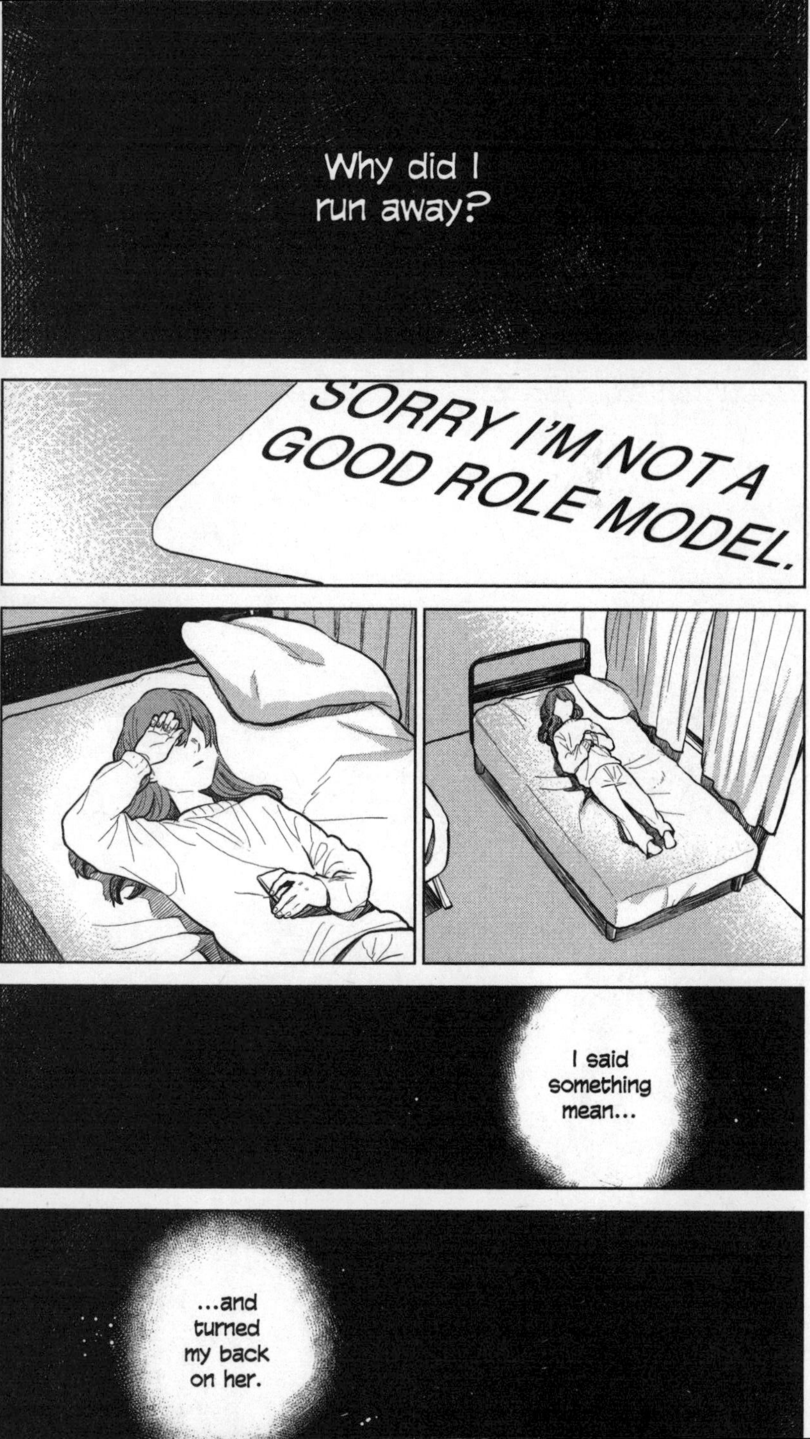
Why did I run away?
SORRY I'M NOT A GOOD ROLE MODEL.
I said something mean...
...and turned my back on her.

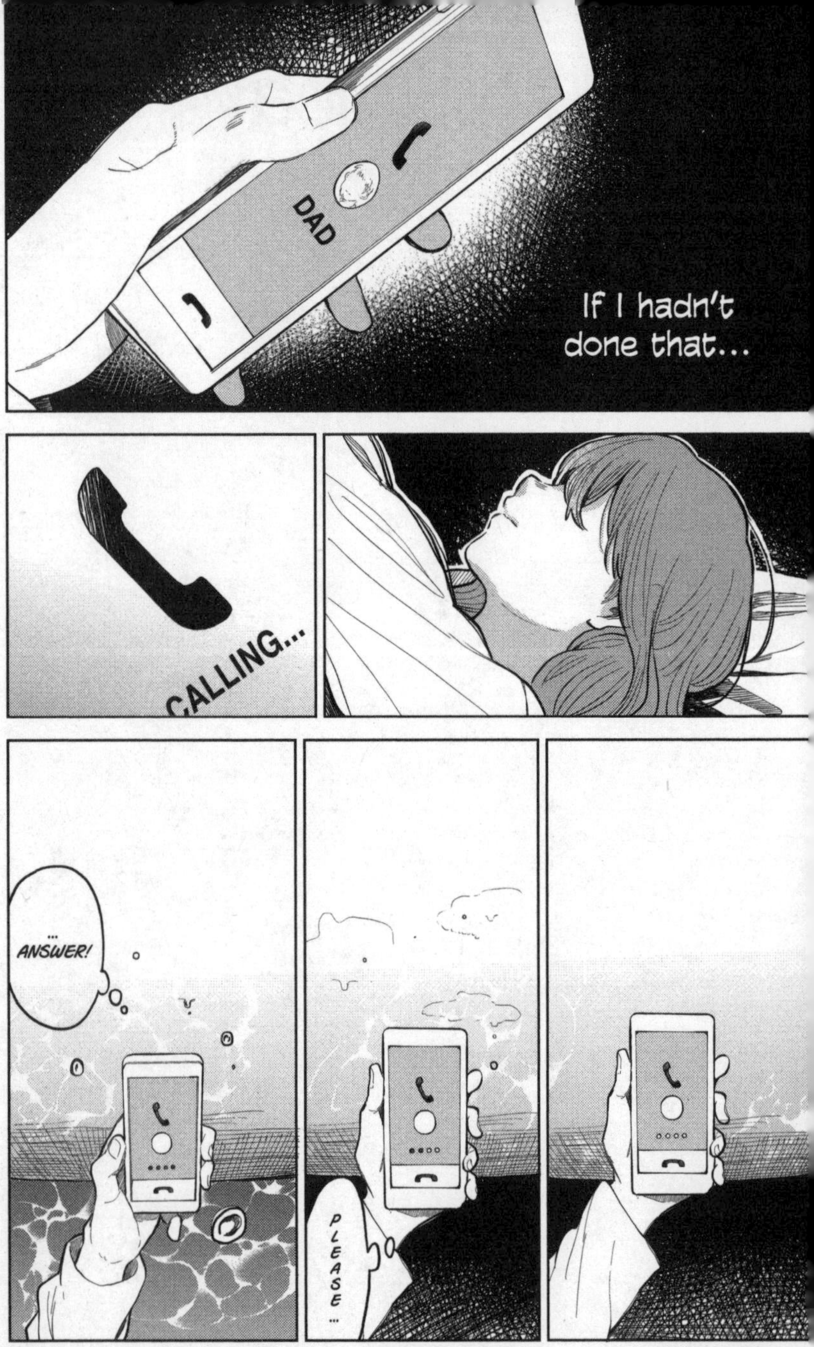
DAD
If I hadn't done that...
CALLING...
PLEASE...
...ANSWER!

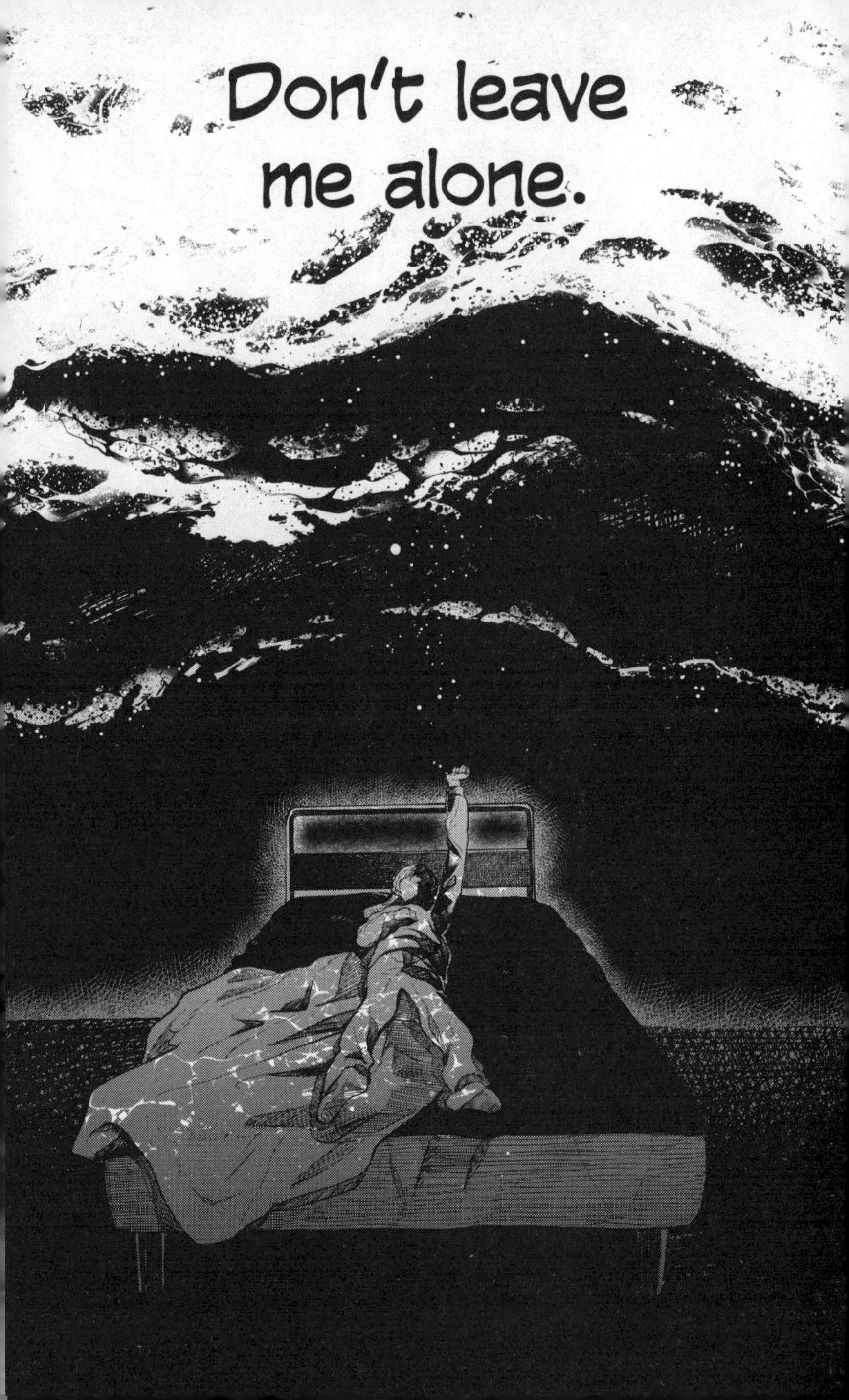
Don't leave me alone.

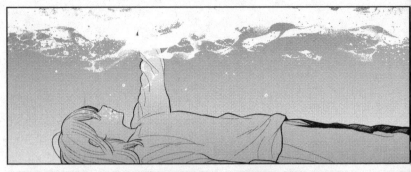

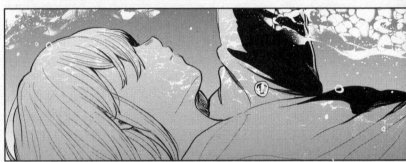

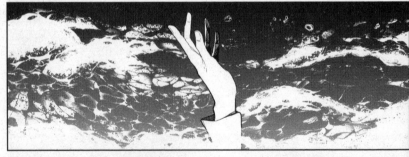

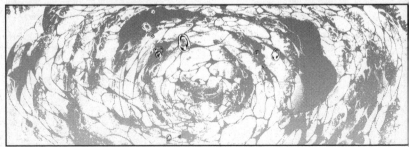

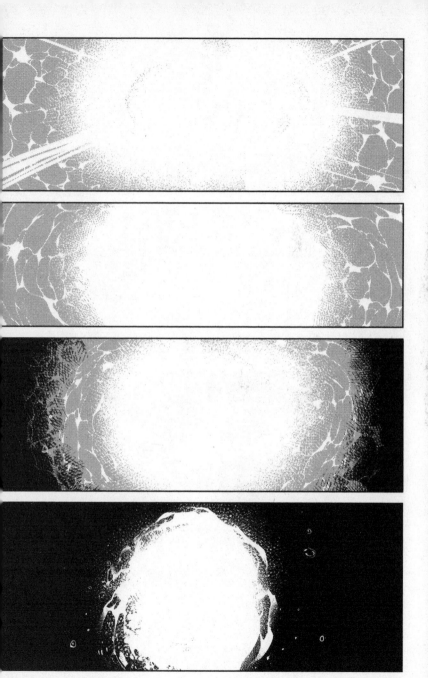

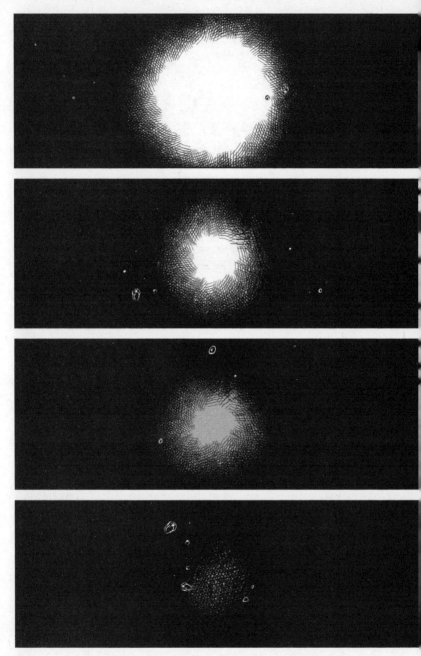

59

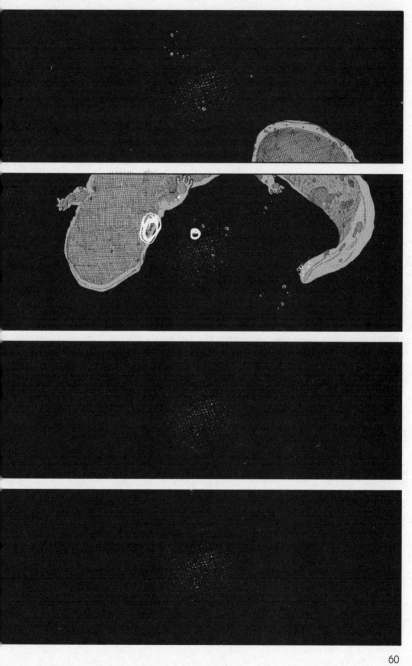

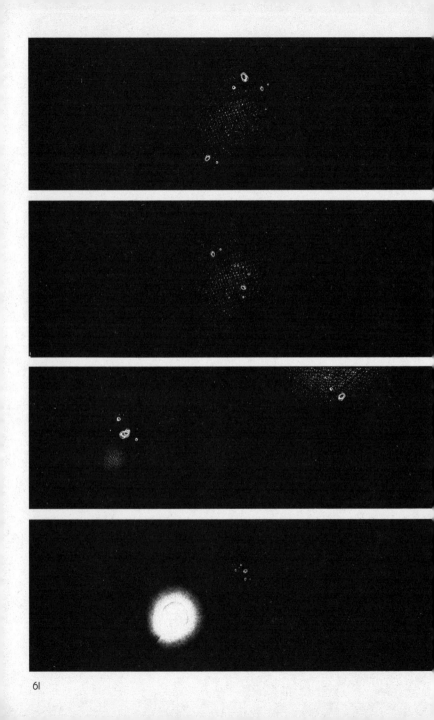

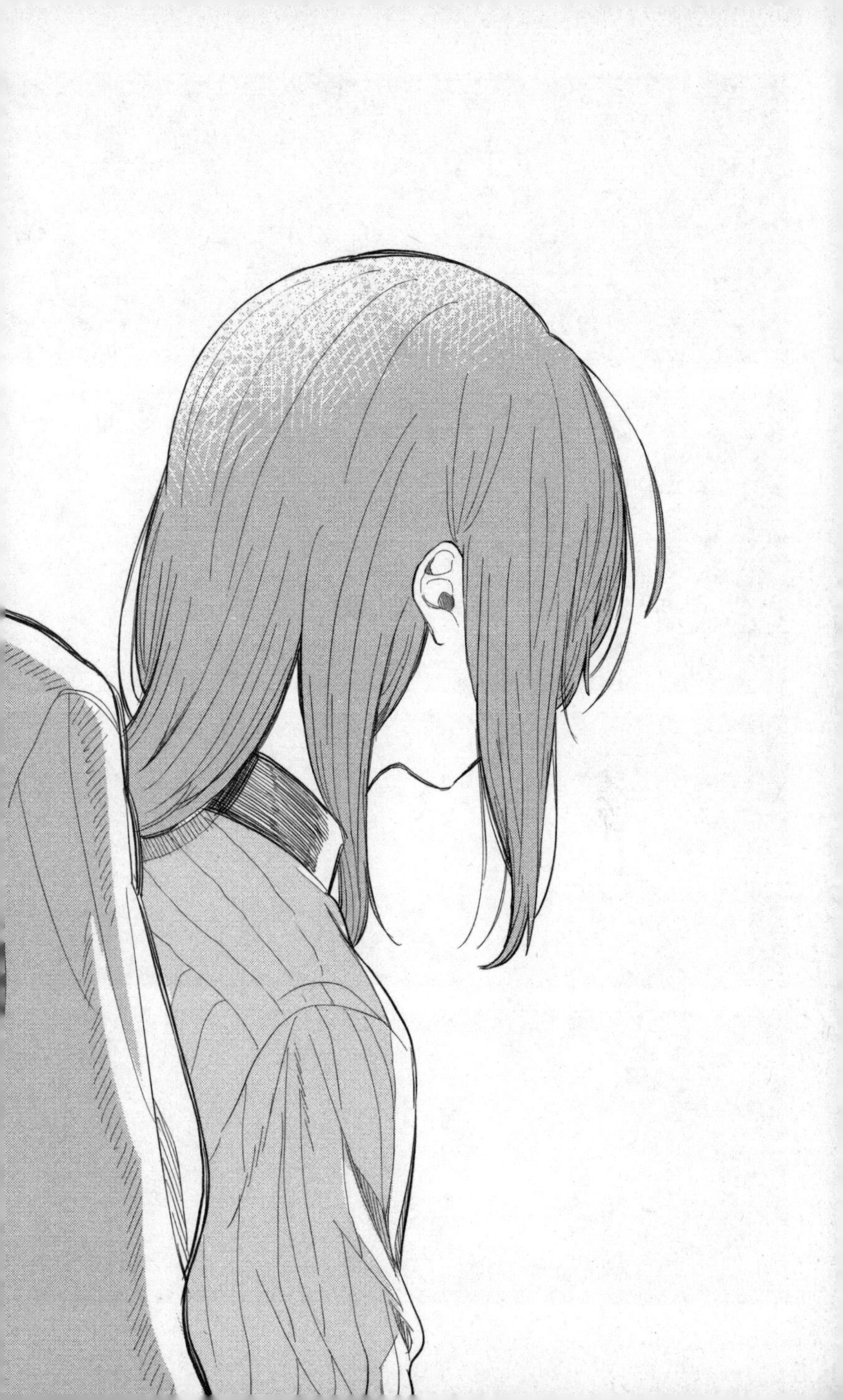

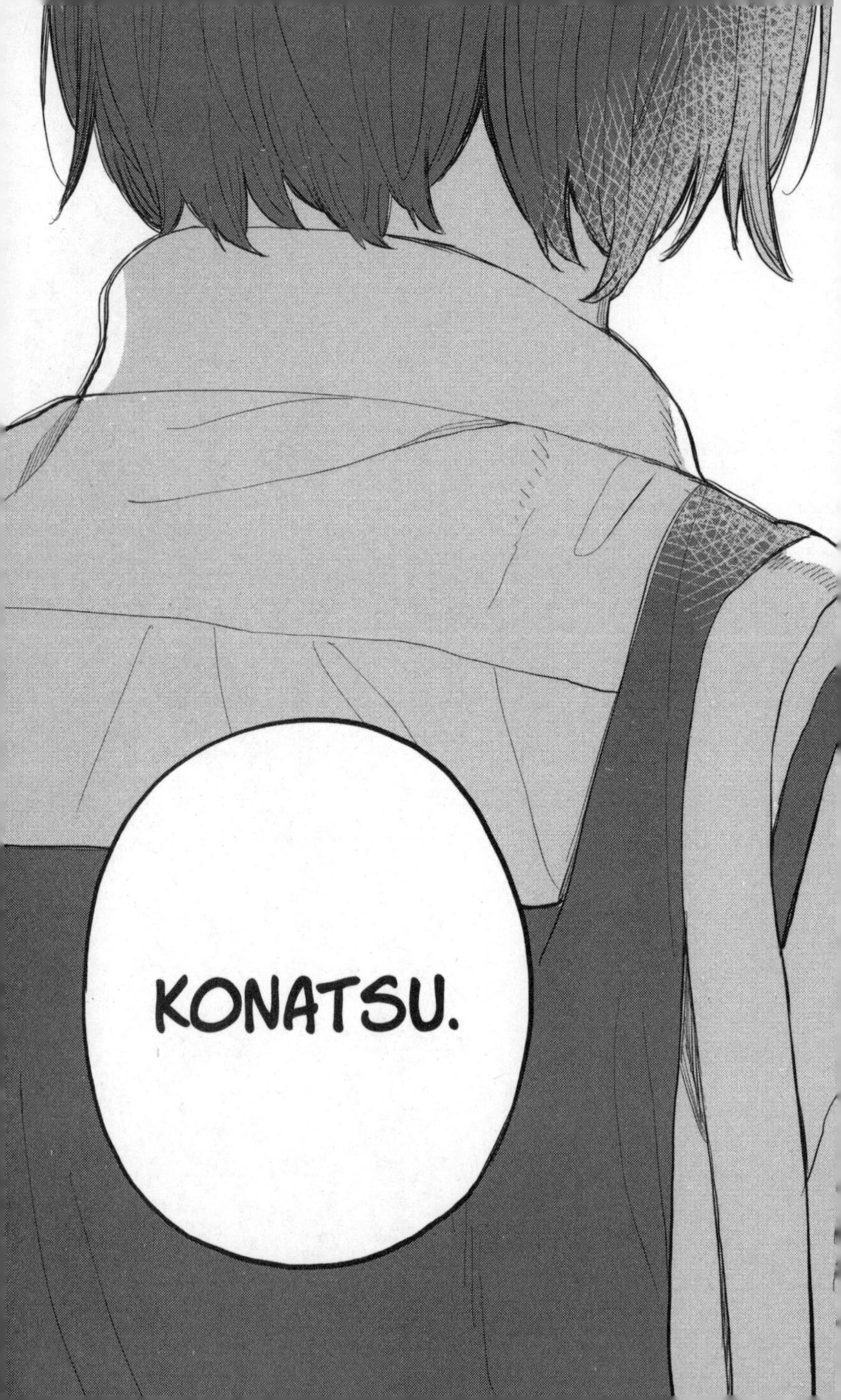
KONATSU.

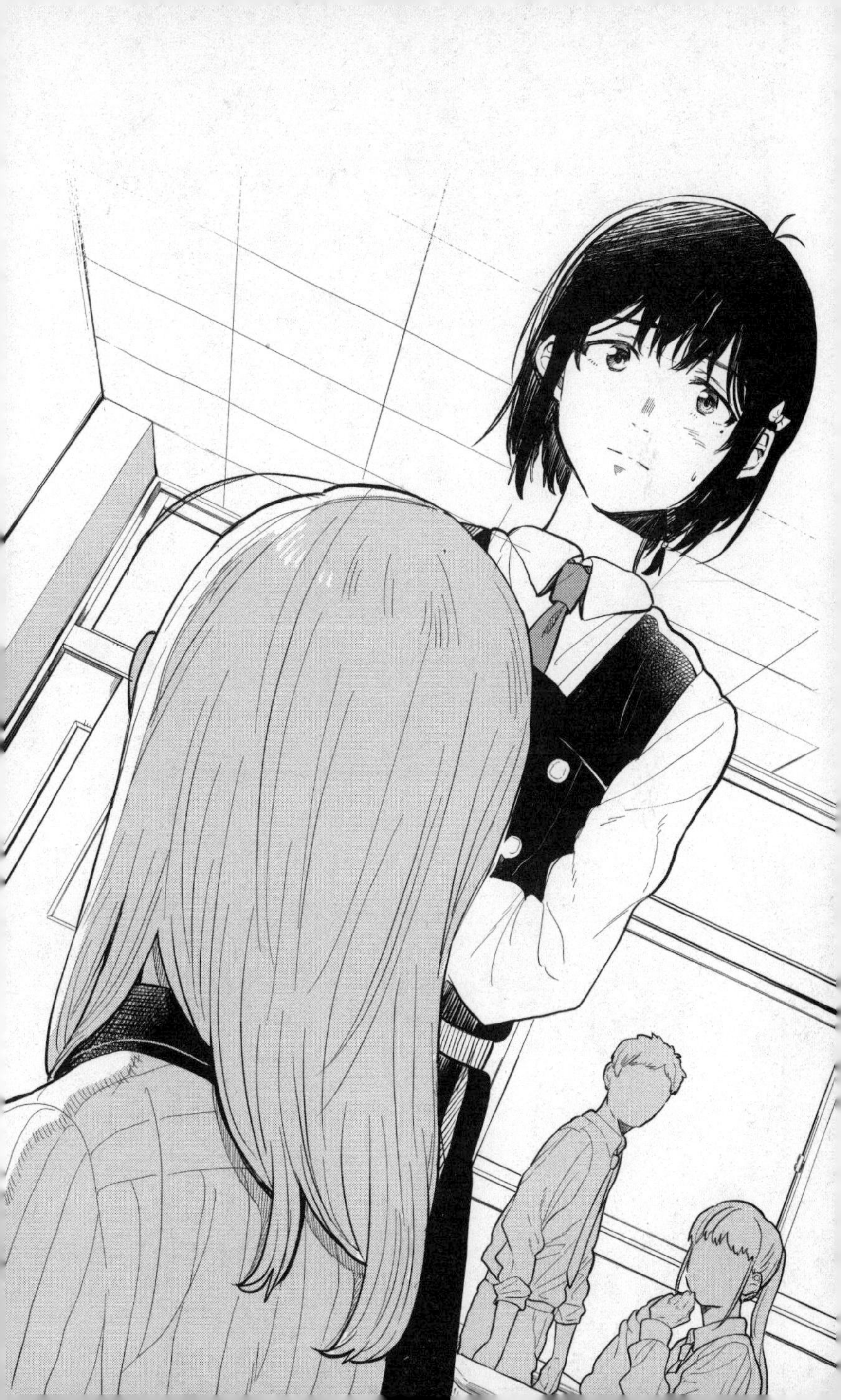

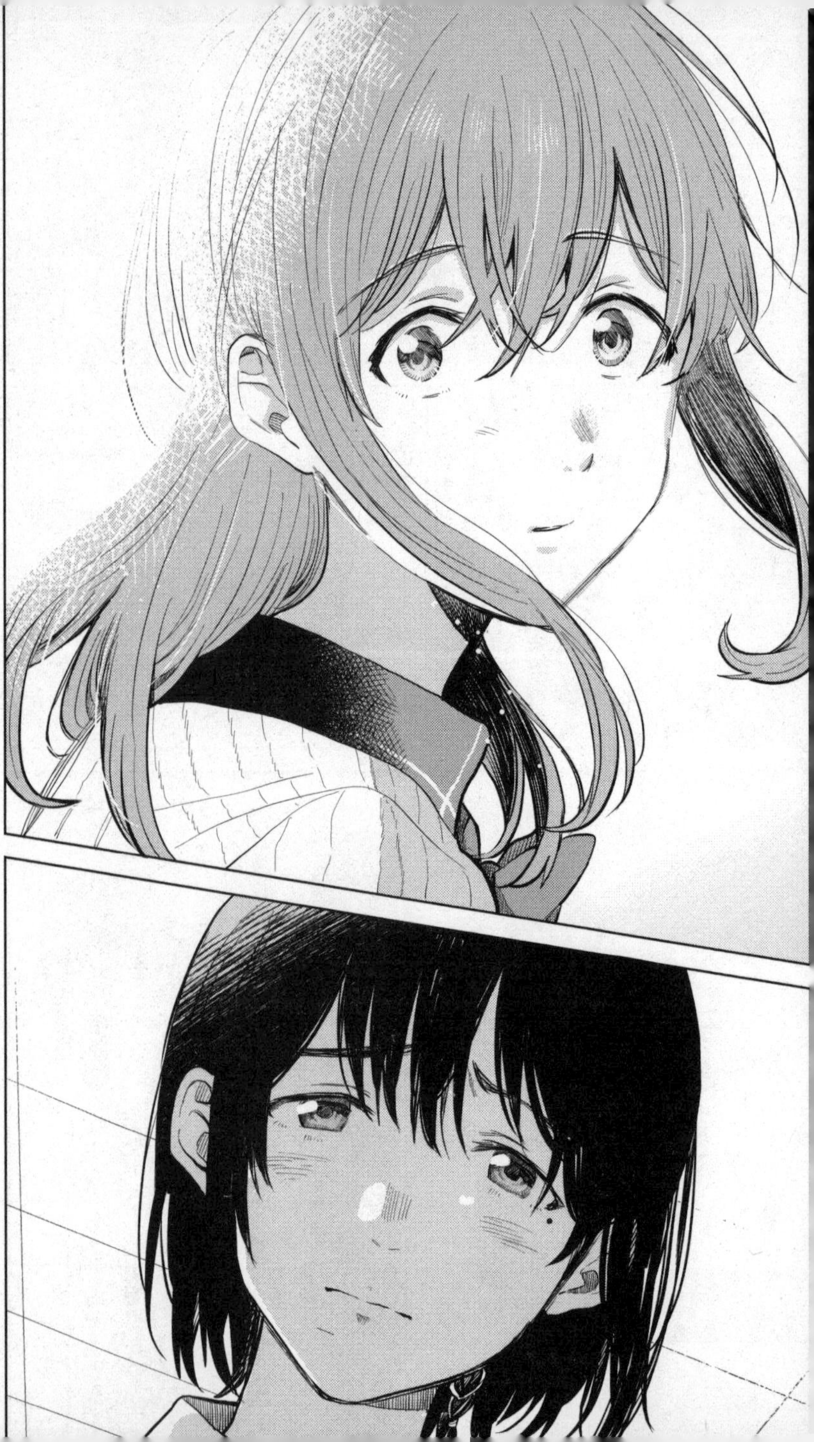

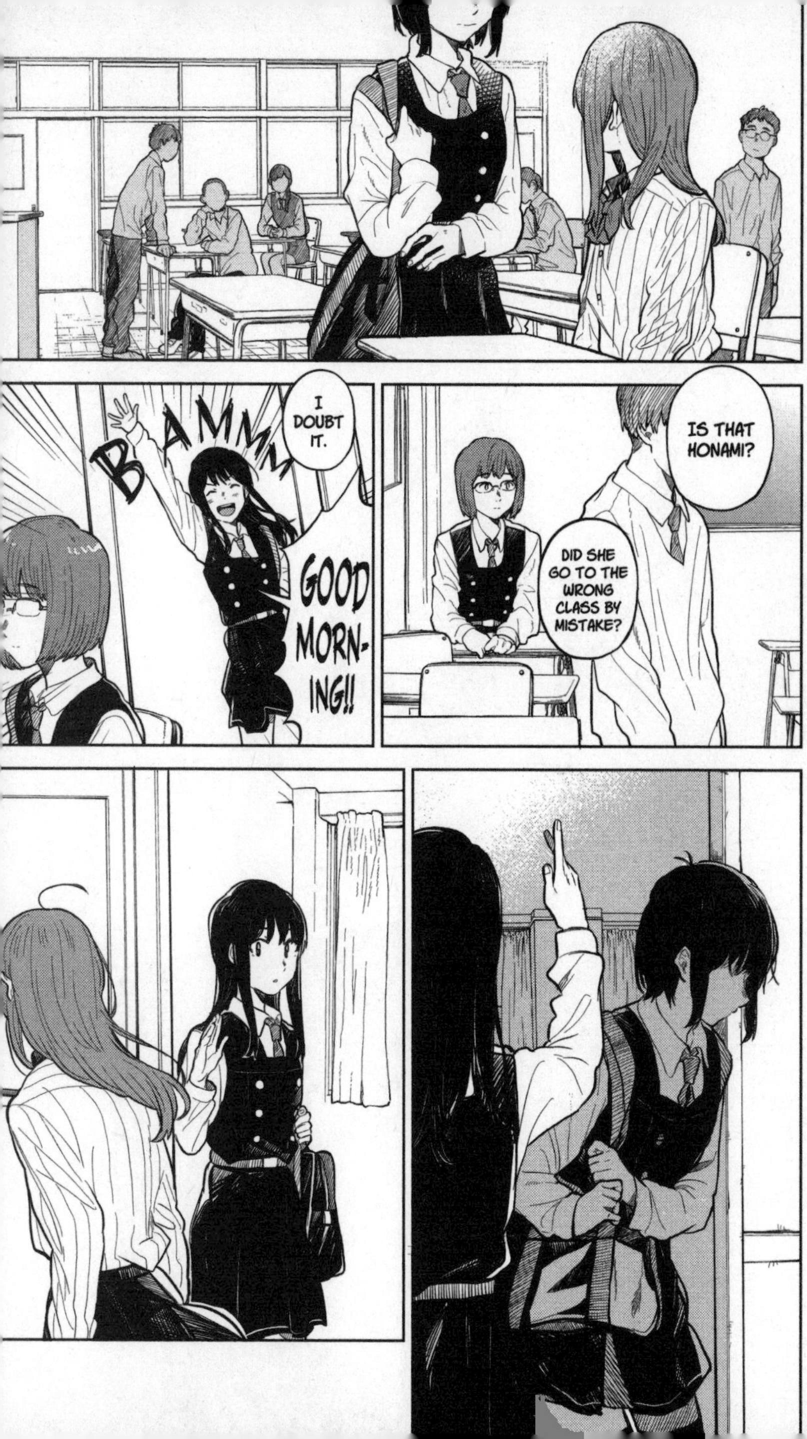
IS THAT HONAMI?
DID SHE GO TO THE WRONG CLASS BY MISTAKE?
I DOUBT IT.
BAMMM
GOOD MORN-ING!!

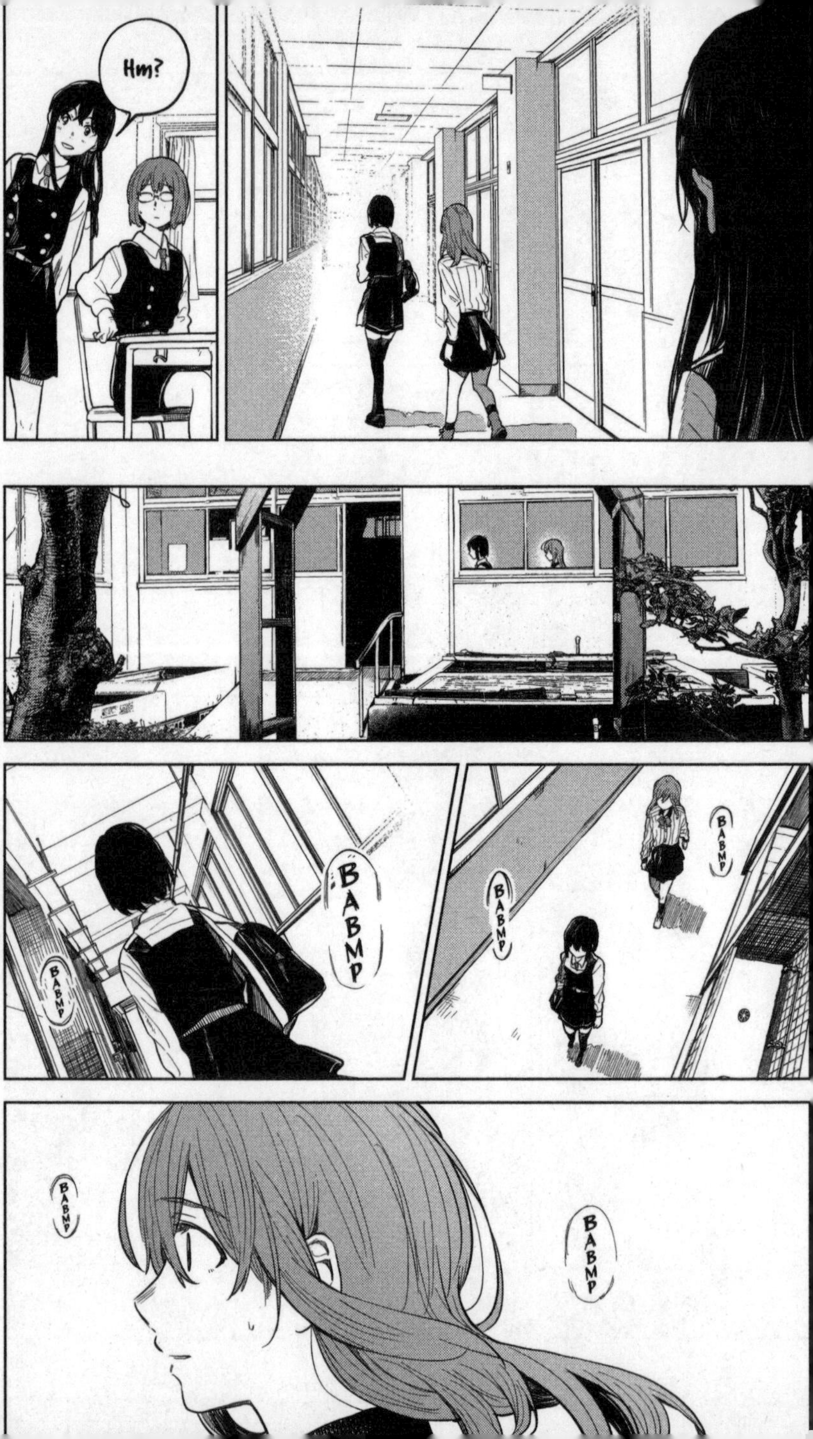
Hm?
BABMP
BABMP
BABMP
BABMP
BABMP
BABMP

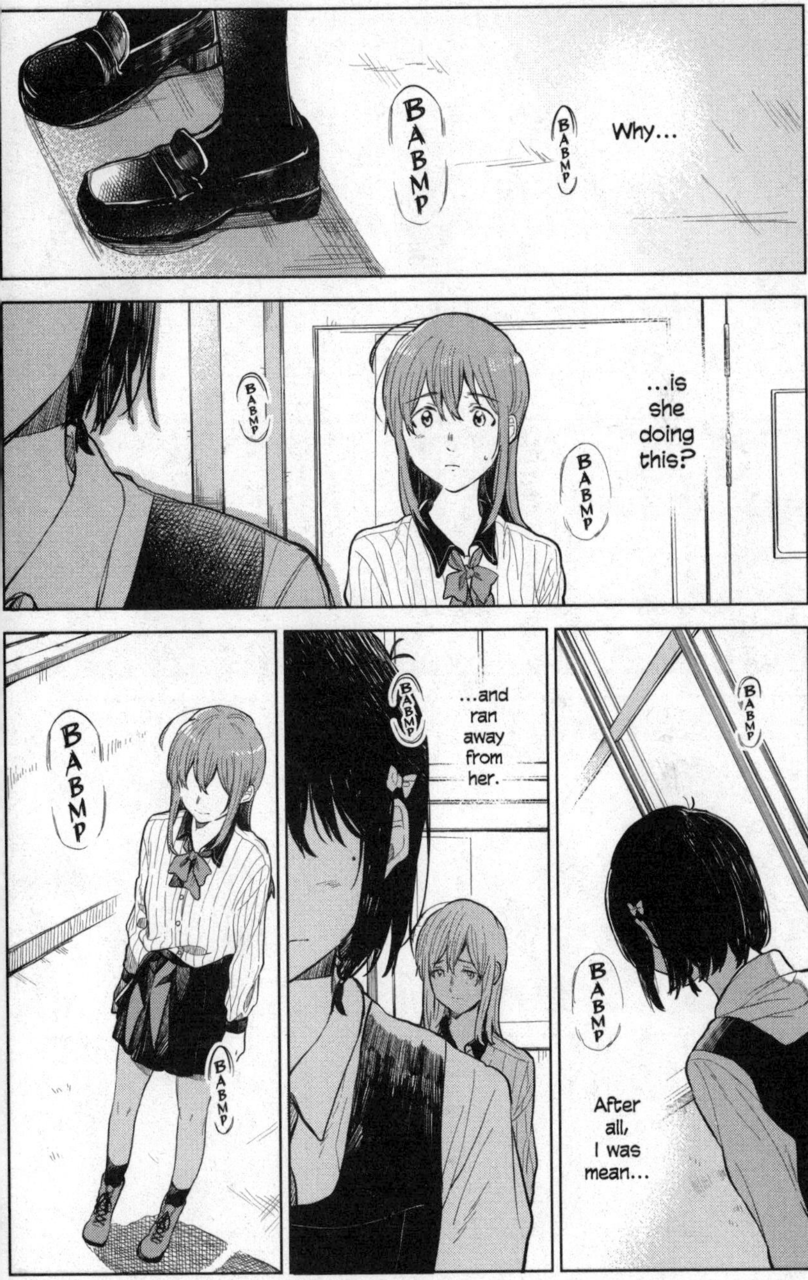
Why...
BABMP
BABMP
...is she doing this?
BABMP
BABMP
BABMP
After all, I was mean...
BABMP
...and ran away from her.
BABMP
BABMP
BABMP

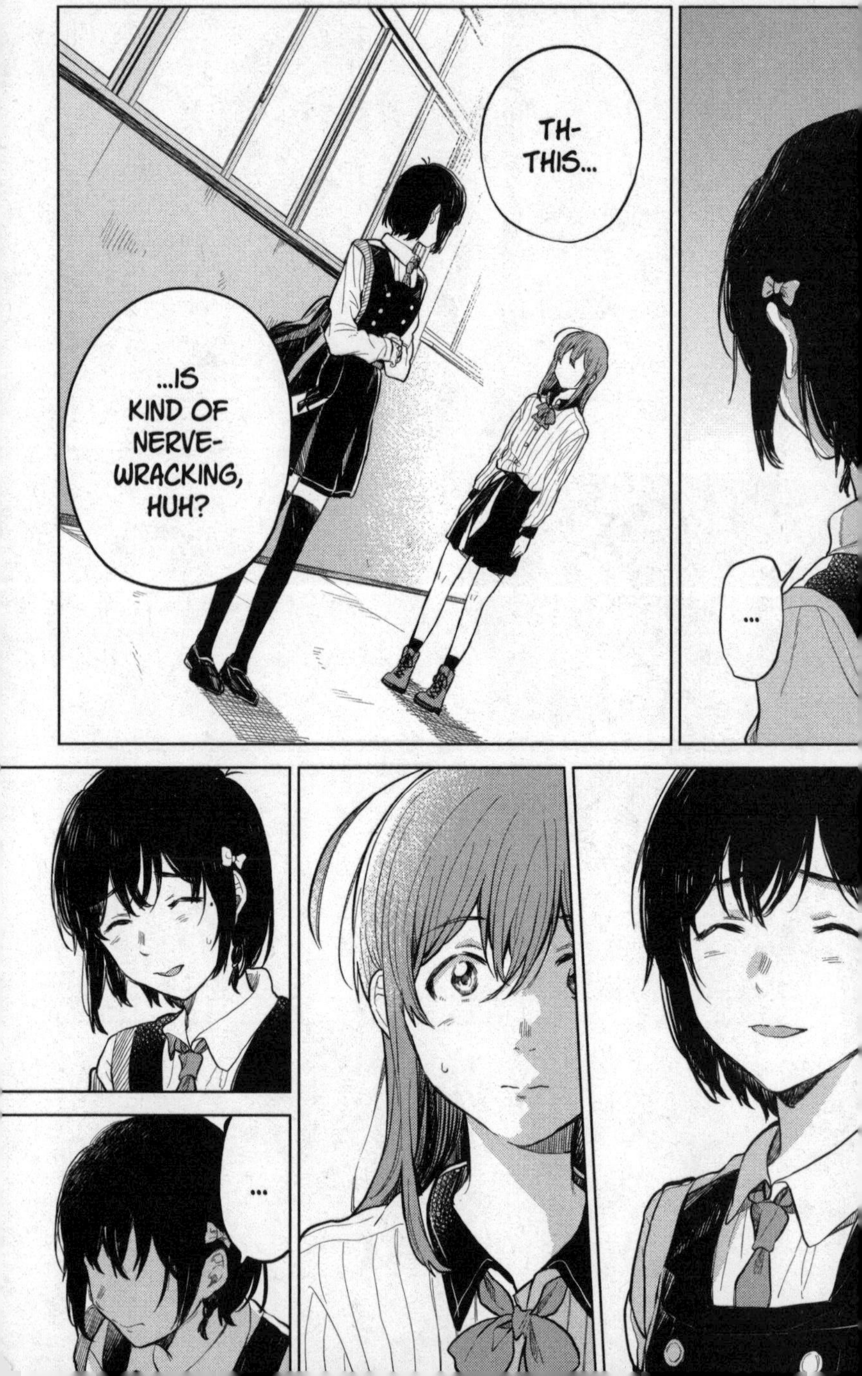
...
TH- THIS...
...IS KIND OF NERVE-WRACKING, HUH?
...

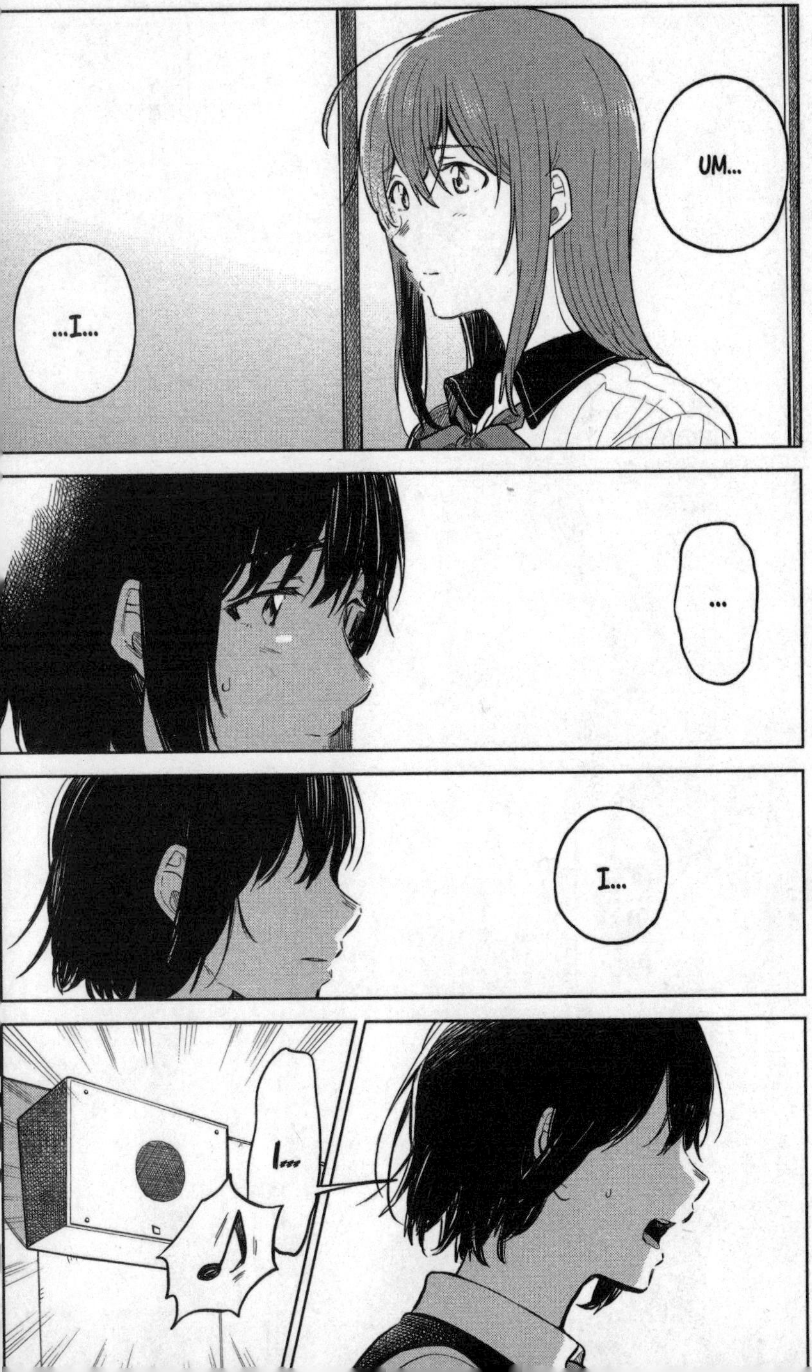
UM...
...I...
...
I...
I...

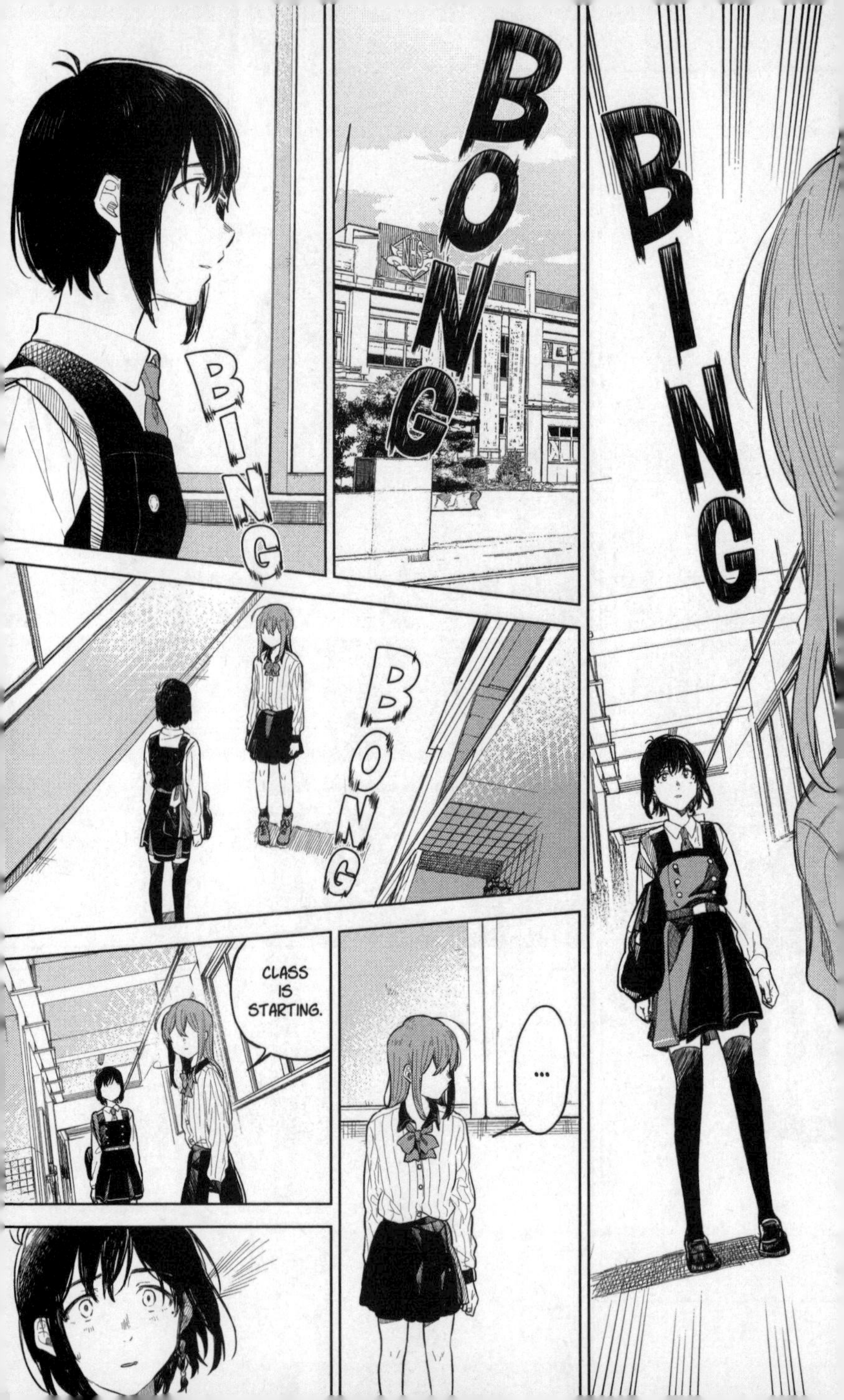
BING
BONG
BING
BONG
...
CLASS IS STARTING.

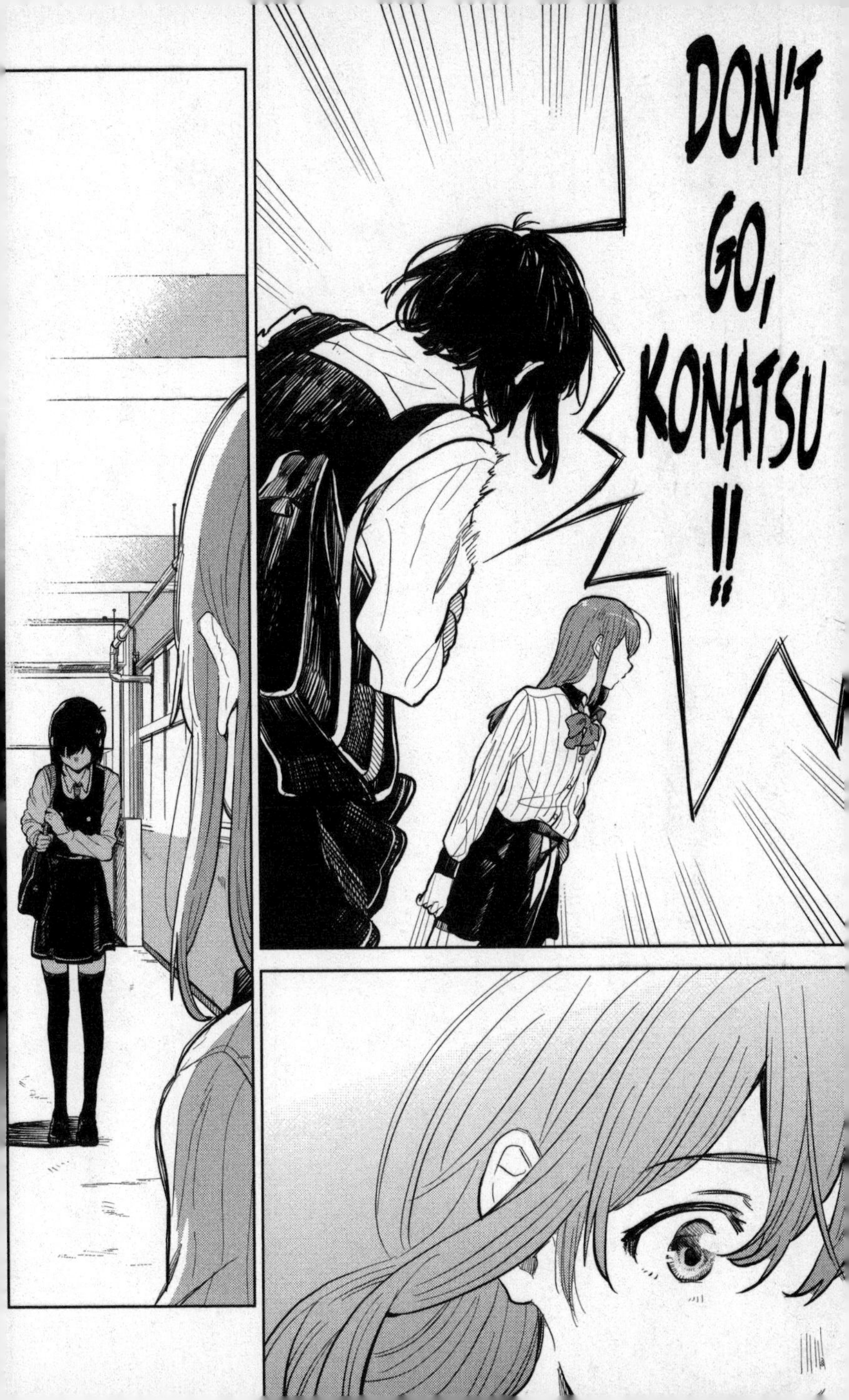
DON'T GO, KONATSU!!

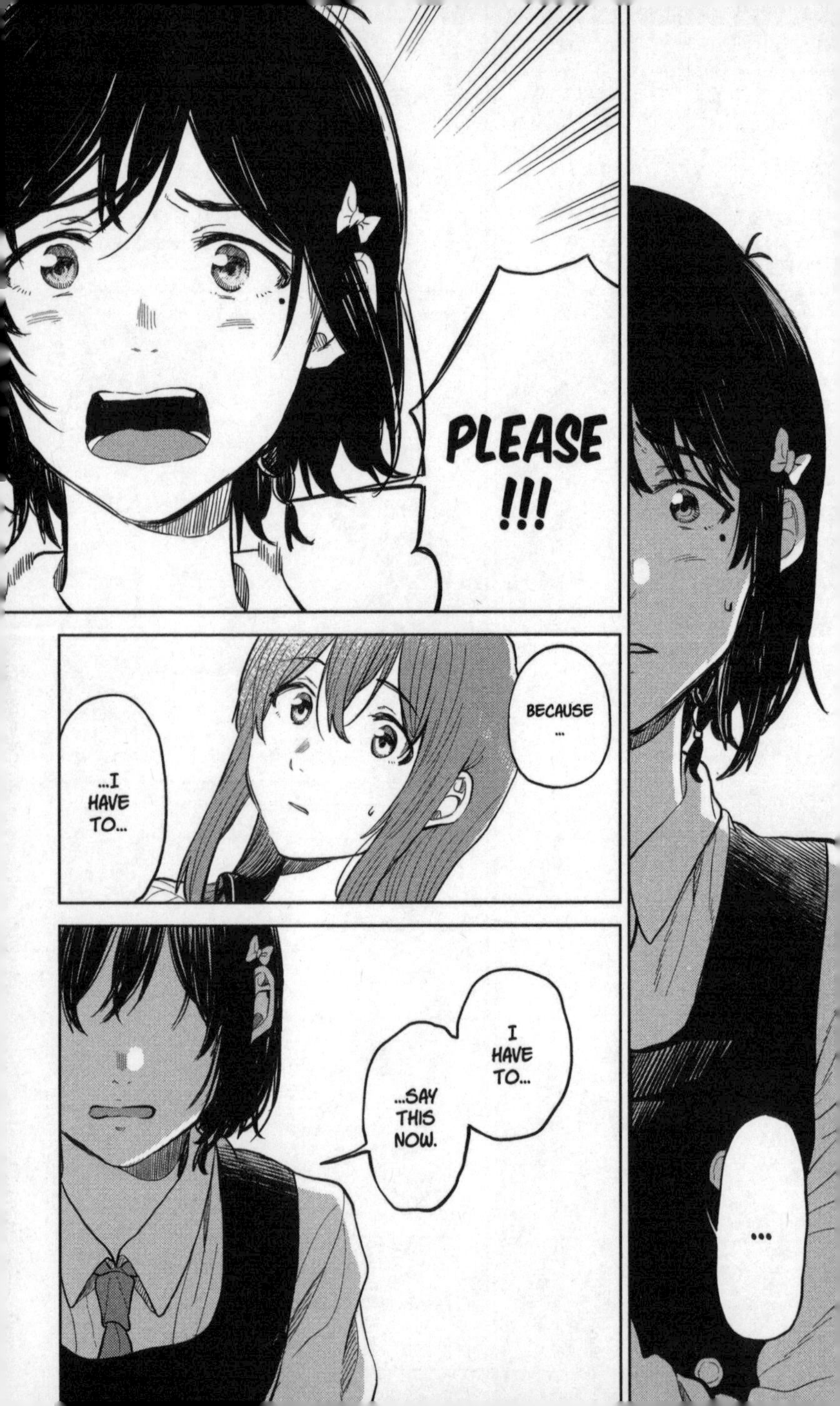
...
PLEASE !!!
BECAUSE ...
...I HAVE TO...
I HAVE TO...
...SAY THIS NOW.

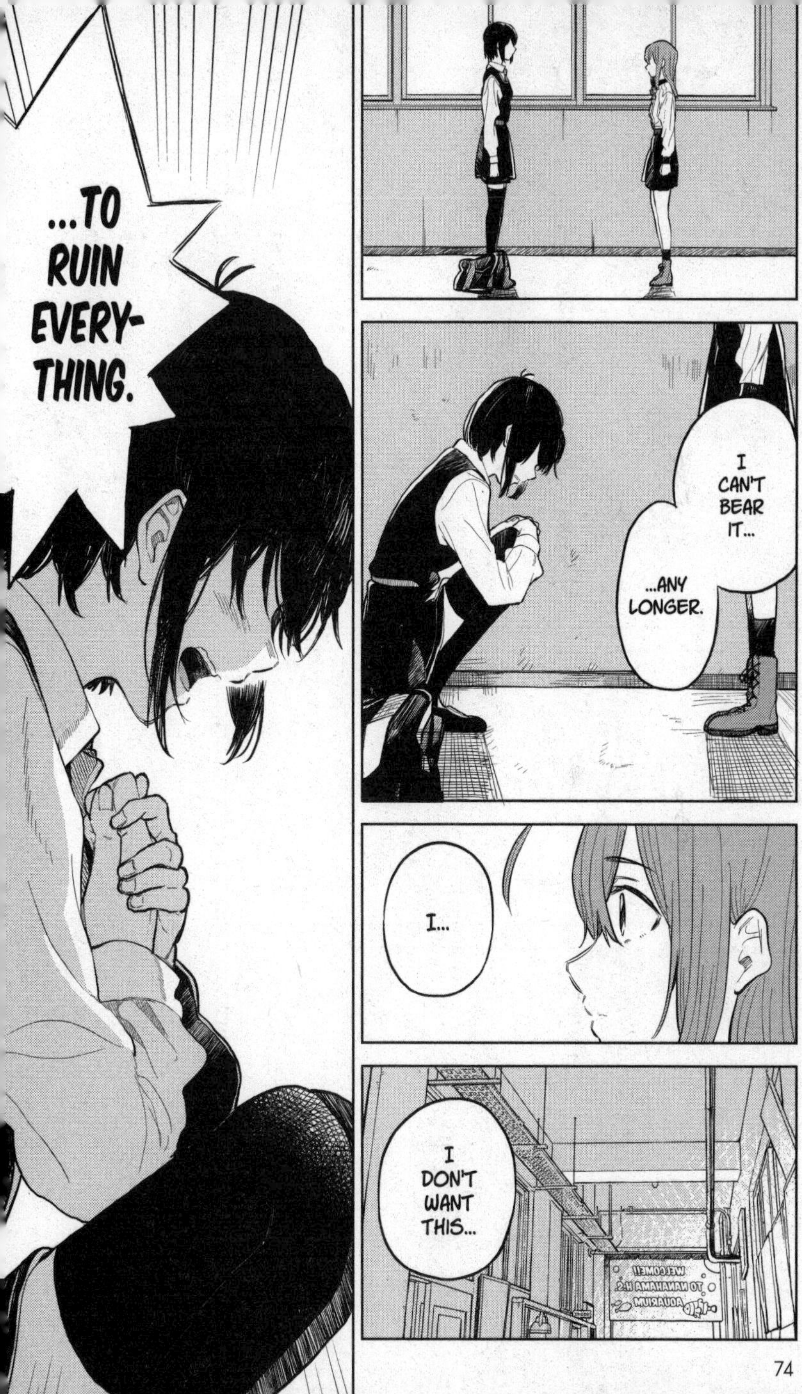
I CAN'T BEAR IT...
...ANY LONGER.
I...
I DON'T WANT THIS...
WELCOME!! TO NANAHAMA H.S. AQUARIUM
...TO RUIN EVERYTHING.

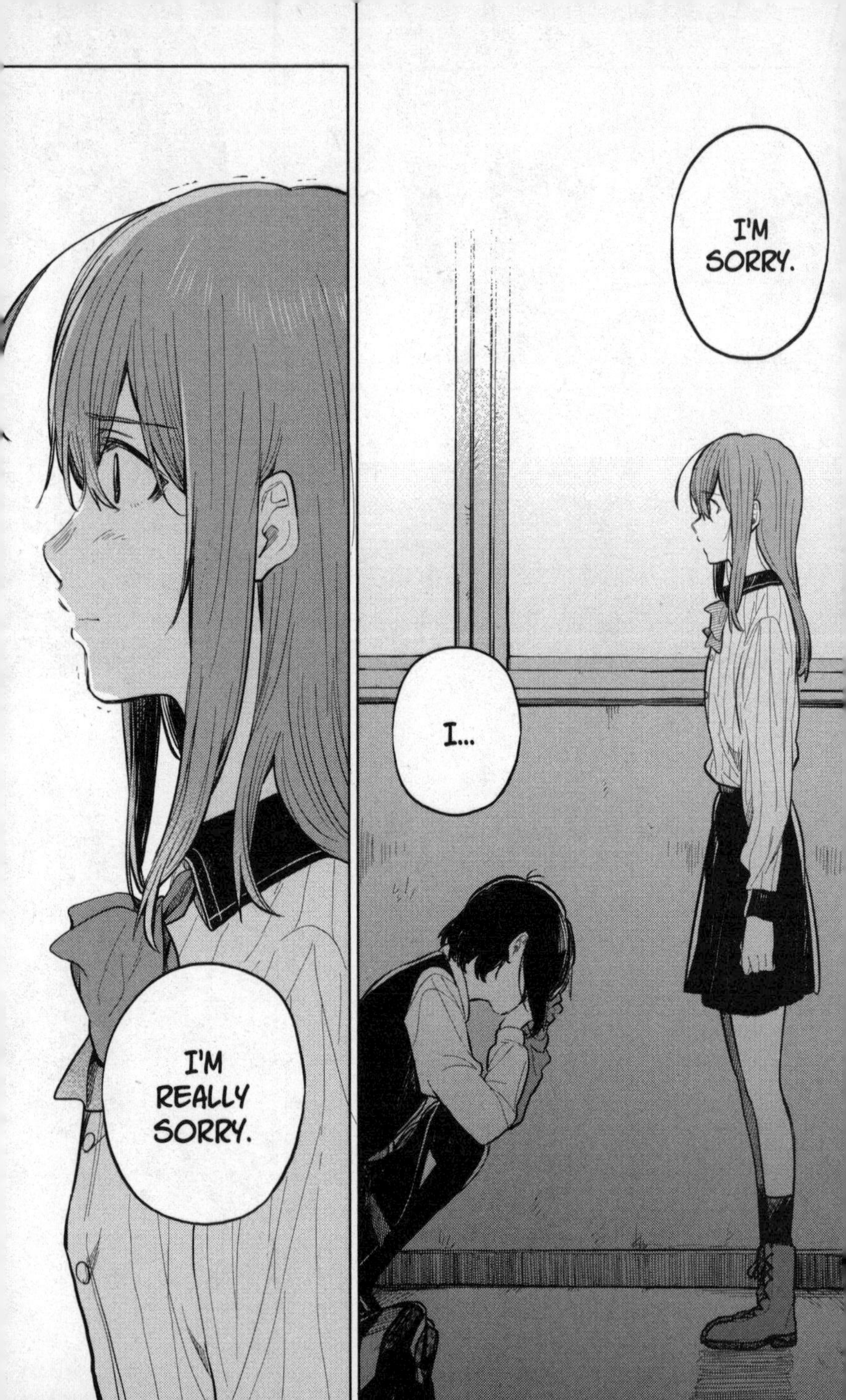
I'M SORRY.
I...
I'M REALLY SORRY.

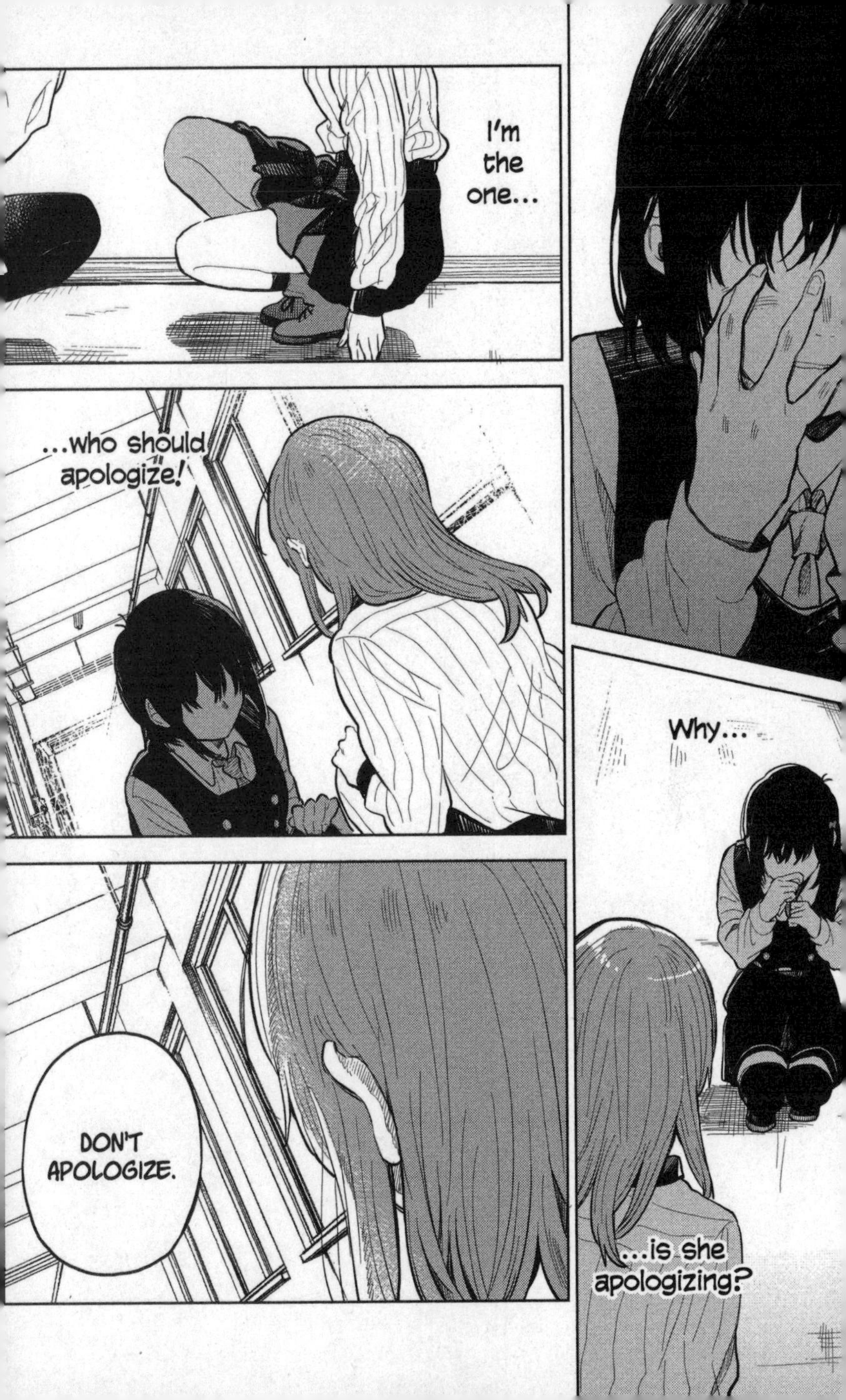
Why...
...is she apologizing?
I'm the one...
...who should apologize!
DON'T APOLOGIZE.

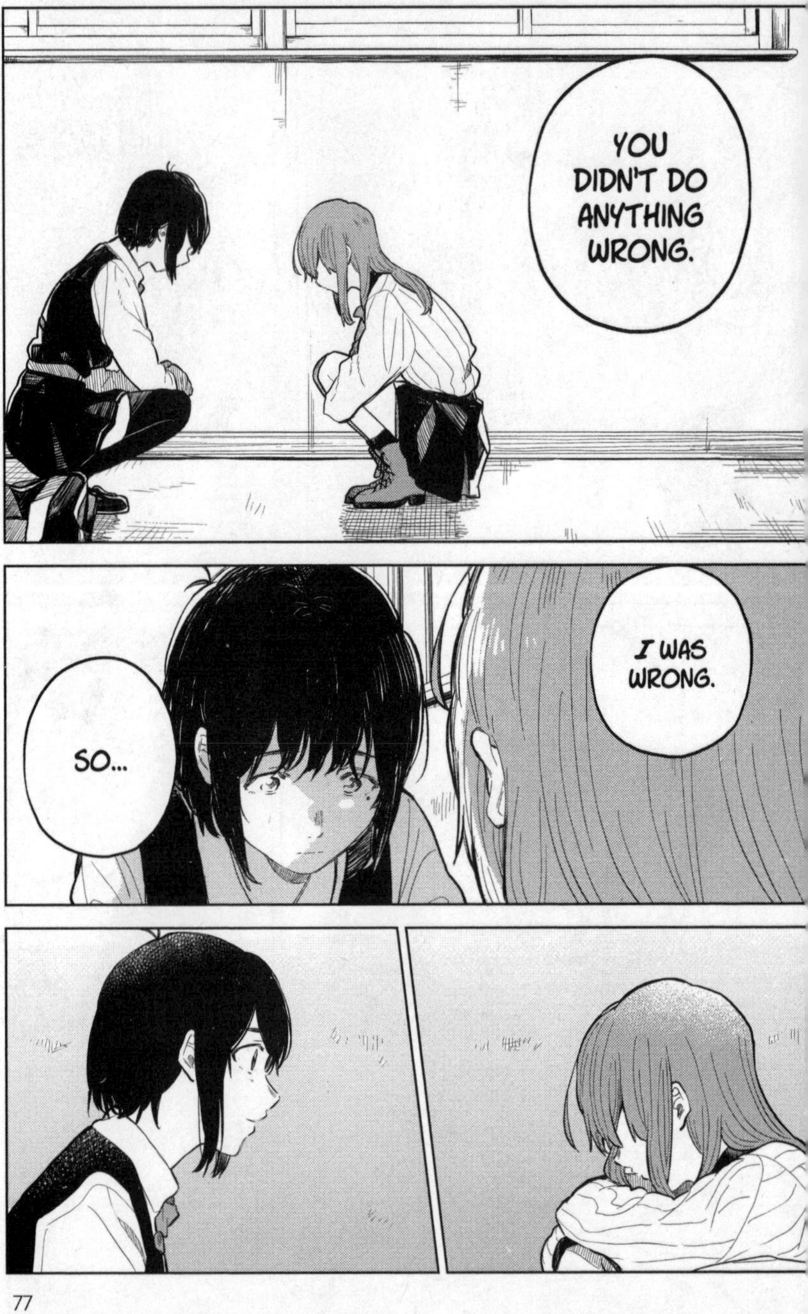
YOU DIDN'T DO ANYTHING WRONG.
I WAS WRONG.
SO...

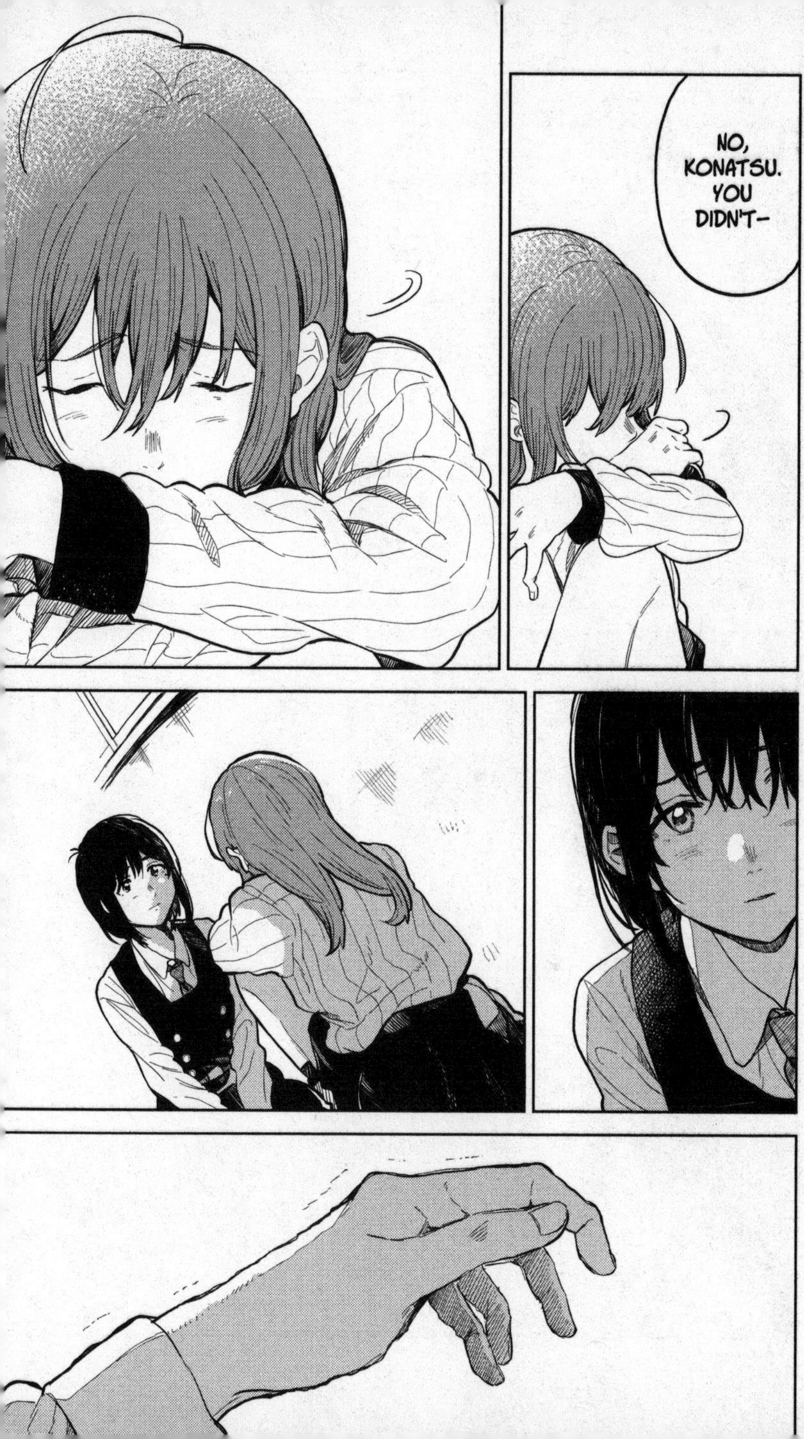
NO, KONATSU. YOU DIDN'T-

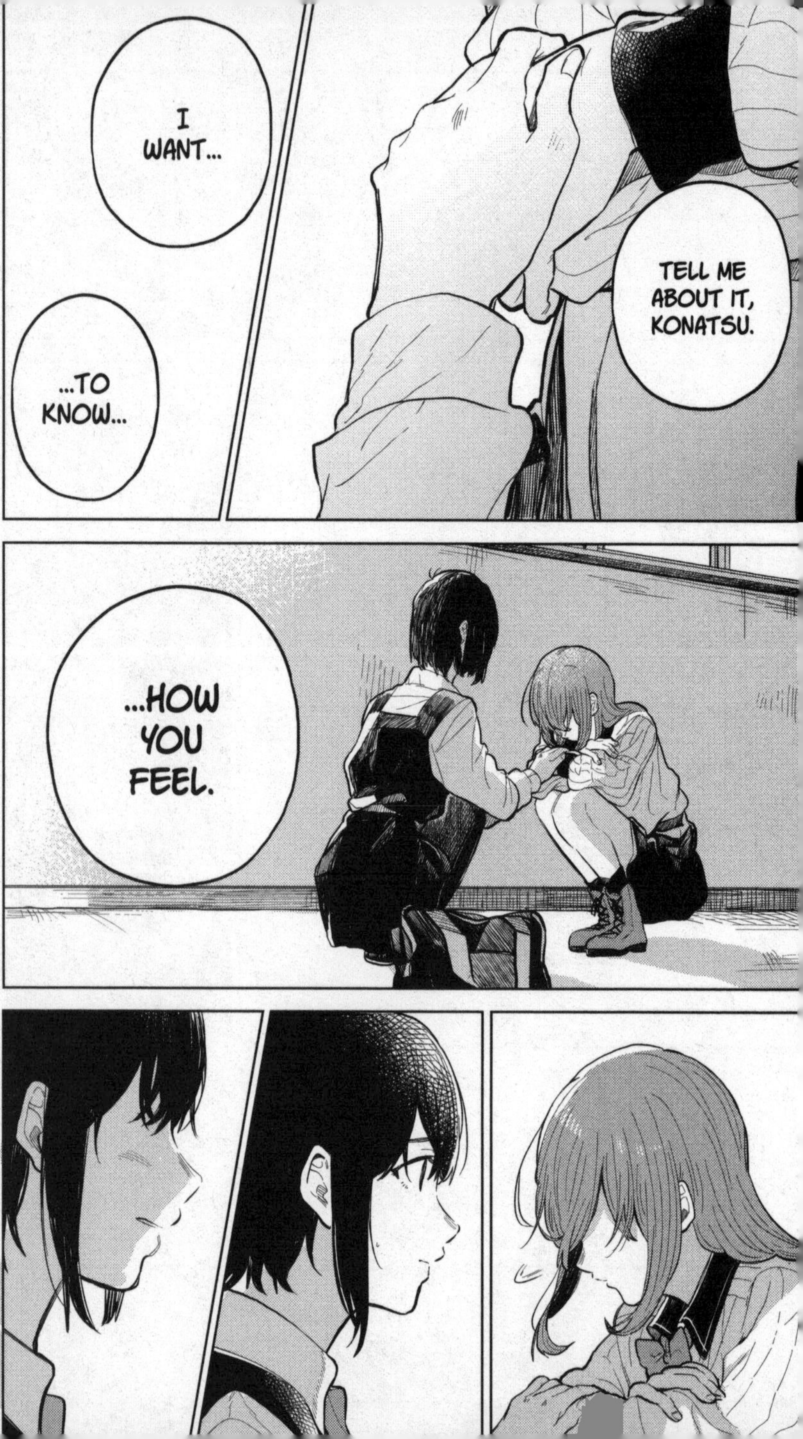
TELL ME ABOUT IT, KONATSU.
I WANT...
...TO KNOW...
...HOW YOU FEEL.

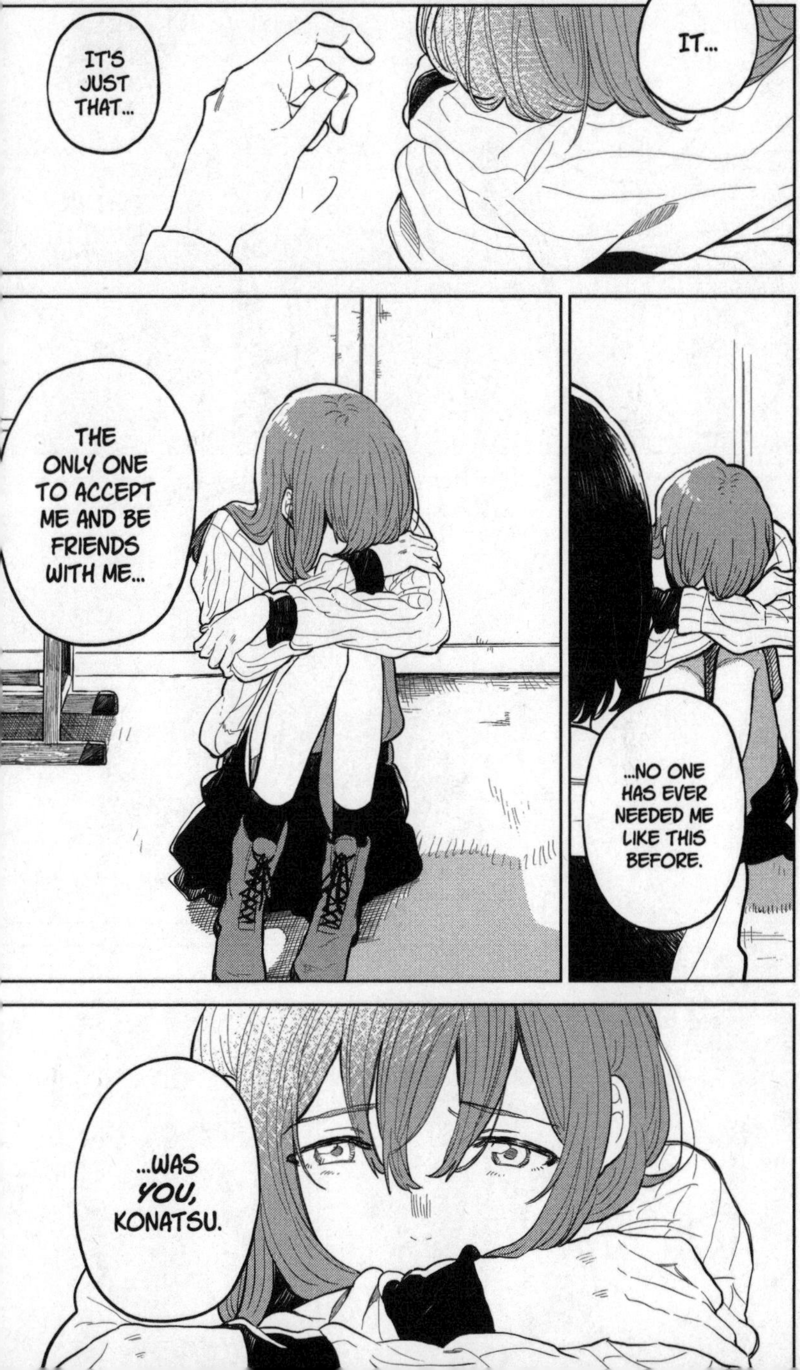
IT...
IT'S JUST THAT...
...NO ONE HAS EVER NEEDED ME LIKE THIS BEFORE.
THE ONLY ONE TO ACCEPT ME AND BE FRIENDS WITH ME...
...WAS *YOU*, KONATSU.

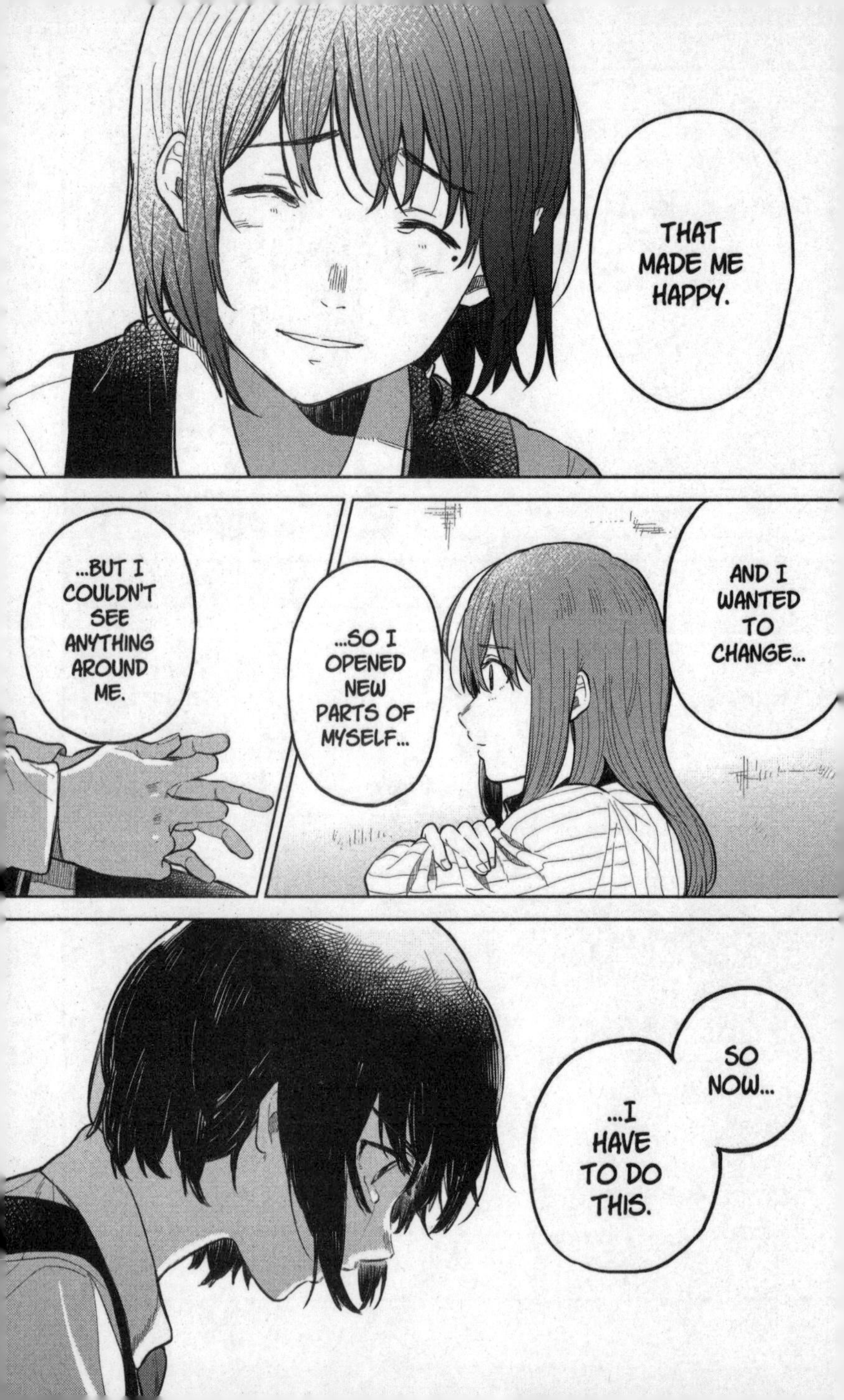
THAT MADE ME HAPPY.
AND I WANTED TO CHANGE...
...SO I OPENED NEW PARTS OF MYSELF...
...BUT I COULDN'T SEE ANYTHING AROUND ME.
SO NOW...
...I HAVE TO DO THIS.

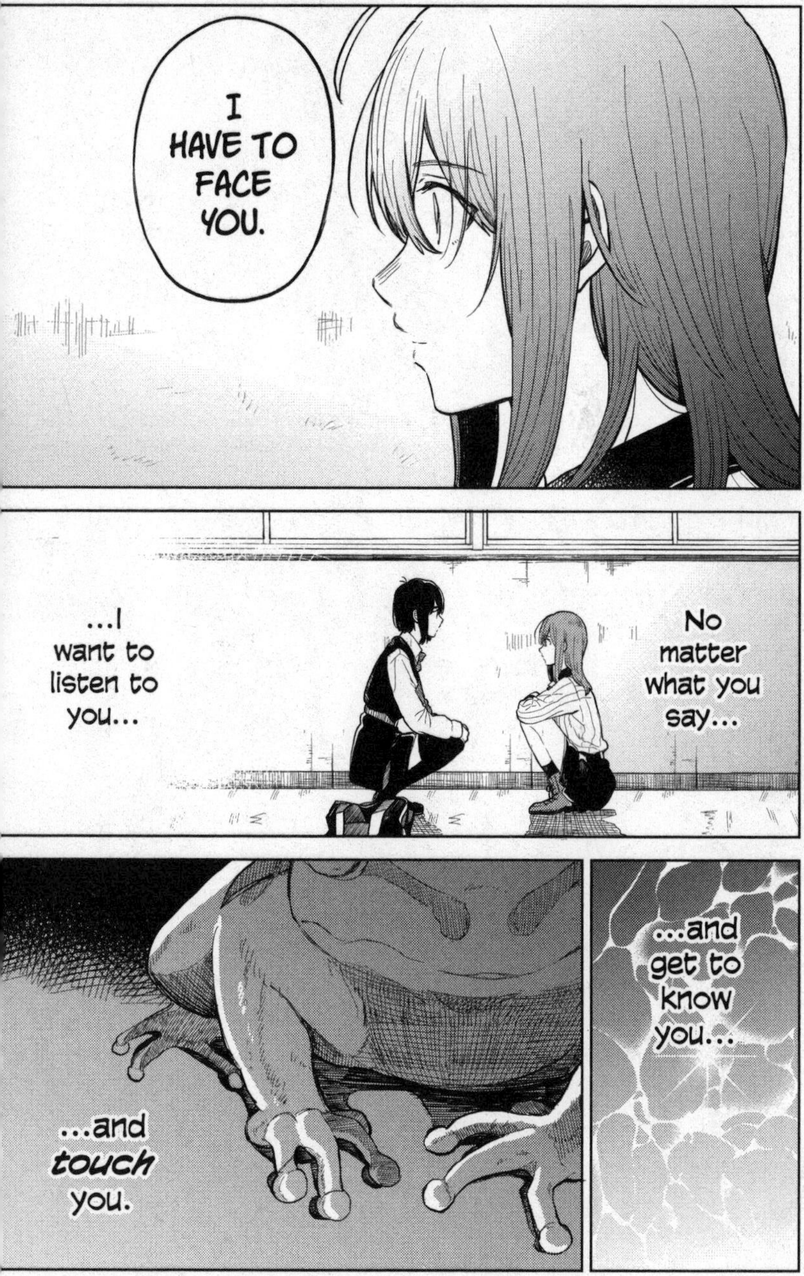
I HAVE TO FACE YOU.
No matter what you say...
...I want to listen to you...
...and get to know you...
...and *touch* you.

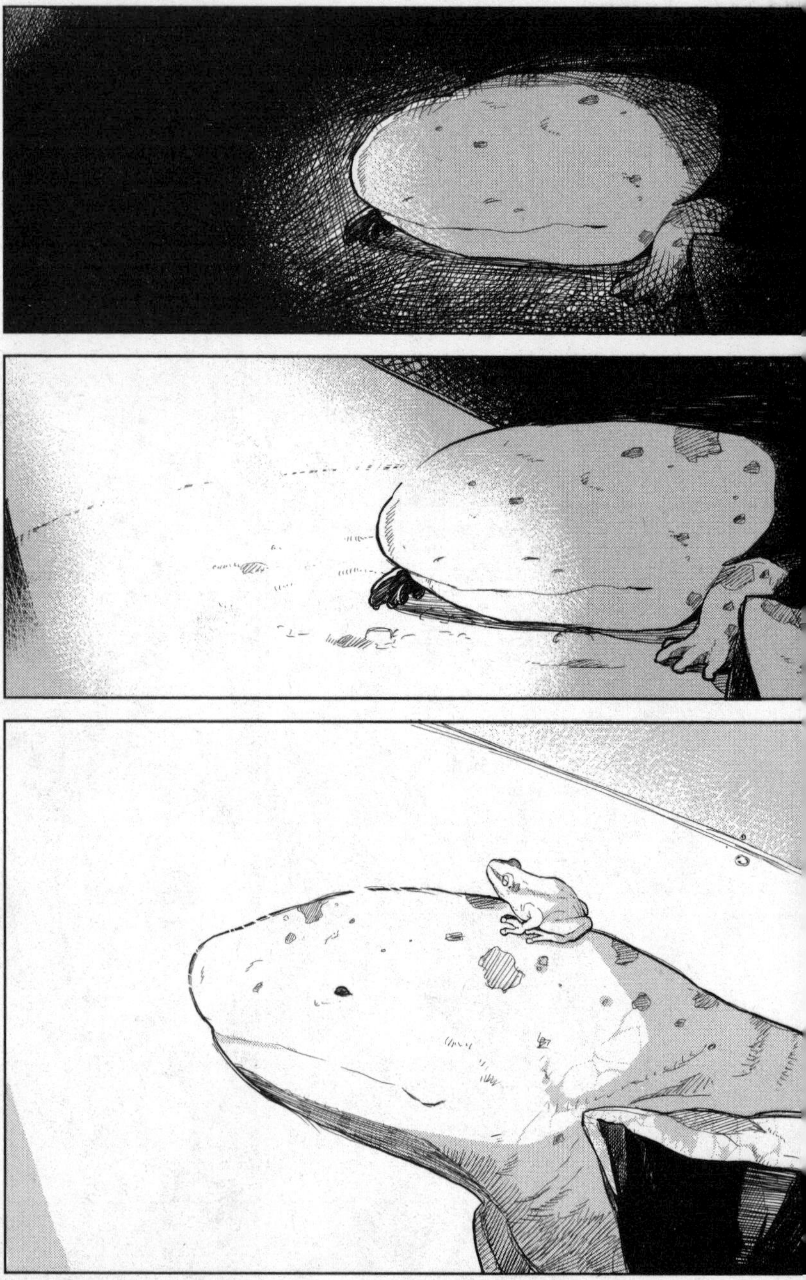

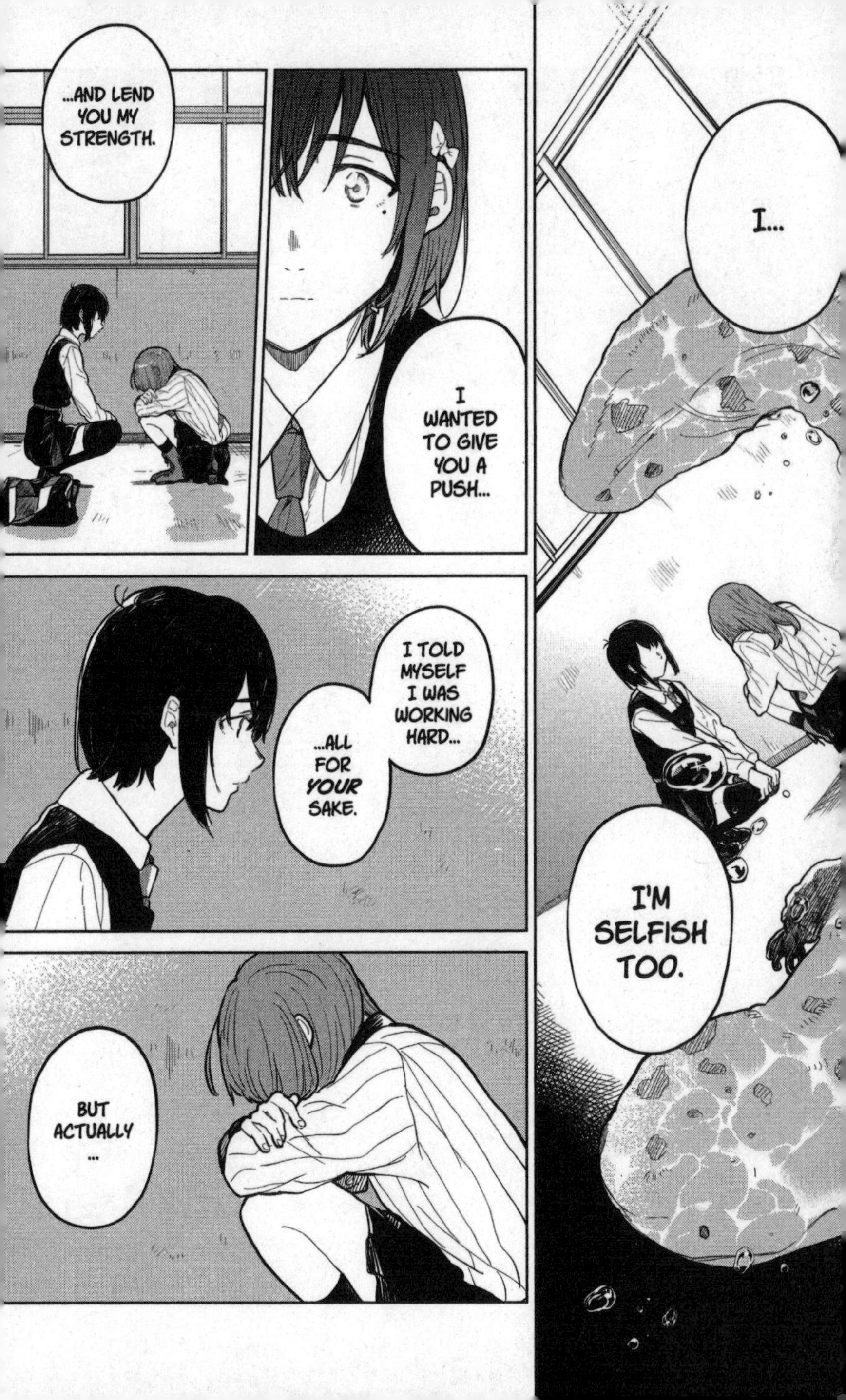
I WANTED TO GIVE YOU A PUSH...
...AND LEND YOU MY STRENGTH.
I TOLD MYSELF I WAS WORKING HARD...
...ALL FOR *YOUR* SAKE.
BUT ACTUALLY ...
I...
I'M SELFISH TOO.

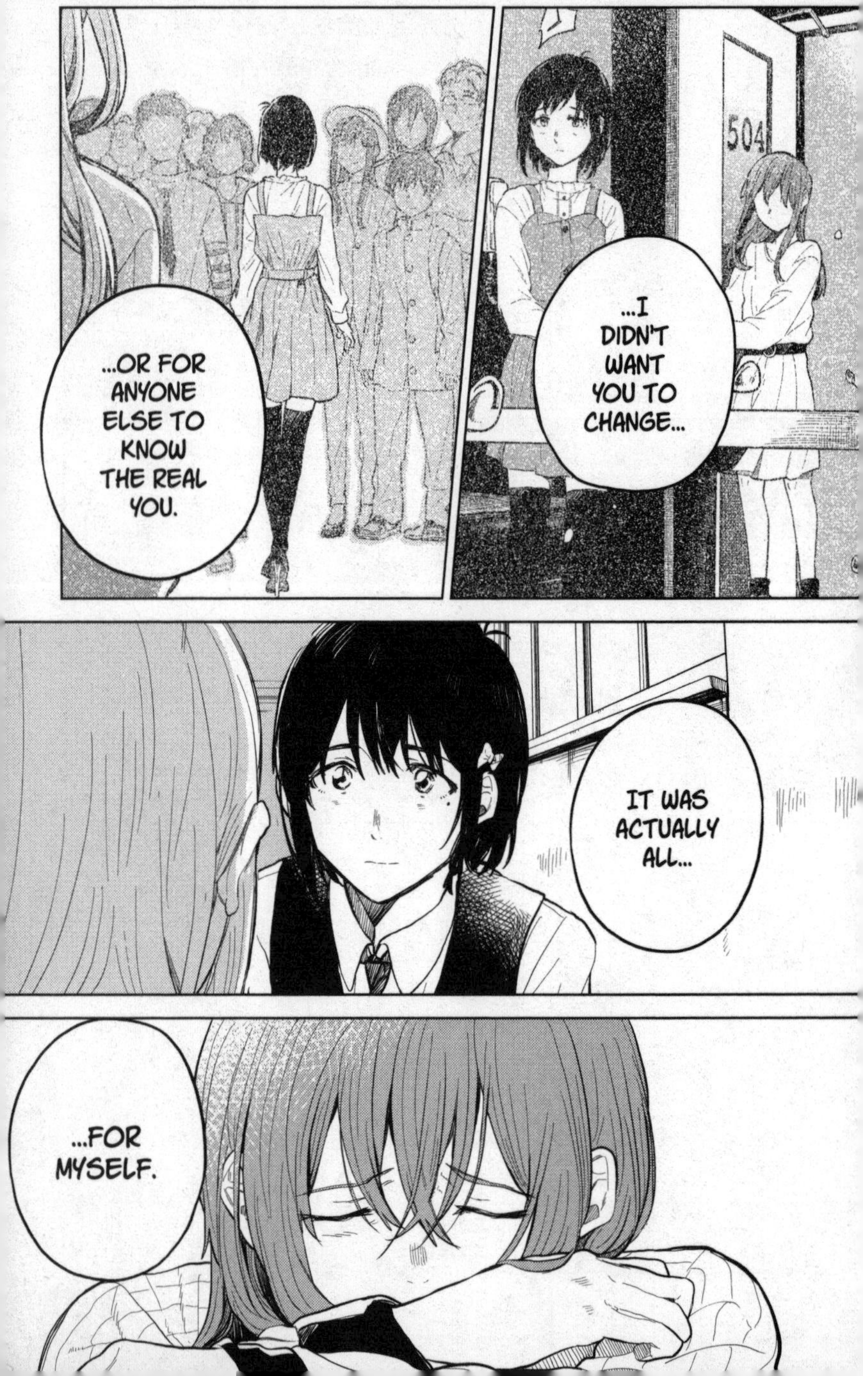
...I DIDN'T WANT YOU TO CHANGE...
...OR FOR ANYONE ELSE TO KNOW THE REAL YOU.
IT WAS ACTUALLY ALL...
...FOR MYSELF.

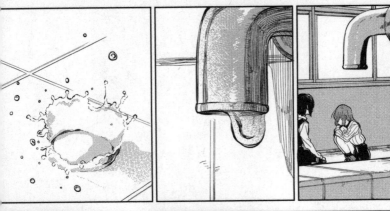

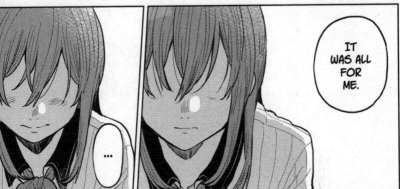

...

IT WAS ALL FOR ME.

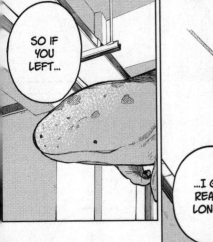

SO IF YOU LEFT...

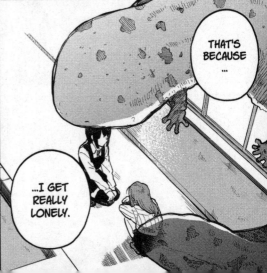

THAT'S BECAUSE ...

...I GET REALLY LONELY.

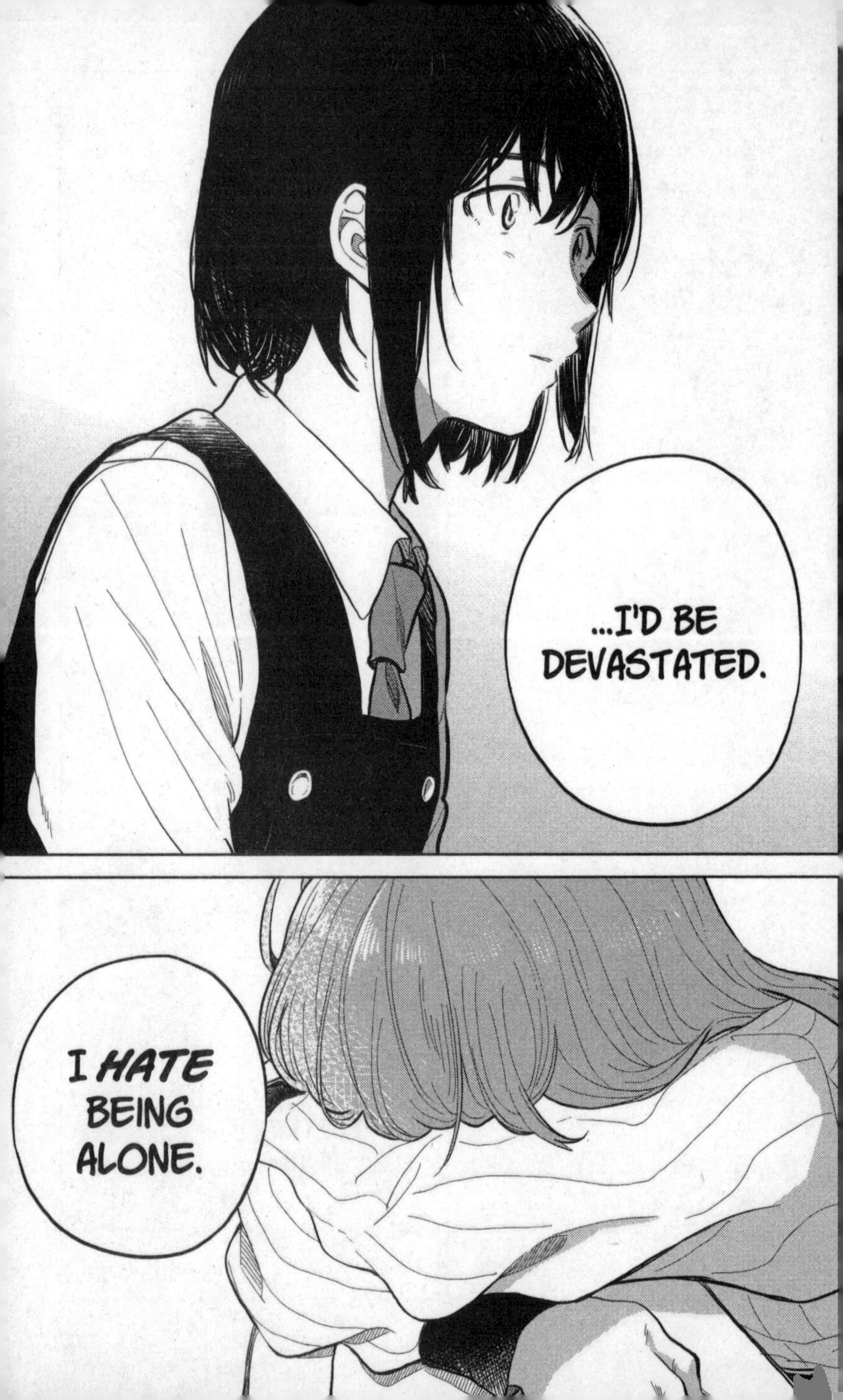
...I'D BE DEVASTATED.
I HATE BEING ALONE.

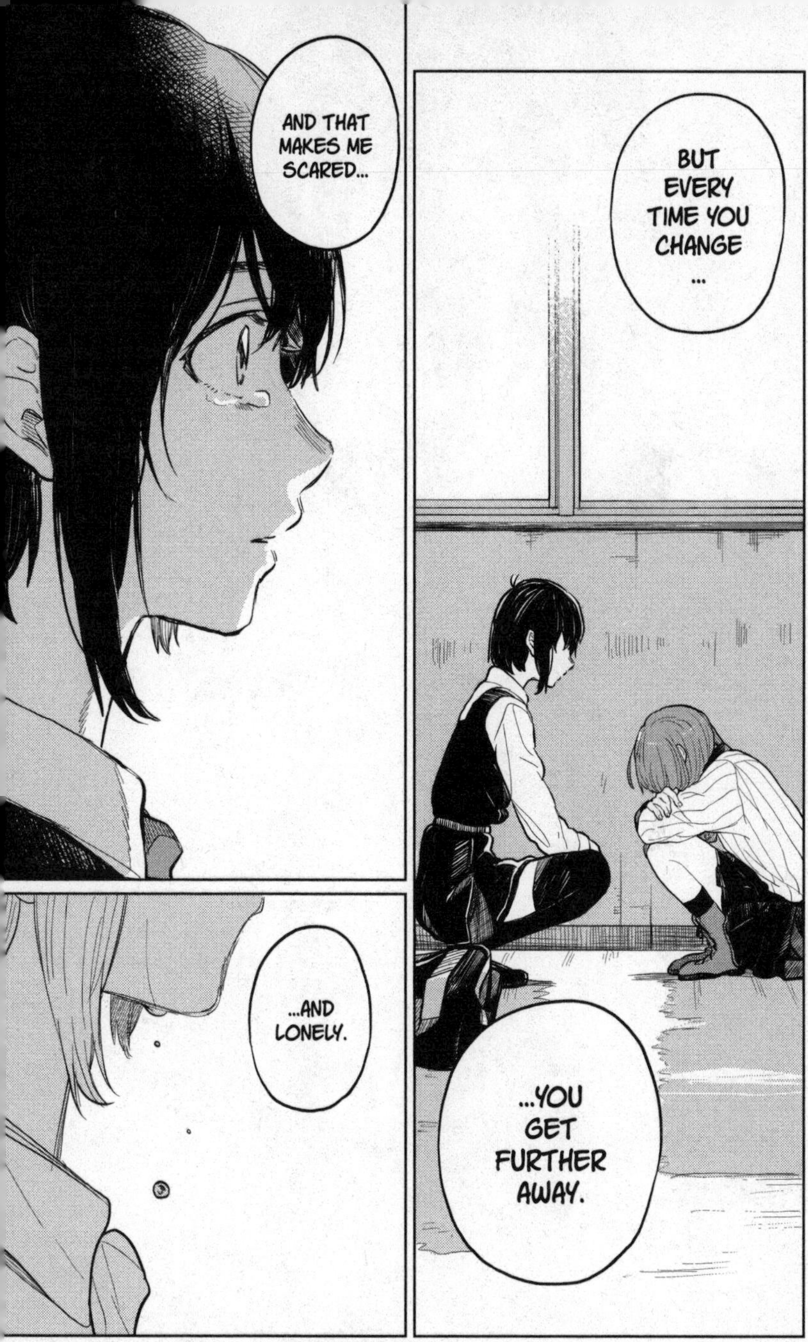
BUT EVERY TIME YOU CHANGE ...
...YOU GET FURTHER AWAY.
AND THAT MAKES ME SCARED...
...AND LONELY.

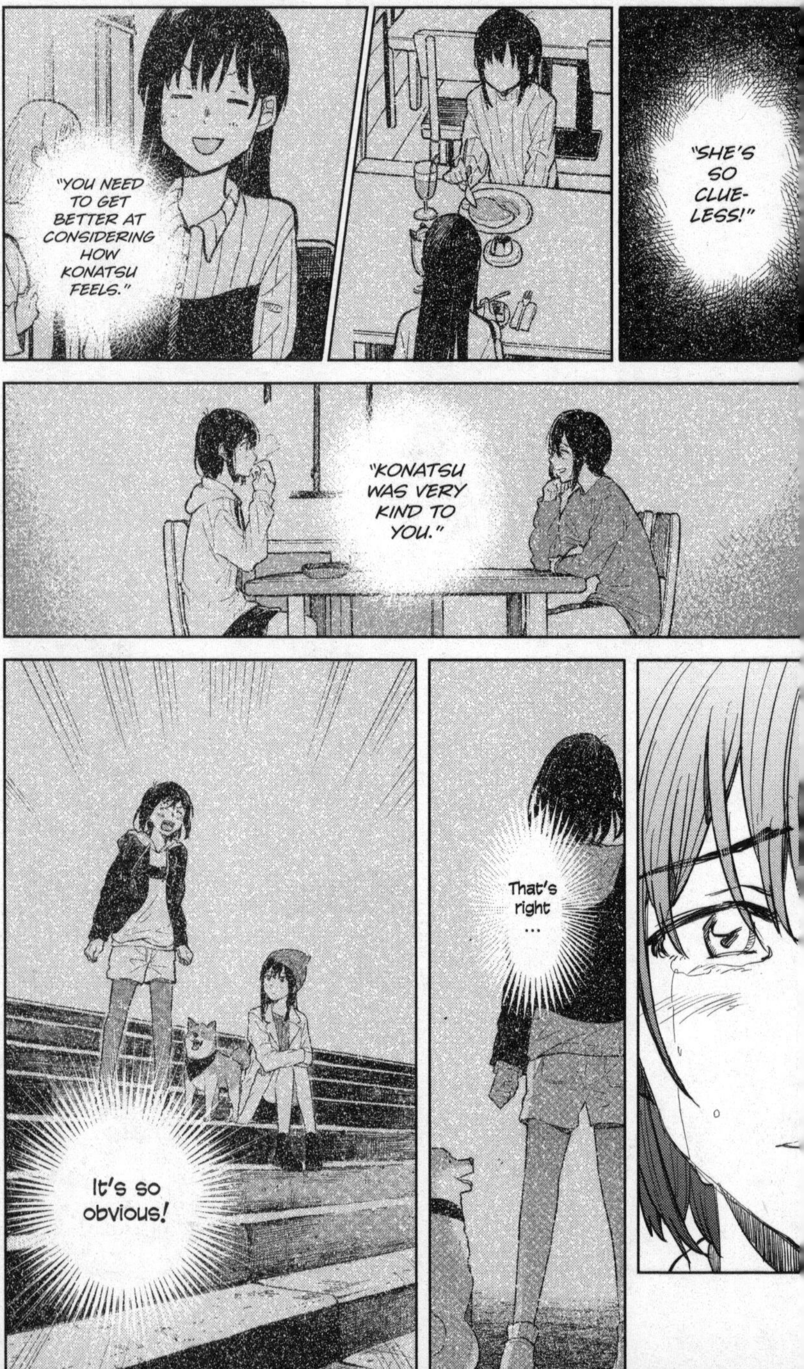
"SHE'S SO CLUE-LESS!"
"YOU NEED TO GET BETTER AT CONSIDERING HOW KONATSU FEELS."
"KONATSU WAS VERY KIND TO YOU."
That's right ...
It's so obvious!

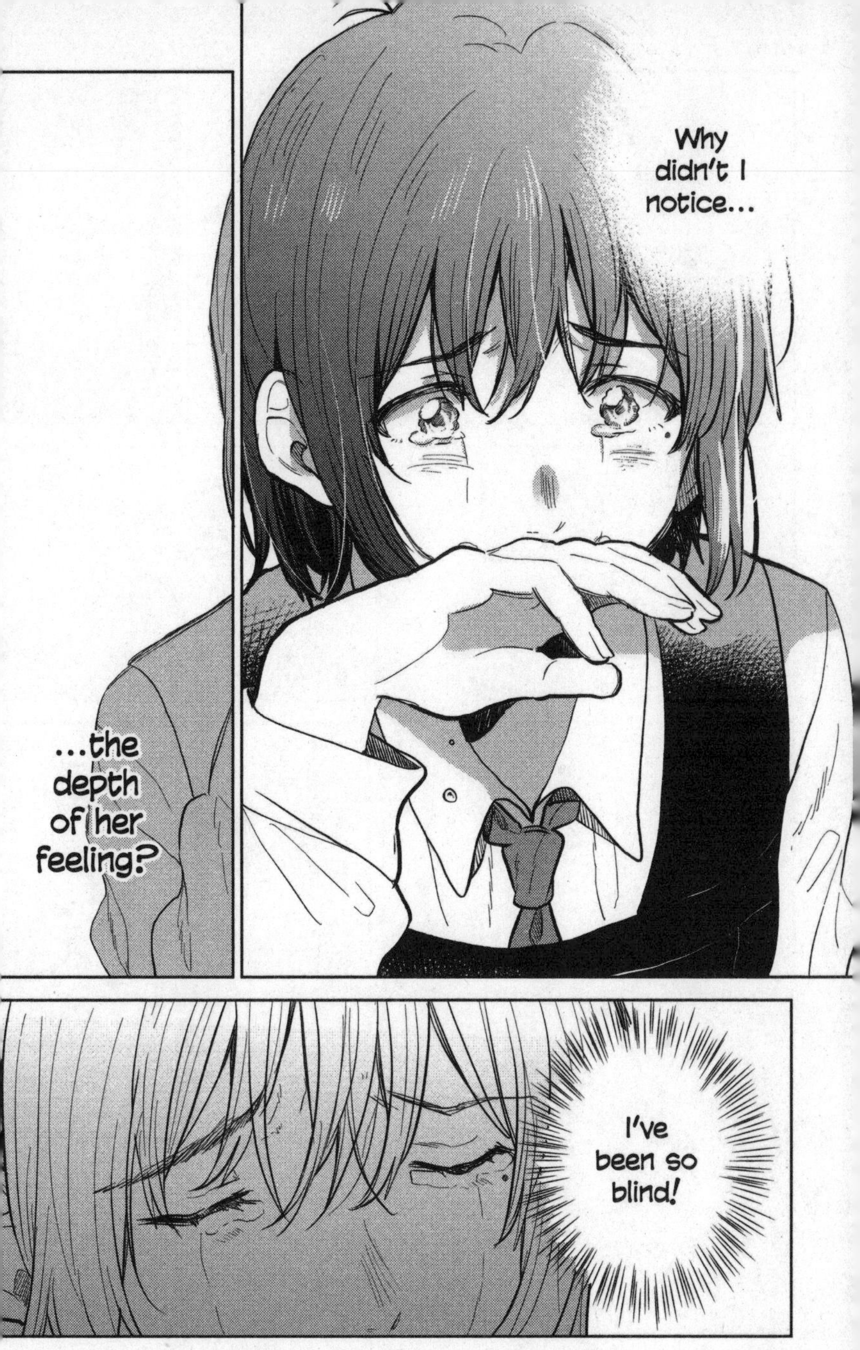
Why didn't I notice...
...the depth of her feeling?
I've been so blind!

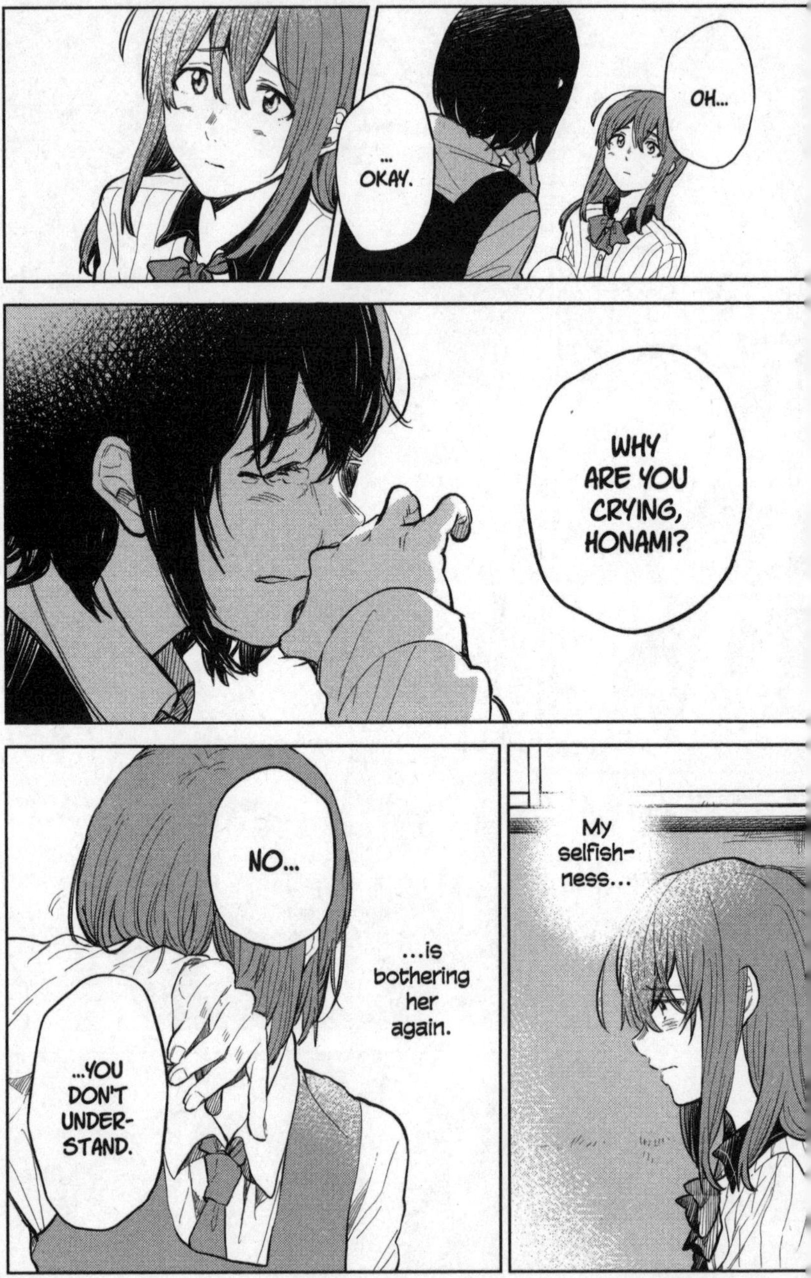
OH...
...OKAY.
WHY ARE YOU CRYING, HONAMI?
My selfish-ness...
NO...
...is bothering her again.
...YOU DON'T UNDER-STAND.

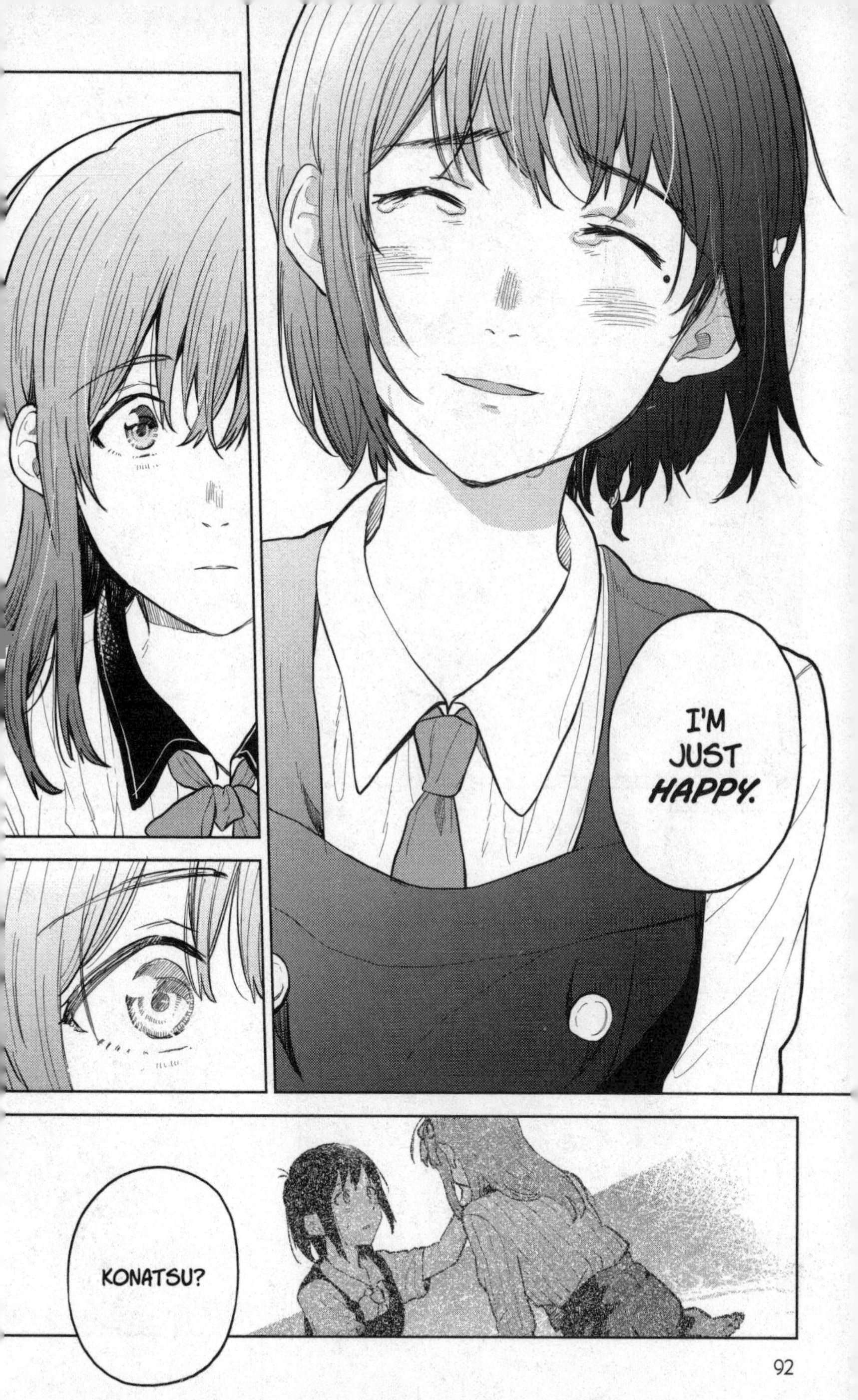
I'M JUST HAPPY.
KONATSU?

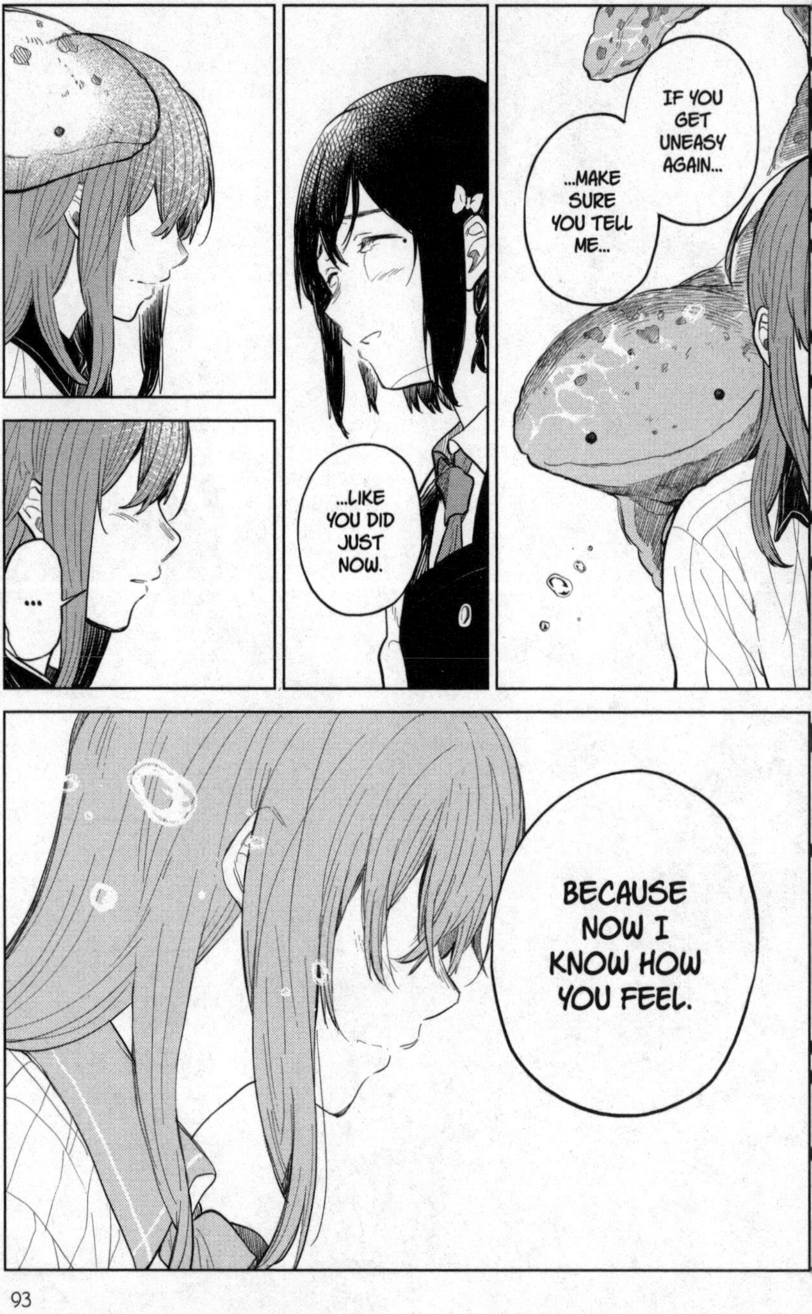
IF YOU GET UNEASY AGAIN...
...MAKE SURE YOU TELL ME...
...LIKE YOU DID JUST NOW.
...
BECAUSE NOW I KNOW HOW YOU FEEL.

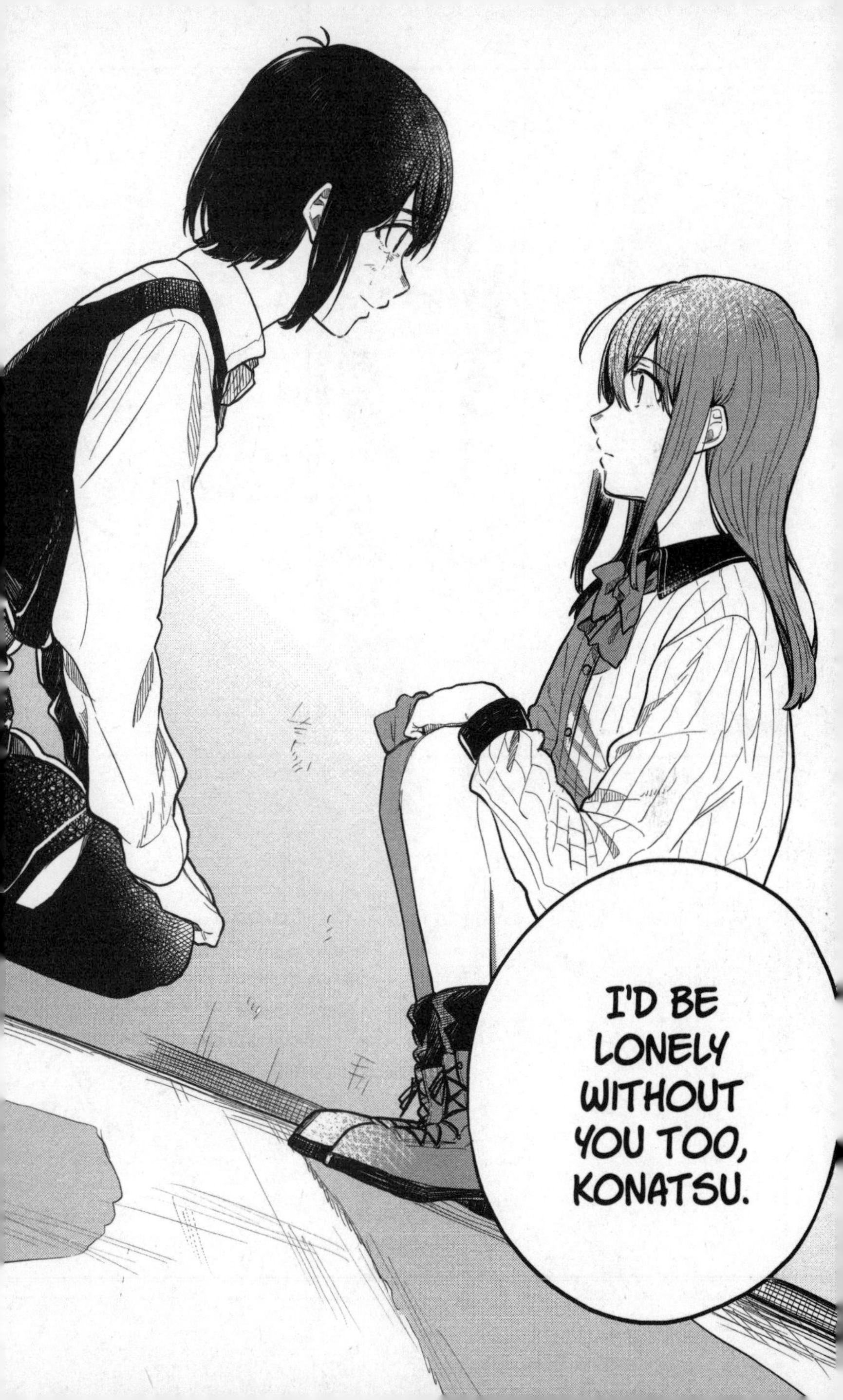
I'D BE LONELY WITHOUT YOU TOO, KONATSU.

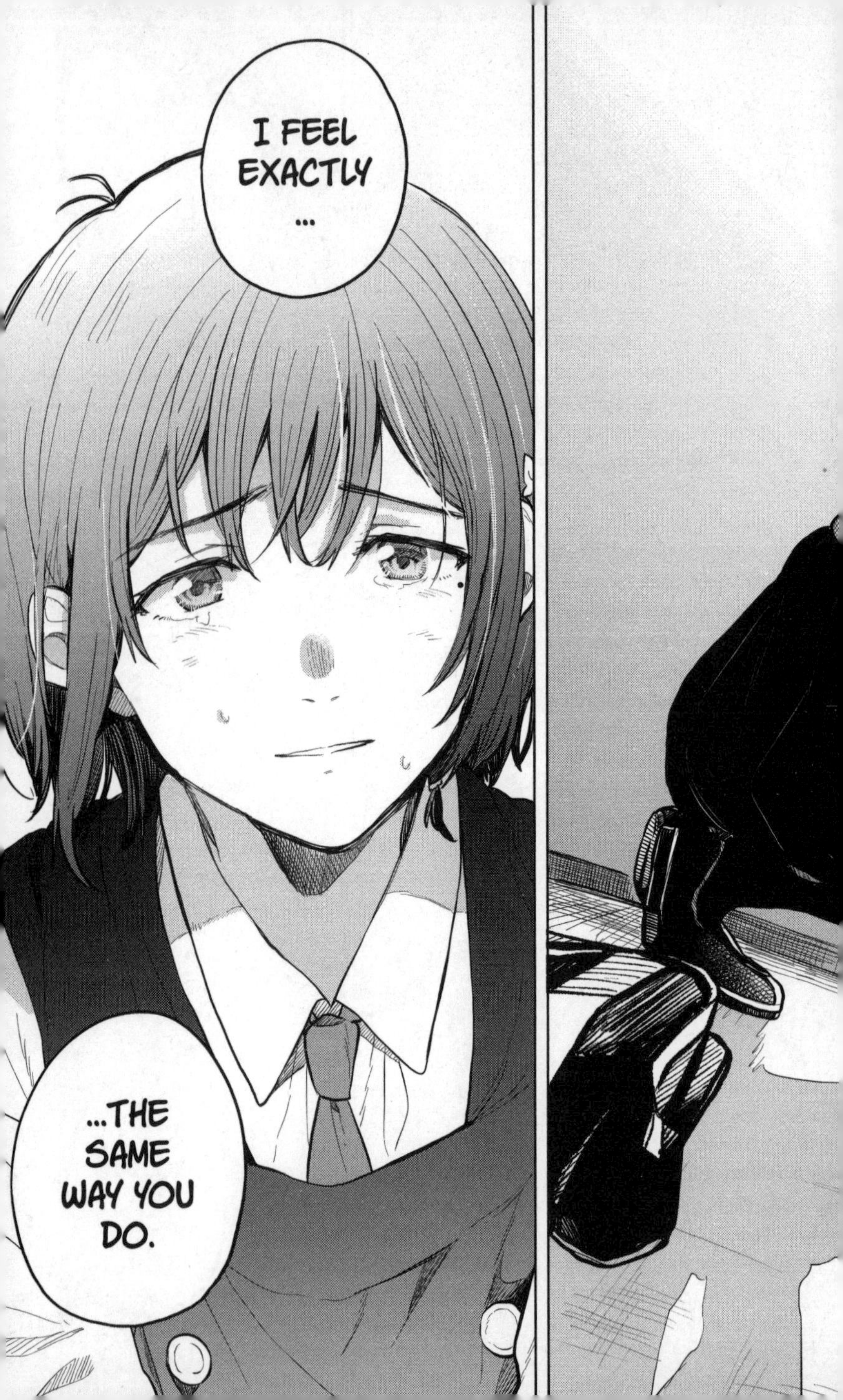
I FEEL EXACTLY ...
...THE SAME WAY YOU DO.

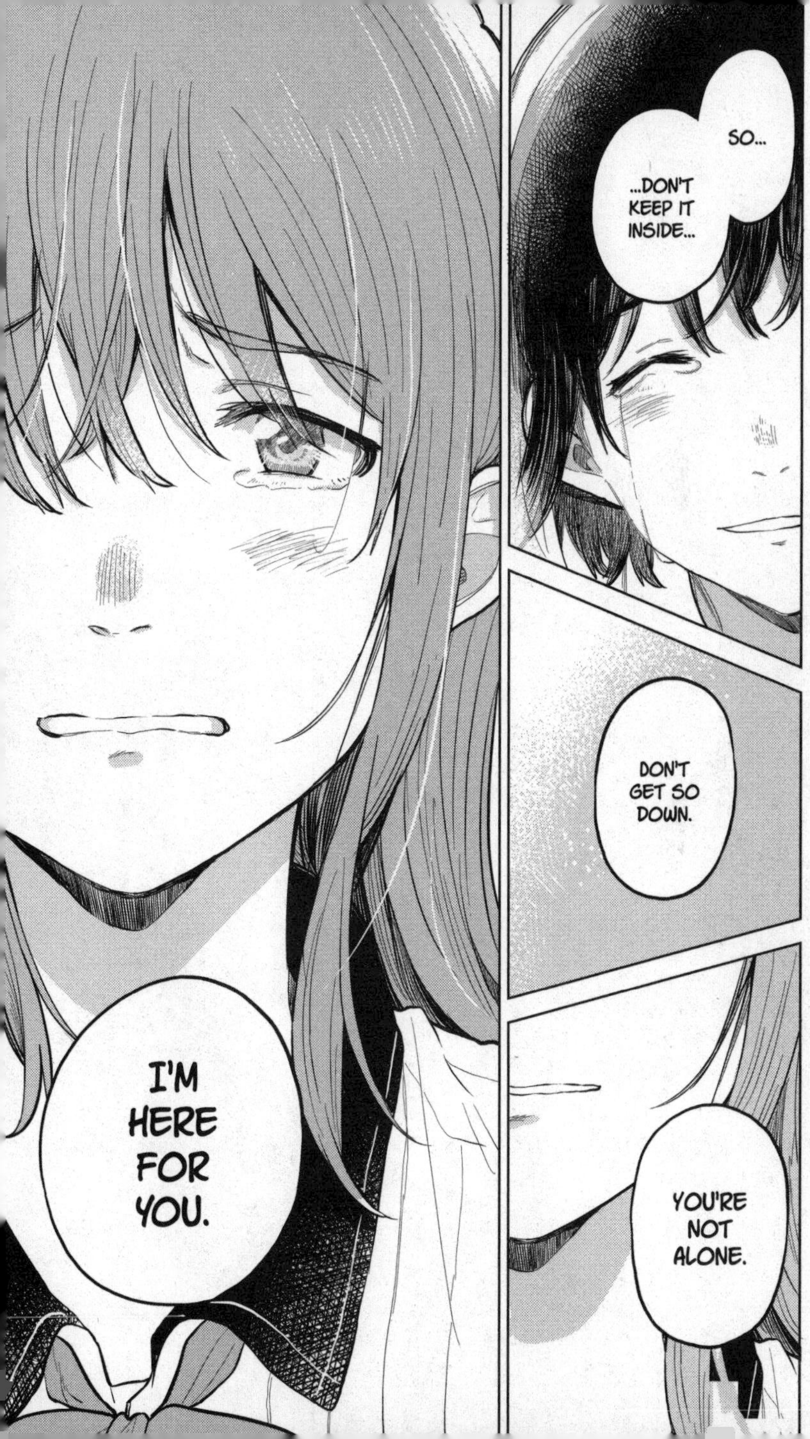
SO...
...DON'T KEEP IT INSIDE...
DON'T GET SO DOWN.
YOU'RE NOT ALONE.
I'M HERE FOR YOU.

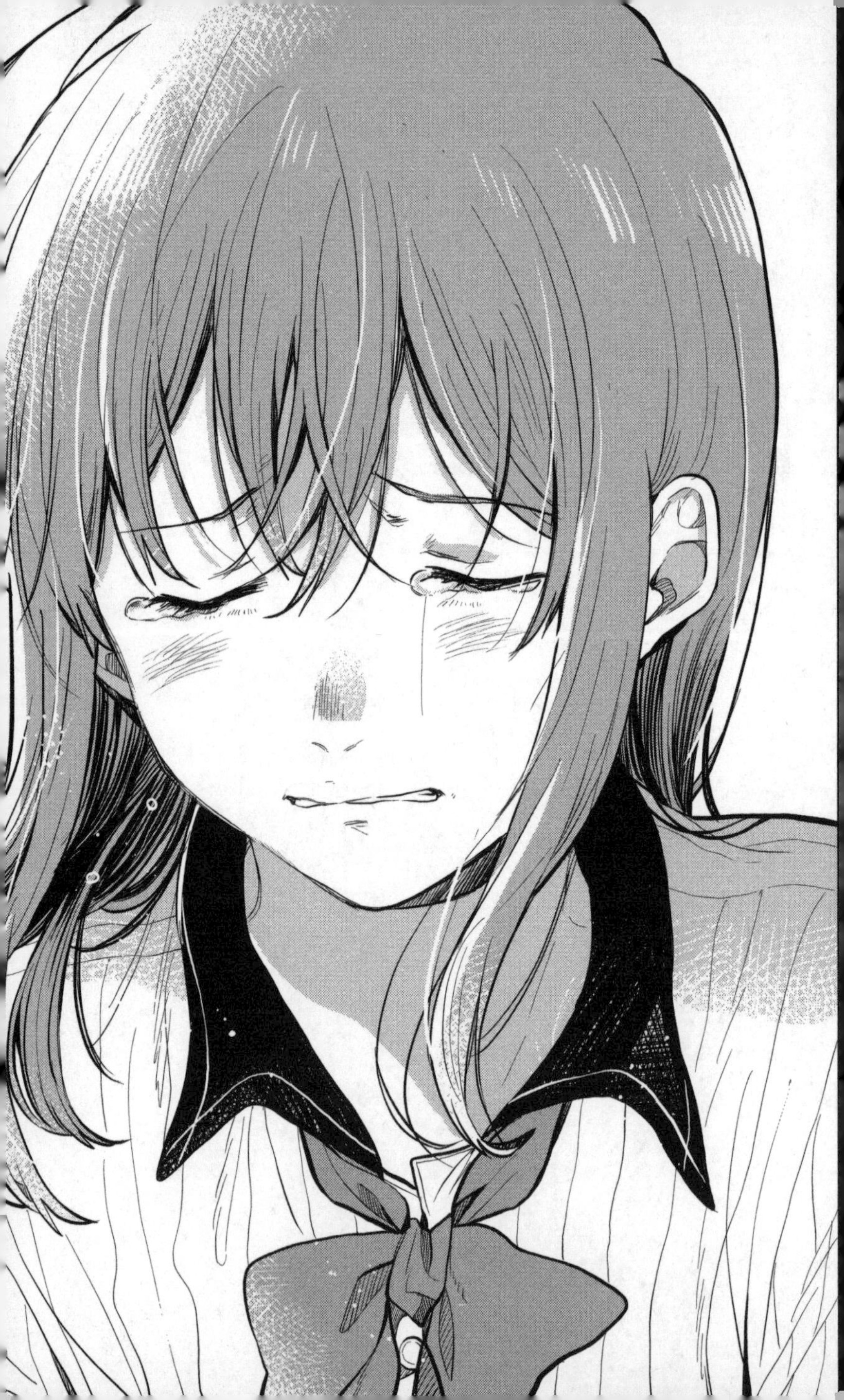

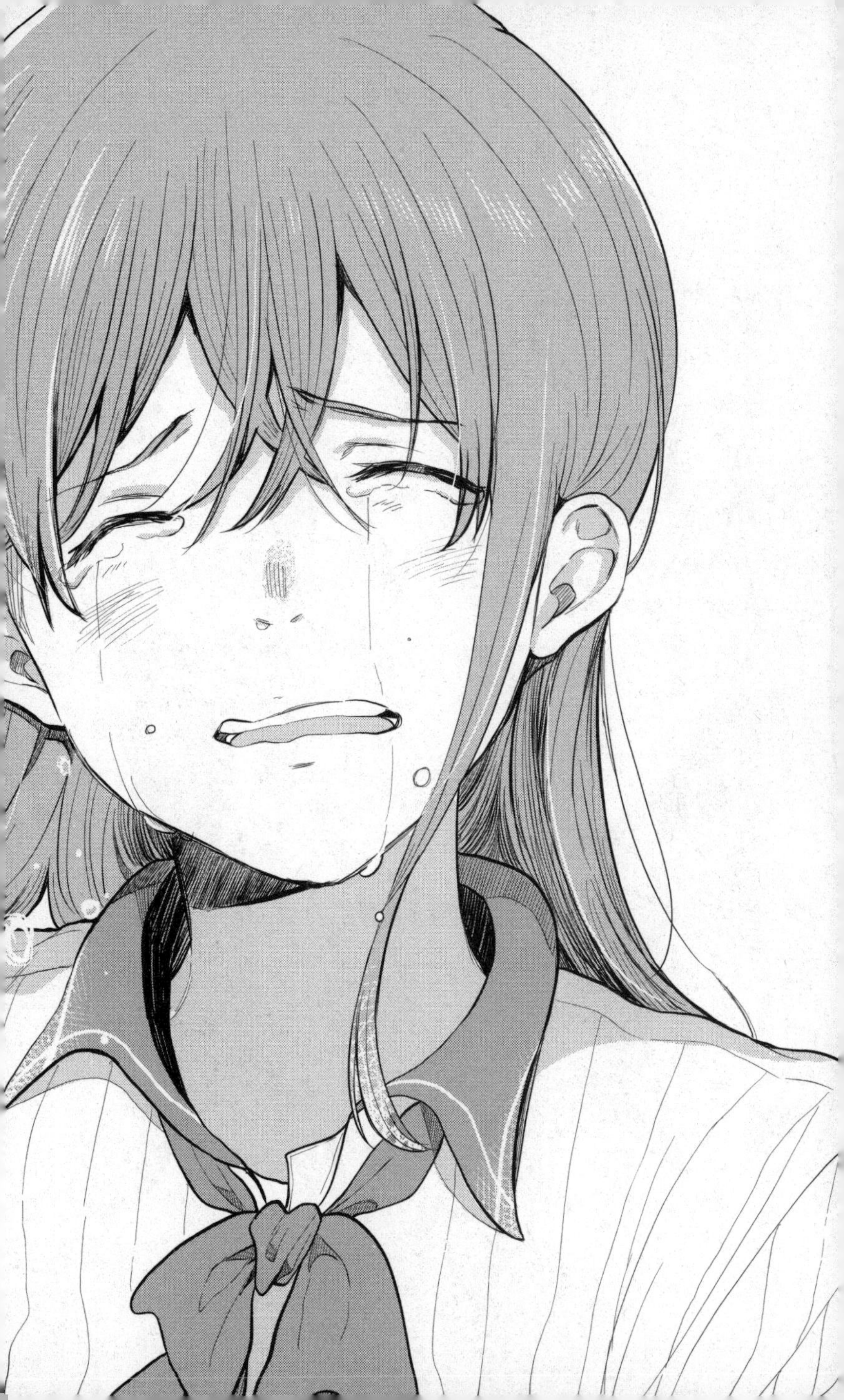

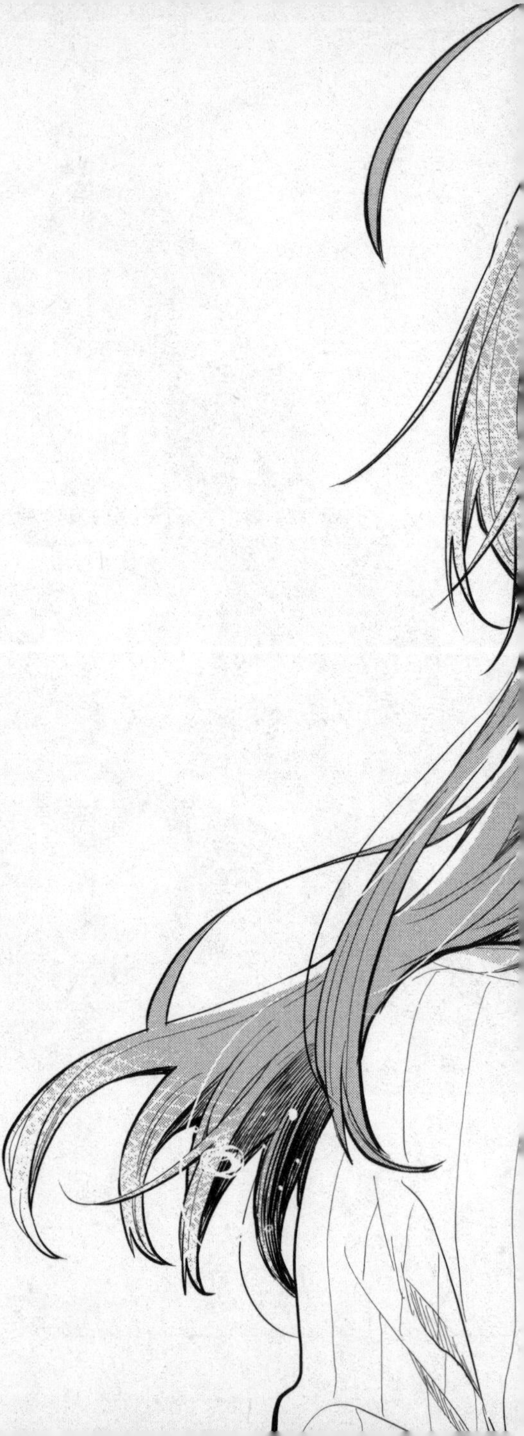

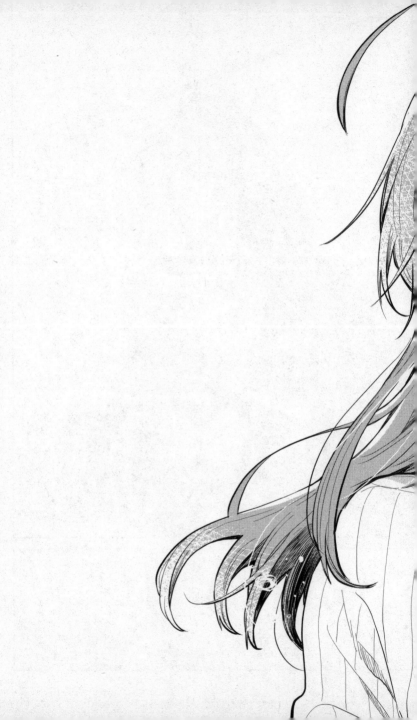

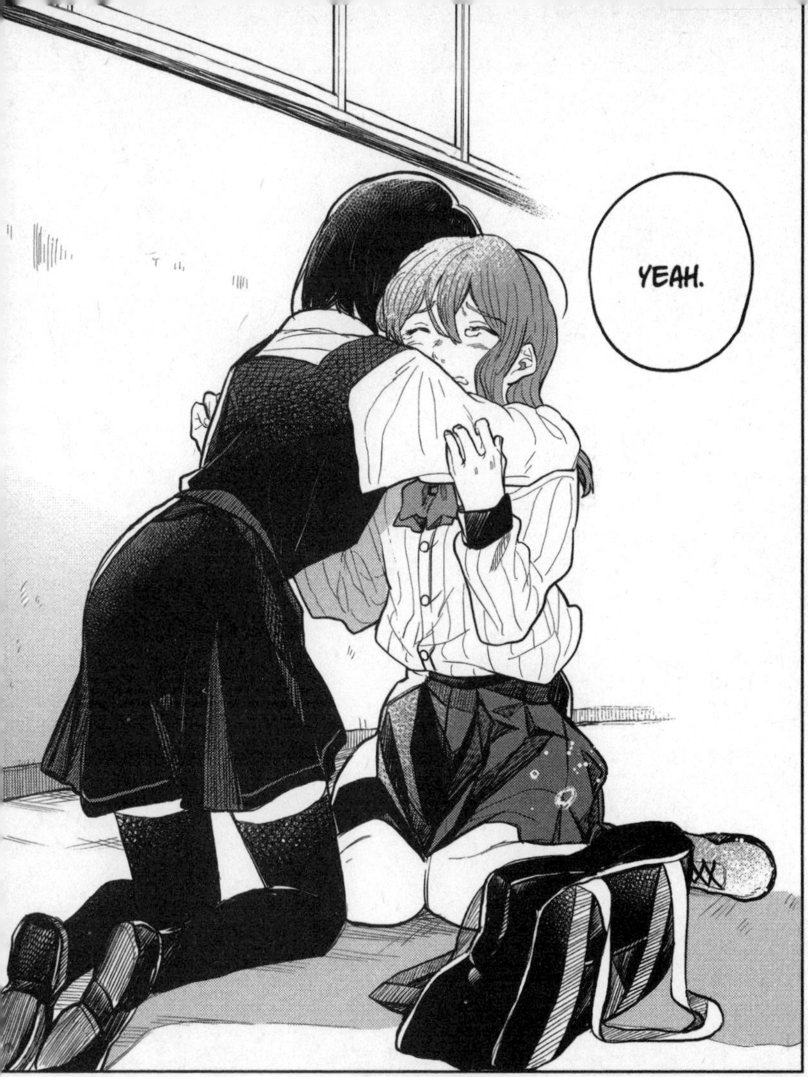
YEAH.
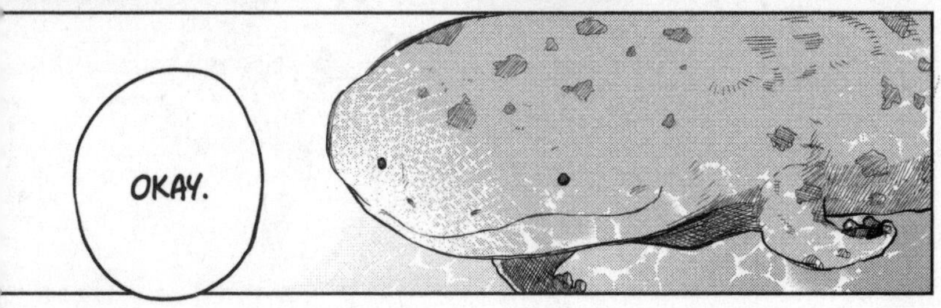
OKAY.

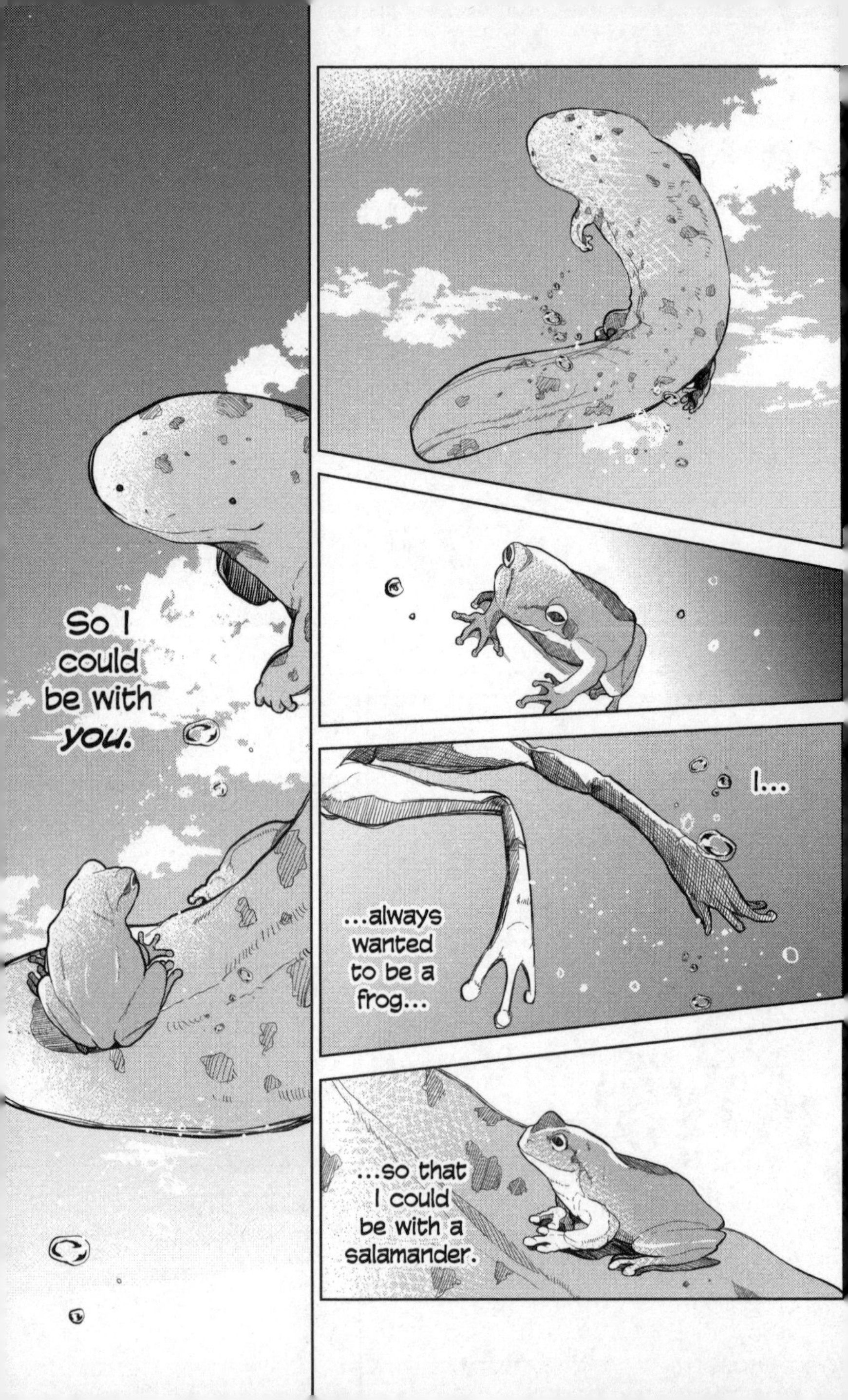
I...
...always wanted to be a frog...
...so that I could be with a salamander.
So I could be with *you.*

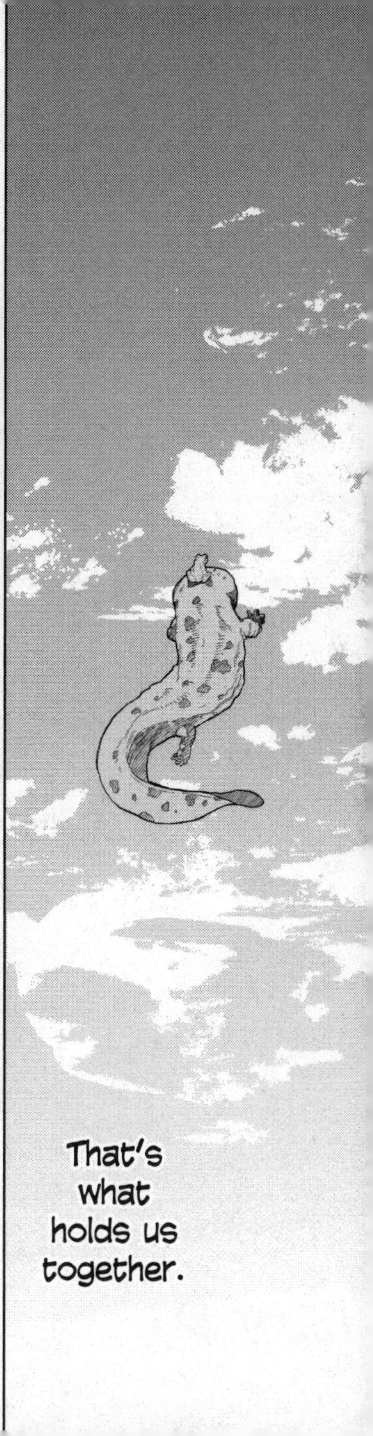
That's what holds us together.

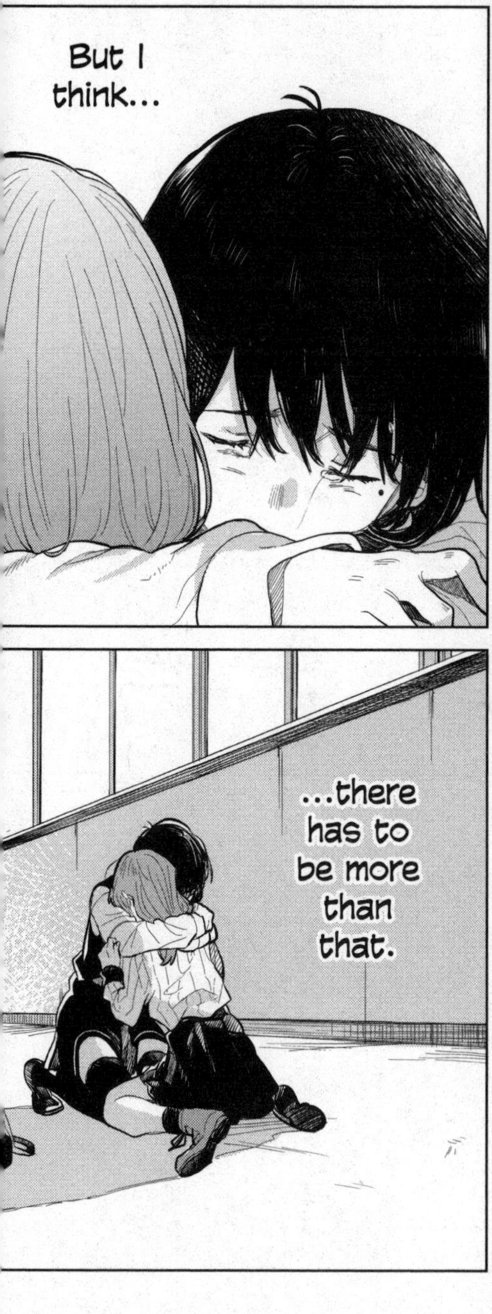
But I think...
...there has to be more than that.

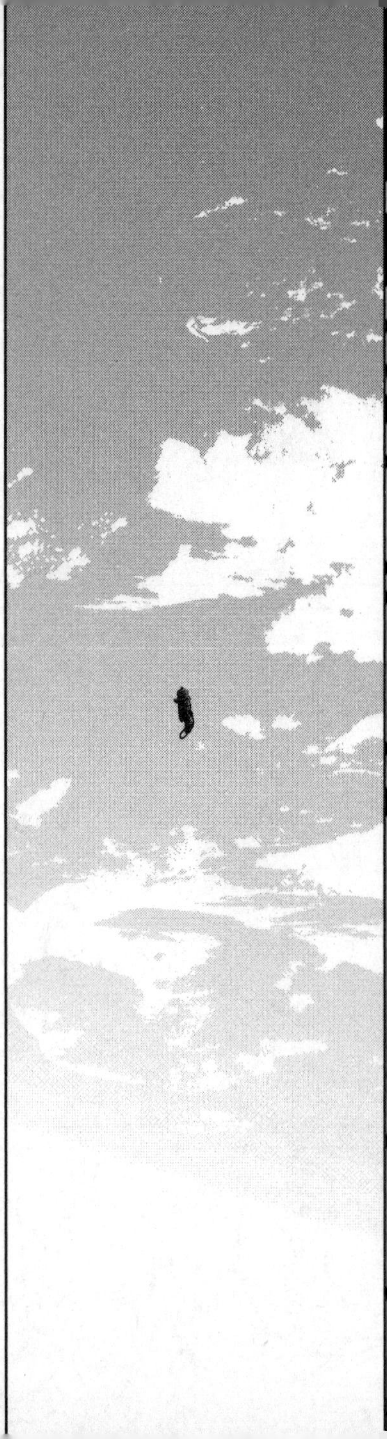

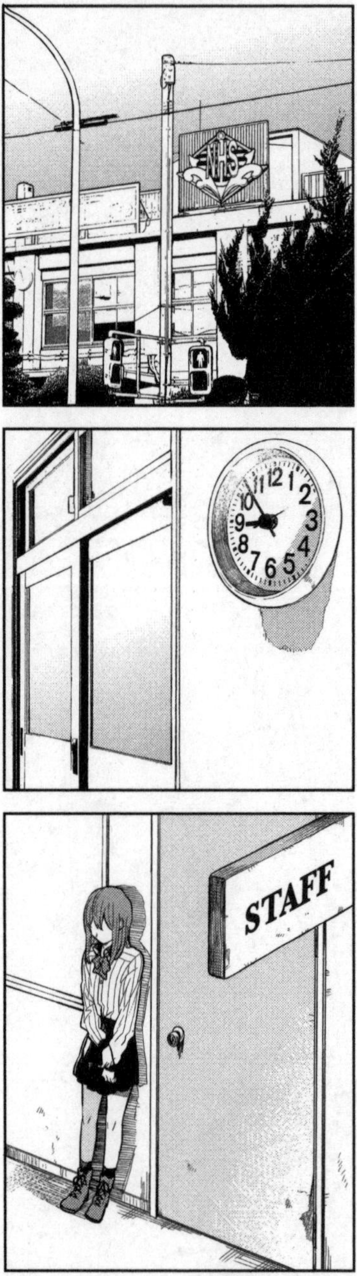
STAFF

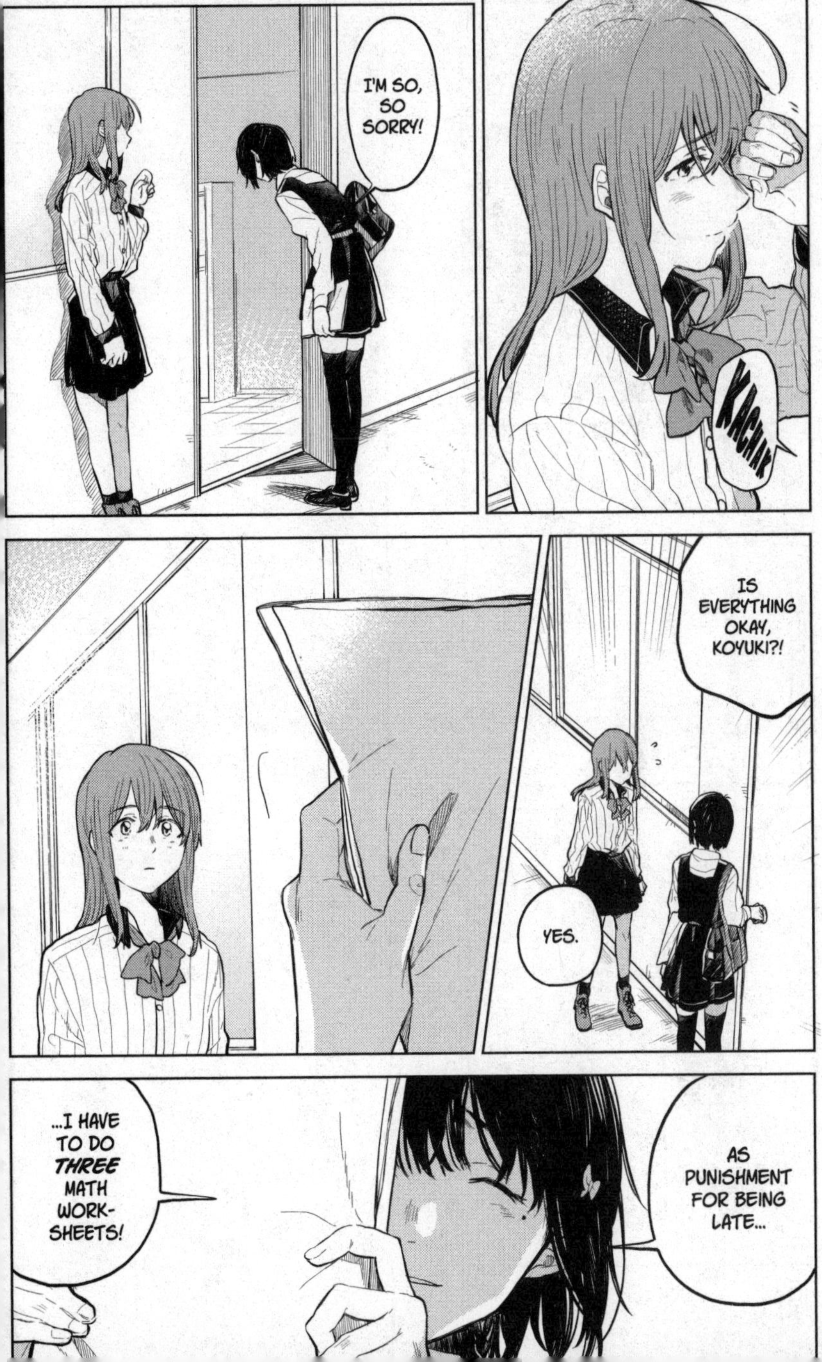
KACHAK
I'M SO, SO SORRY!
IS EVERYTHING OKAY, KOYUKI?!
YES.
AS PUNISHMENT FOR BEING LATE...
...I HAVE TO DO THREE MATH WORK-SHEETS!

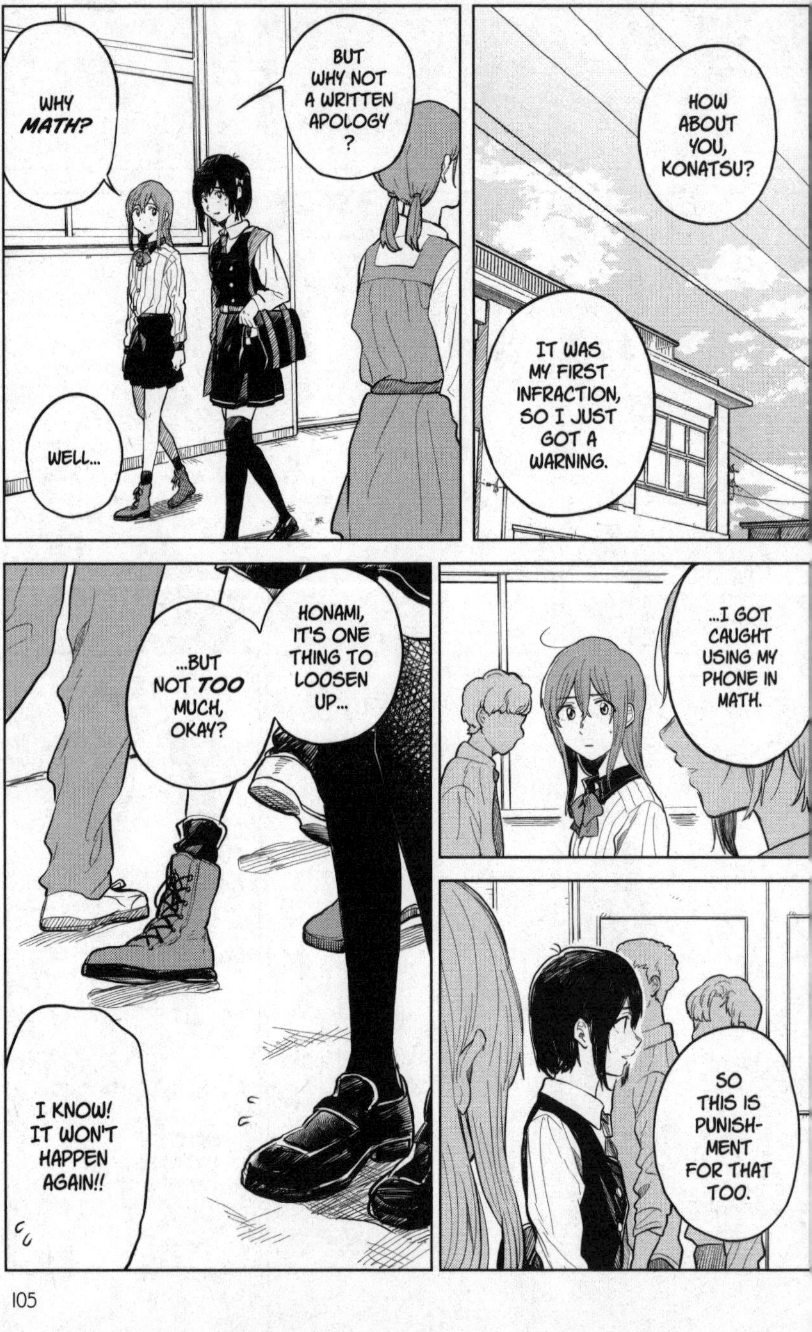
HOW ABOUT YOU, KONATSU?
IT WAS MY FIRST INFRACTION, SO I JUST GOT A WARNING.
BUT WHY NOT A WRITTEN APOLOGY?
WHY *MATH?*
WELL...
...I GOT CAUGHT USING MY PHONE IN MATH.
SO THIS IS PUNISH-MENT FOR THAT TOO.
HONAMI, IT'S ONE THING TO LOOSEN UP...
...BUT NOT *TOO* MUCH, OKAY?
I KNOW! IT WON'T HAPPEN AGAIN!!

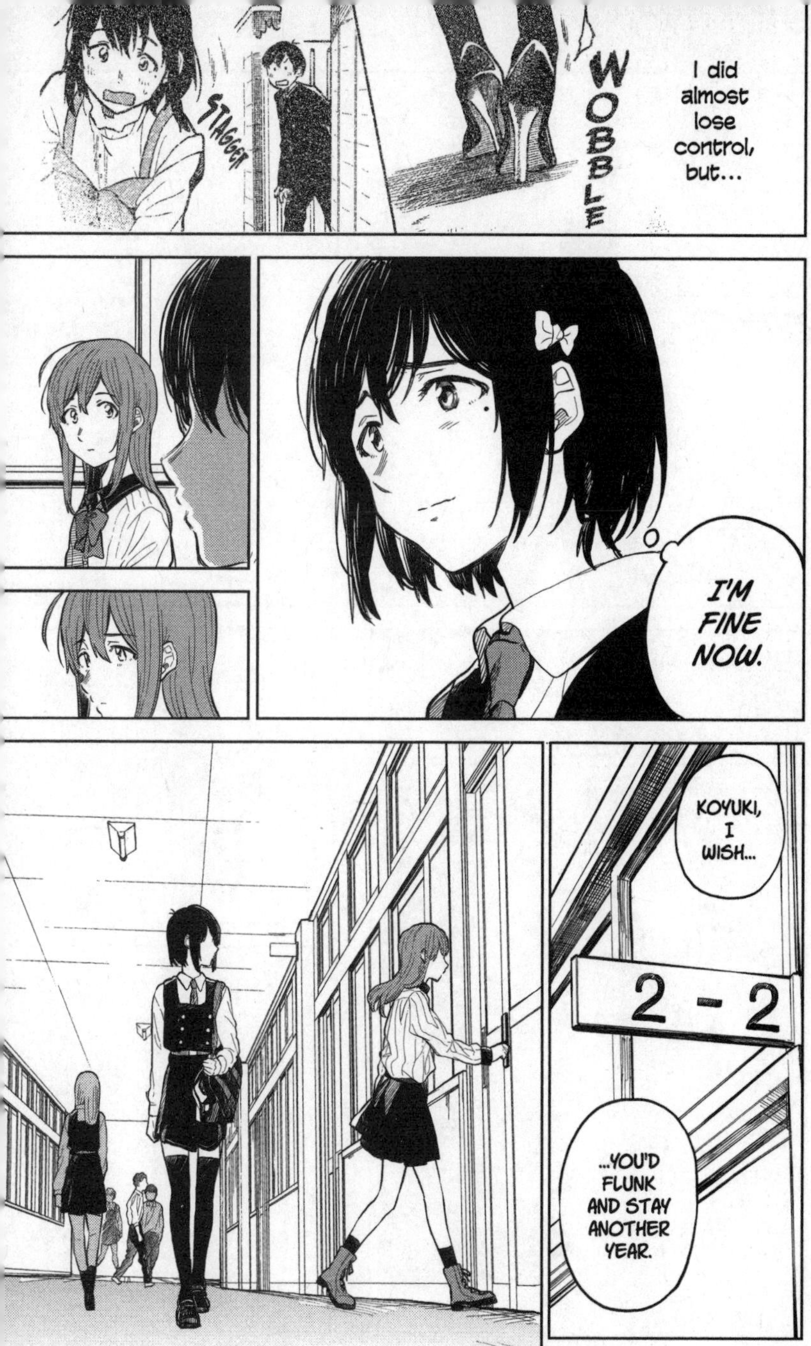
WOBBLE
I did almost lose control, but...
STAGGER
I'M FINE NOW.
KOYUKI, I WISH...
2 - 2
...YOU'D FLUNK AND STAY ANOTHER YEAR.

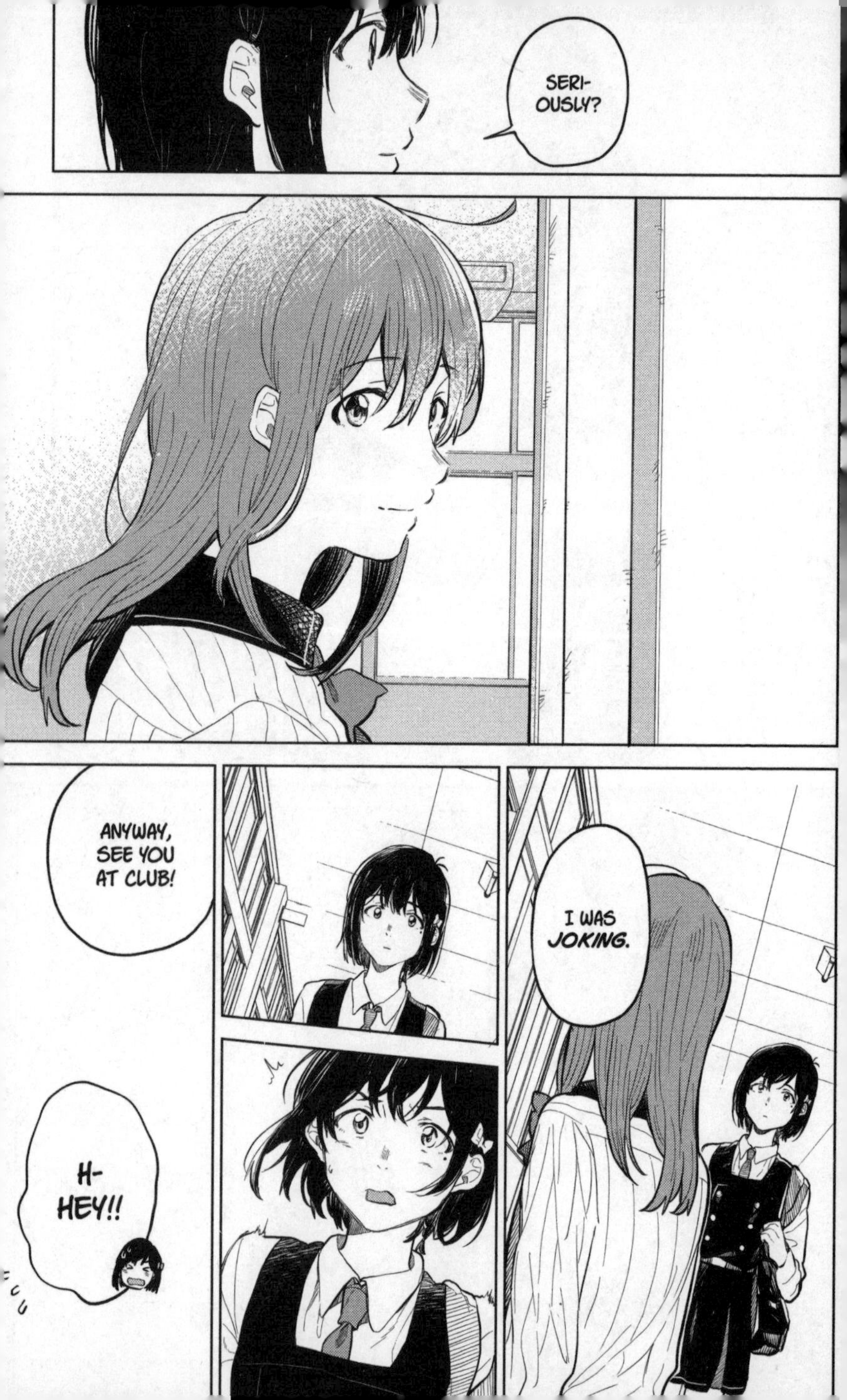
SERI-OUSLY?
I WAS JOKING.
ANYWAY, SEE YOU AT CLUB!
H- HEY!!

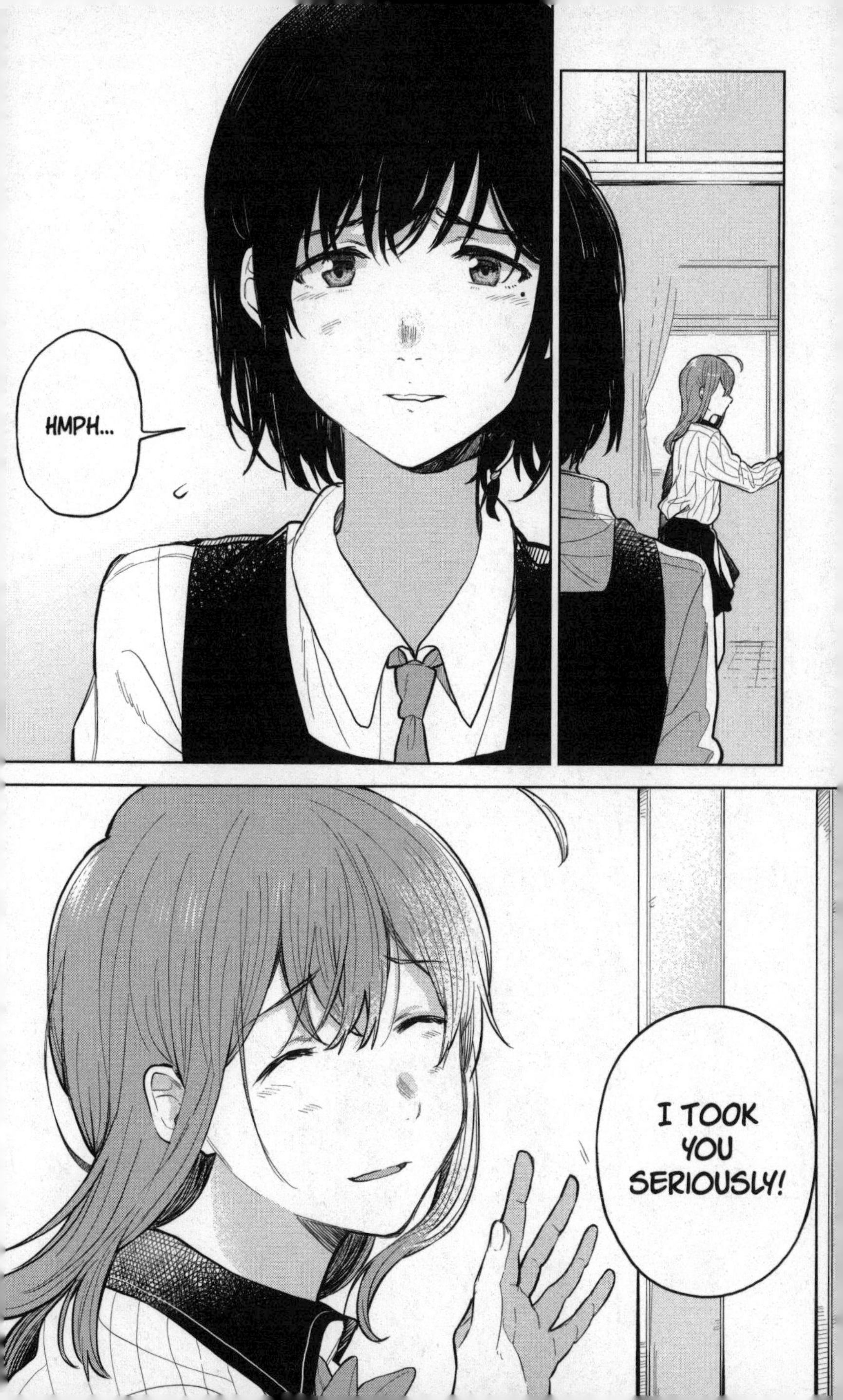
HMPH...
I TOOK YOU SERIOUSLY!

A Tropical Fish
Yearns for Snow

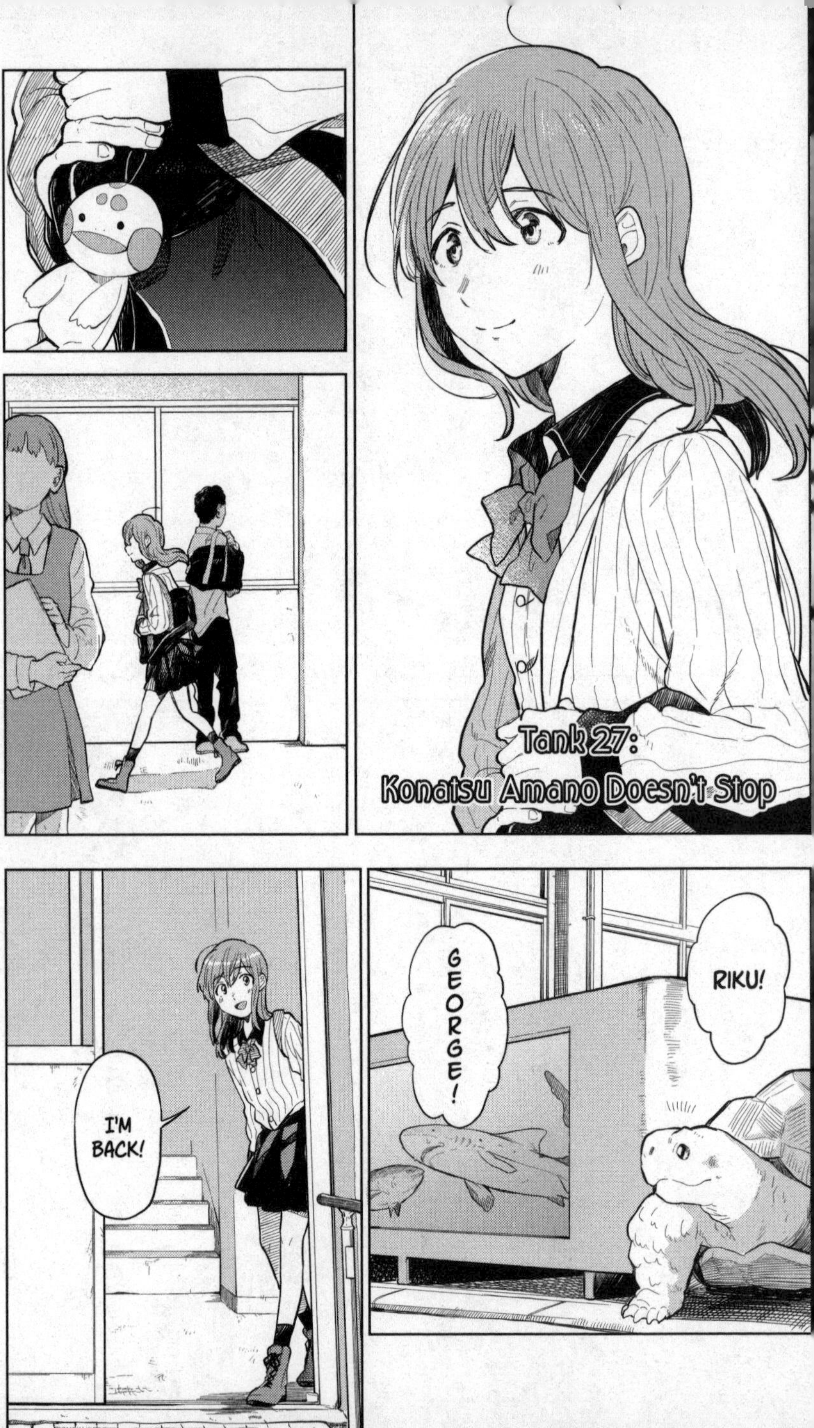
Tank 27:
Konatsu Amano Doesn't Stop
RIKU!
GEORGE!
I'M BACK!

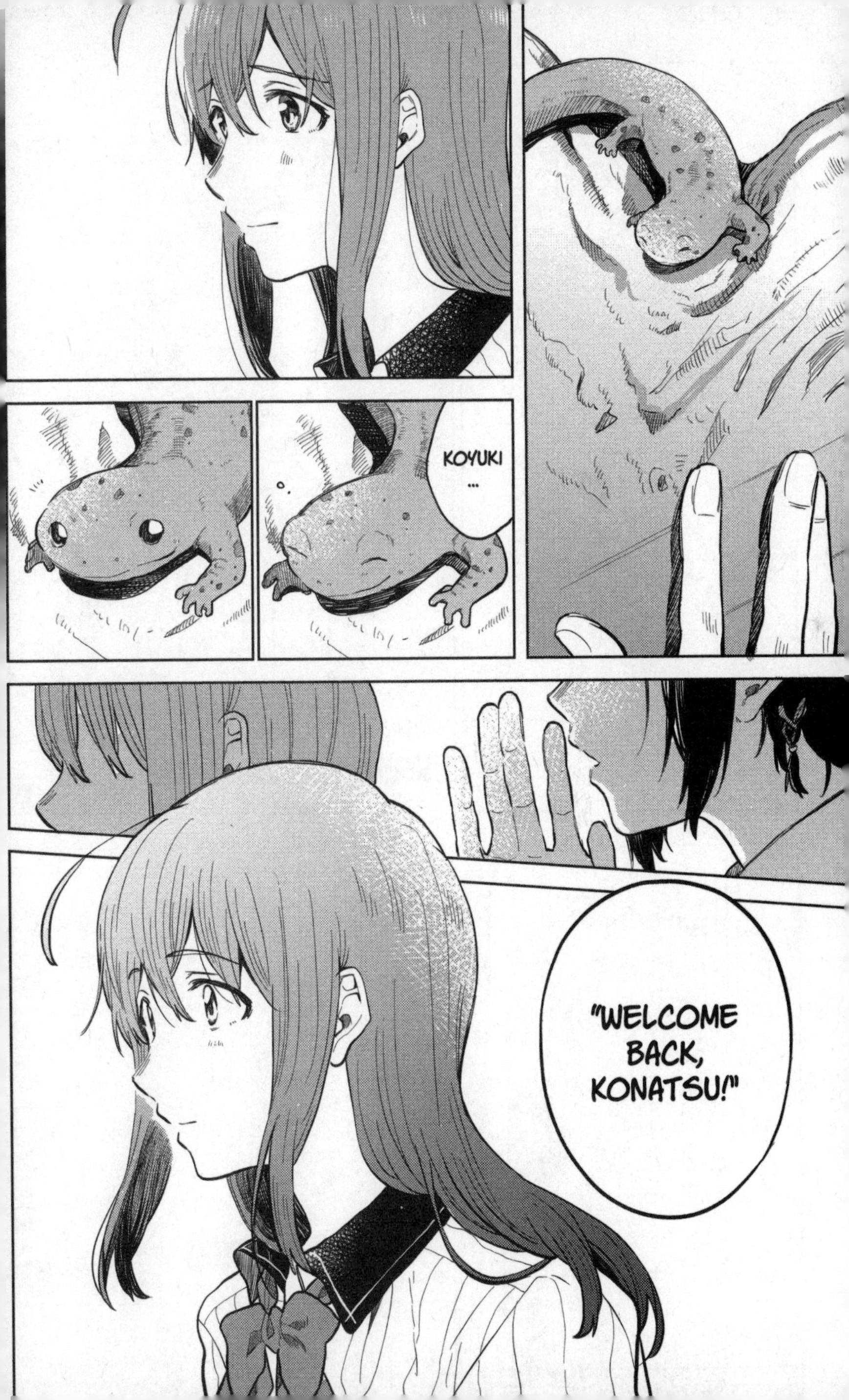
KOYUKI
...
"WELCOME BACK, KONATSU!"

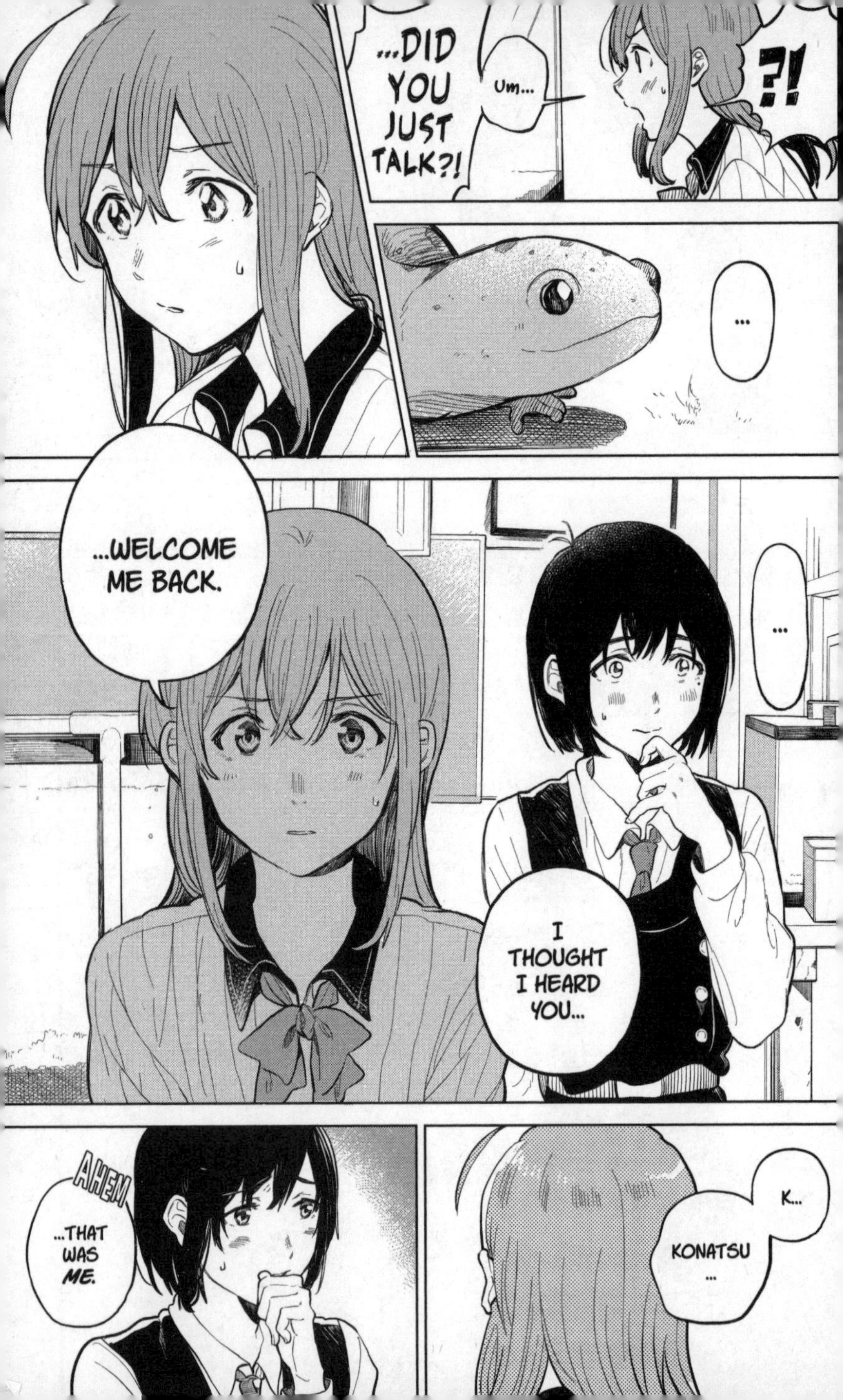
?!
Um...
...DID YOU JUST TALK?!
...
...
I THOUGHT I HEARD YOU...
...WELCOME ME BACK.
K...
KONATSU ...
AHEM
...THAT WAS ME.

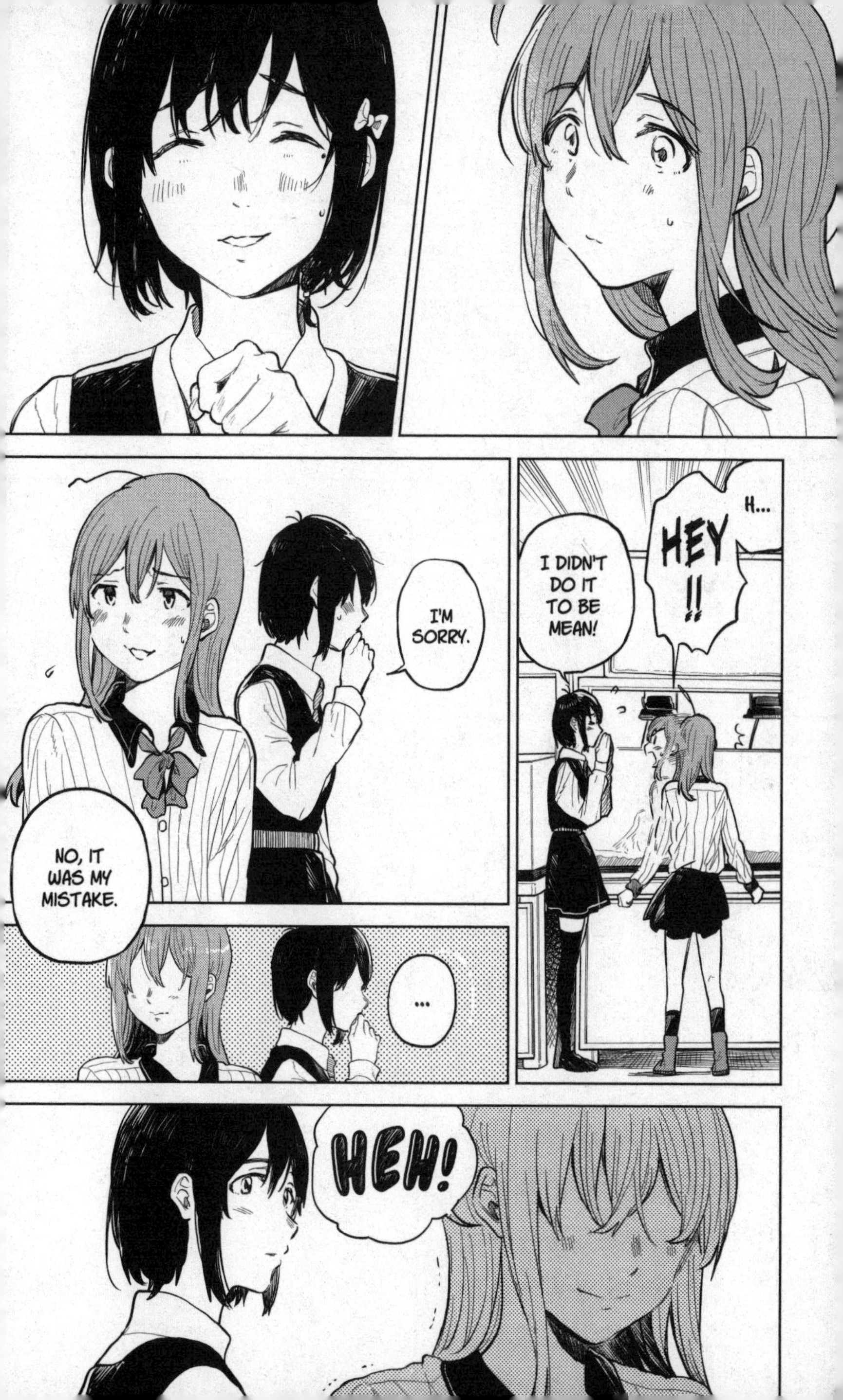
H...
HEY !!
I DIDN'T DO IT TO BE MEAN!
I'M SORRY.
NO, IT WAS MY MISTAKE.
...
HEH!

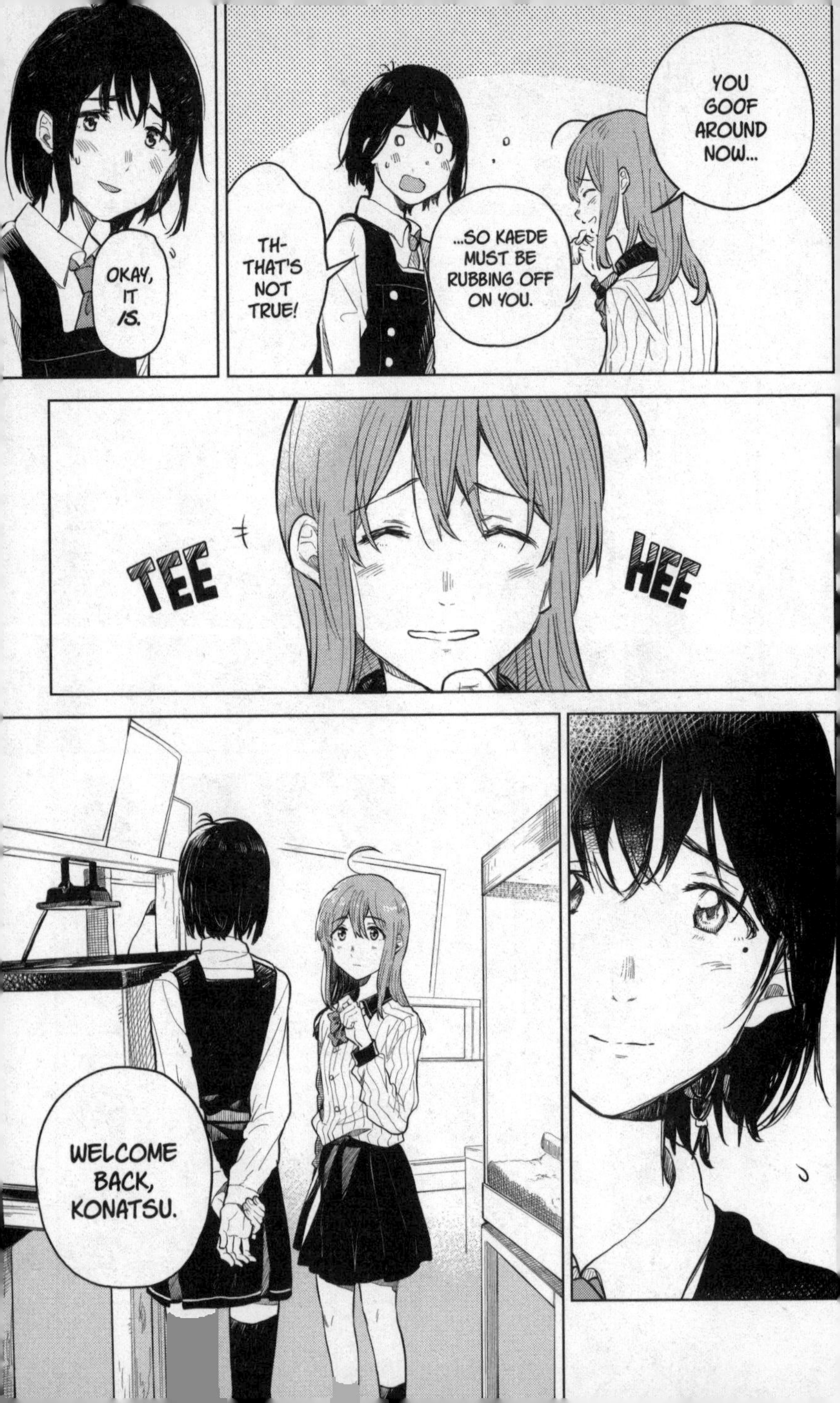
YOU GOOF AROUND NOW...
...SO KAEDE MUST BE RUBBING OFF ON YOU.
TH-THAT'S NOT TRUE!
OKAY, IT IS.
TEE HEE
WELCOME BACK, KONATSU.

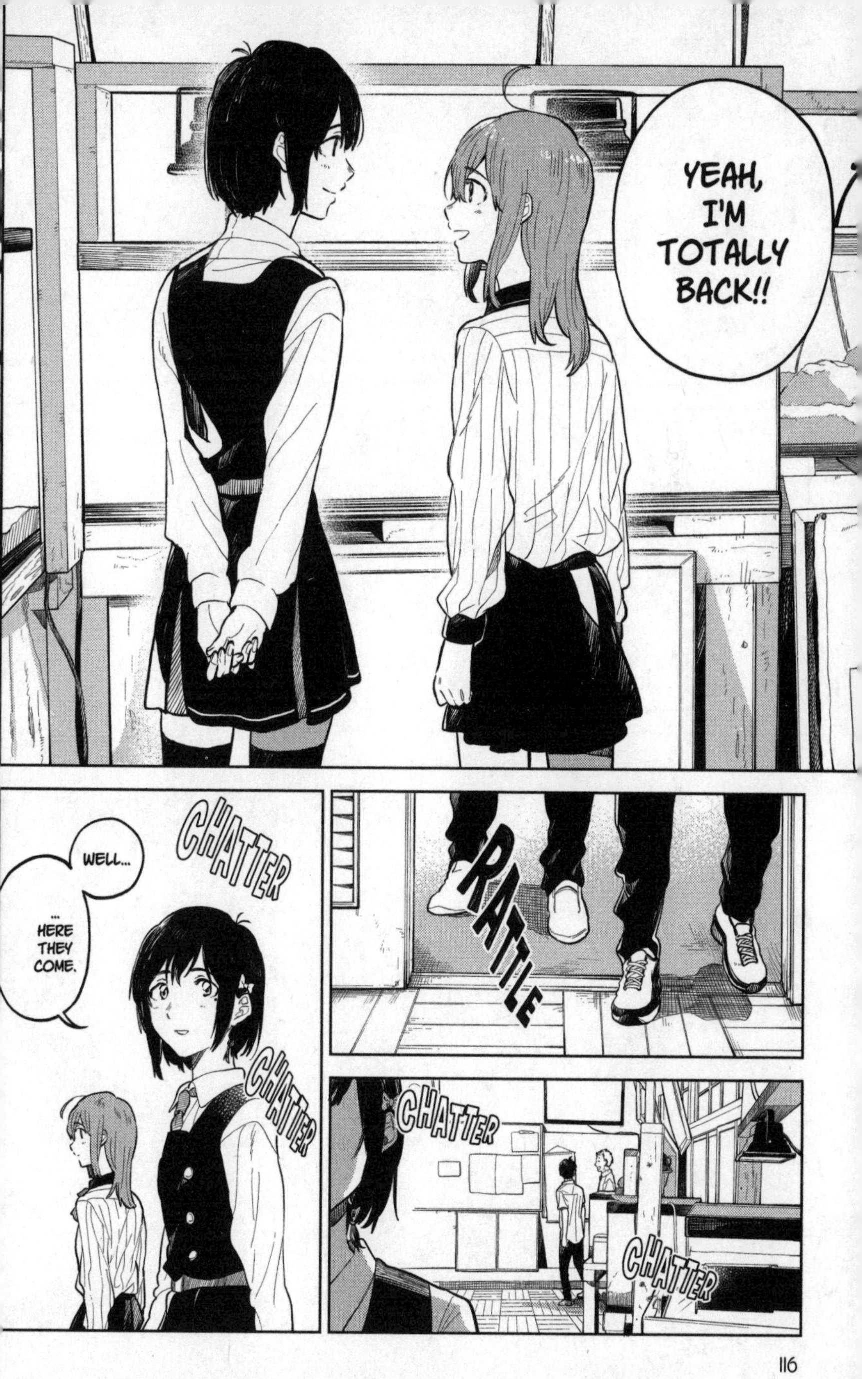
YEAH, I'M TOTALLY BACK!!
RATTLE
CHATTER
CHATTER
CHATTER
WELL...
... HERE THEY COME.
CHATTER

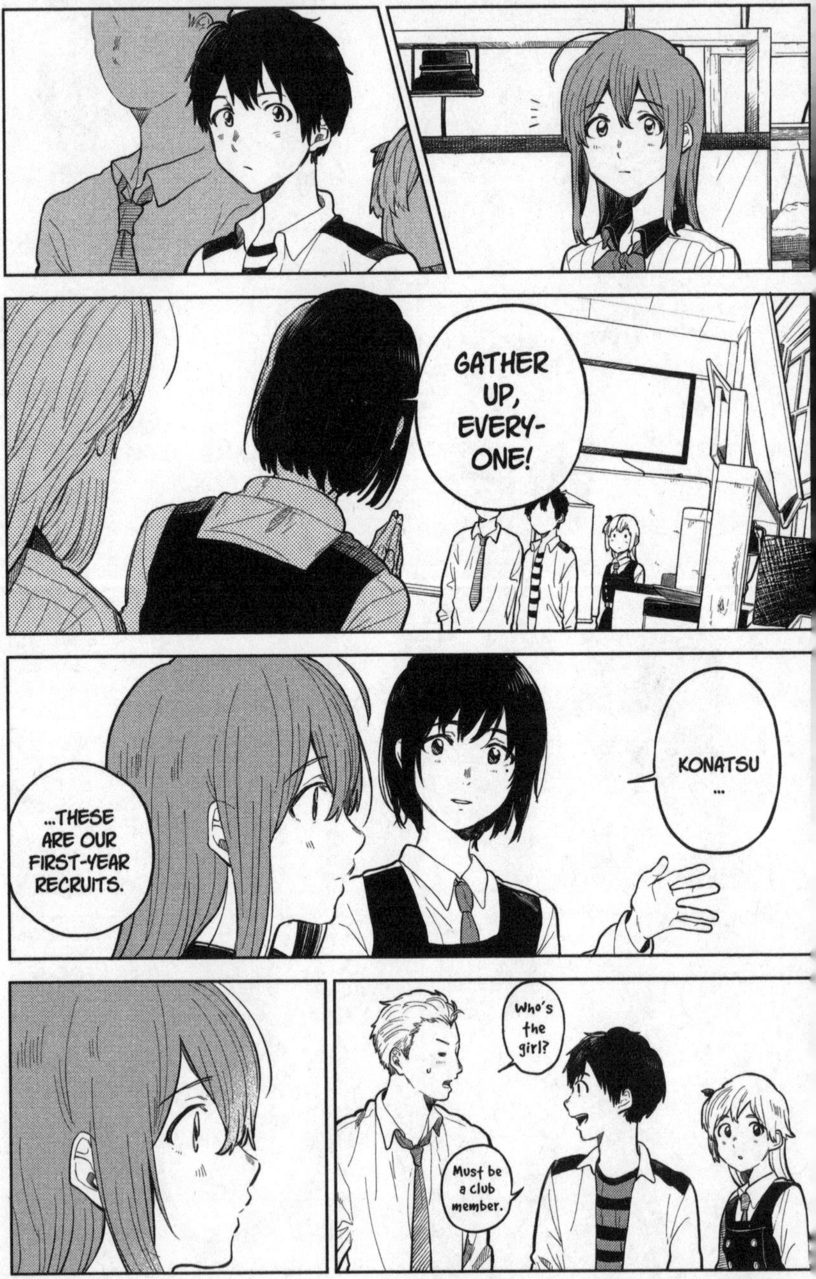
GATHER UP, EVERY-ONE!
KONATSU ...
...THESE ARE OUR FIRST-YEAR RECRUITS.
Who's the girl?
Must be a club member.

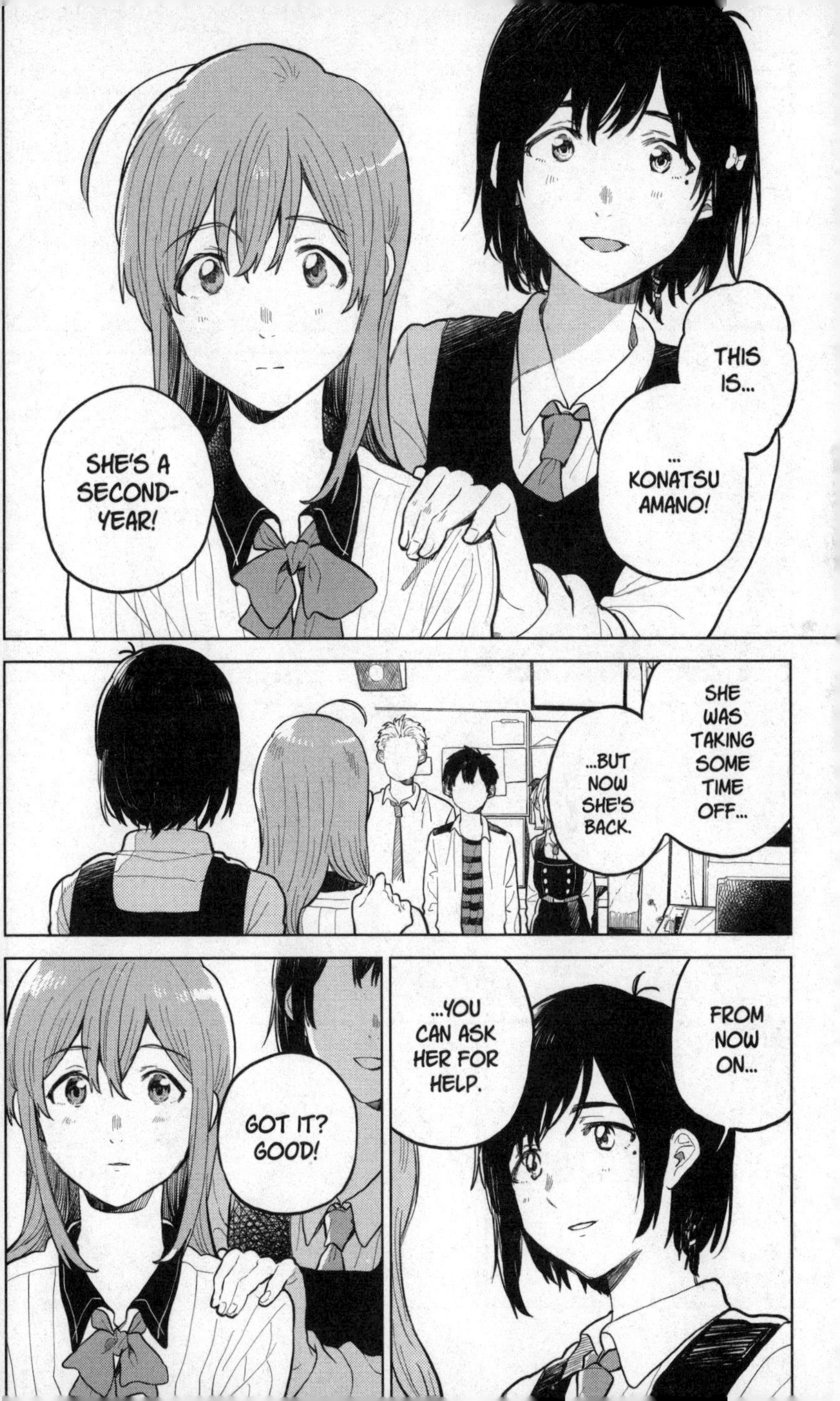
THIS IS...
...KONATSU AMANO!
SHE'S A SECOND-YEAR!
SHE WAS TAKING SOME TIME OFF...
...BUT NOW SHE'S BACK.
FROM NOW ON...
...YOU CAN ASK HER FOR HELP.
GOT IT? GOOD!

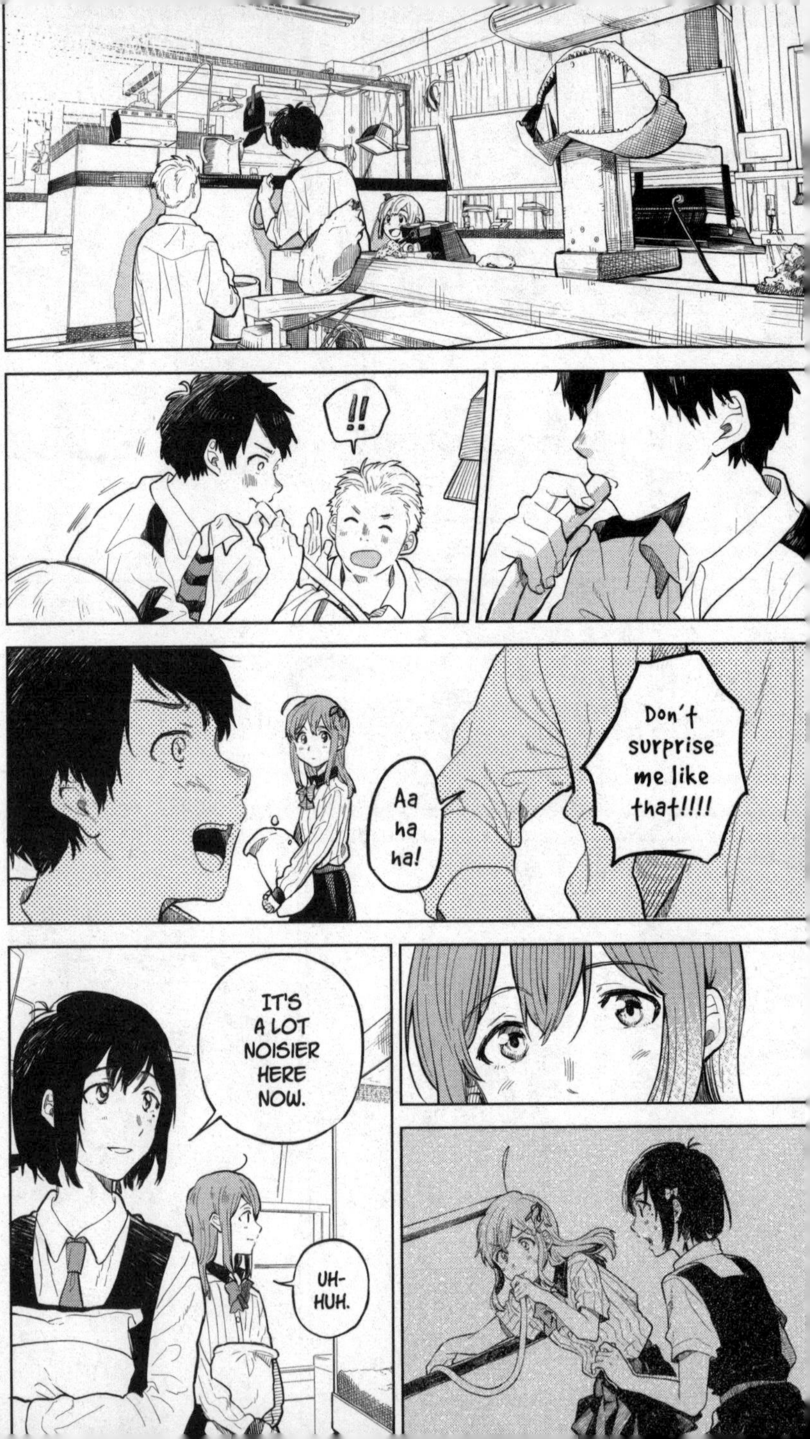
!!
Don't surprise me like that!!!!!
Aa ha ha!
IT'S A LOT NOISIER HERE NOW.
UH-HUH.

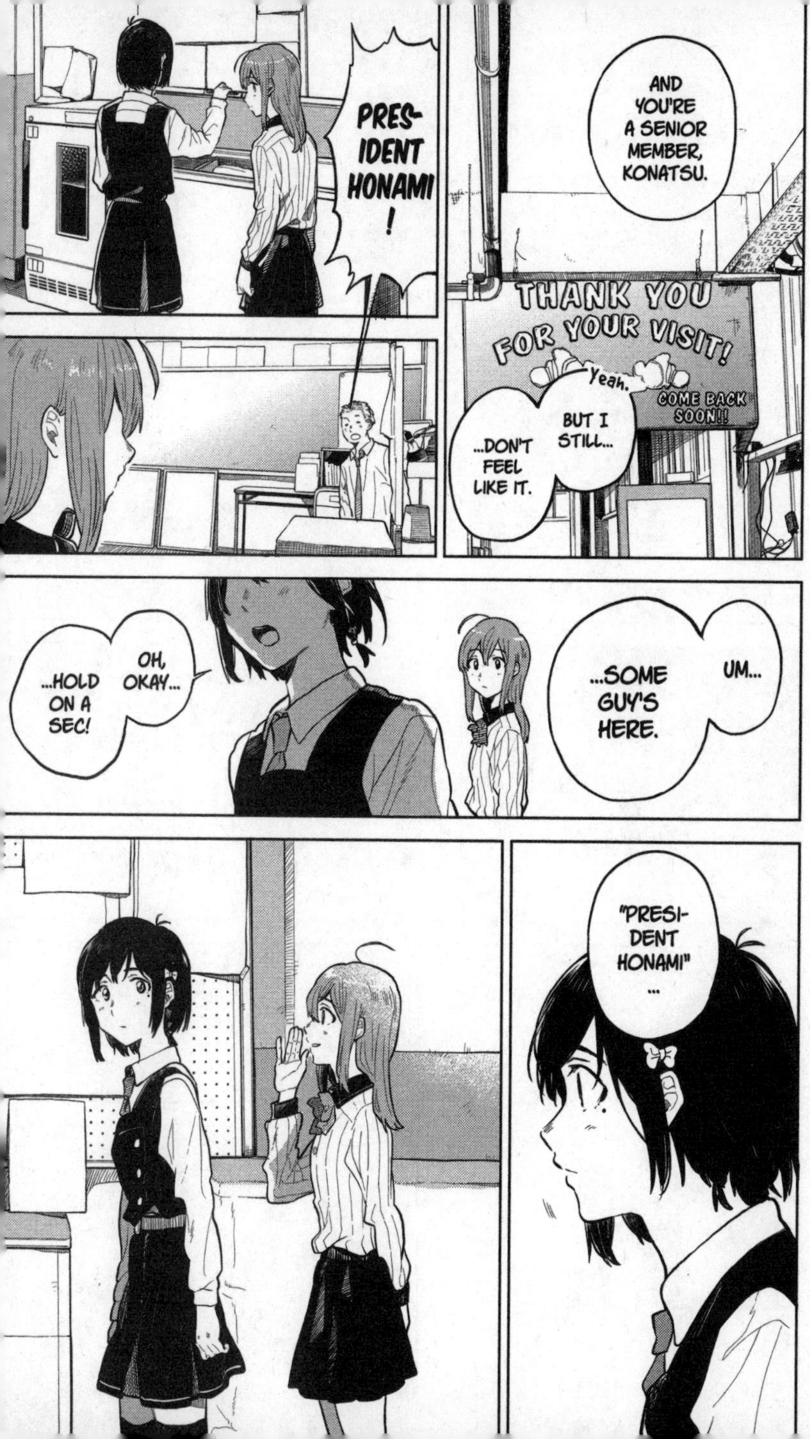
AND YOU'RE A SENIOR MEMBER, KONATSU.
THANK YOU FOR YOUR VISIT!
COME BACK SOON!!
Yeah.
BUT I STILL...
...DON'T FEEL LIKE IT.
PRES-IDENT HONAMI!
UM...
...SOME GUY'S HERE.
OH, OKAY...
...HOLD ON A SEC!
"PRESI-DENT HONAMI"...

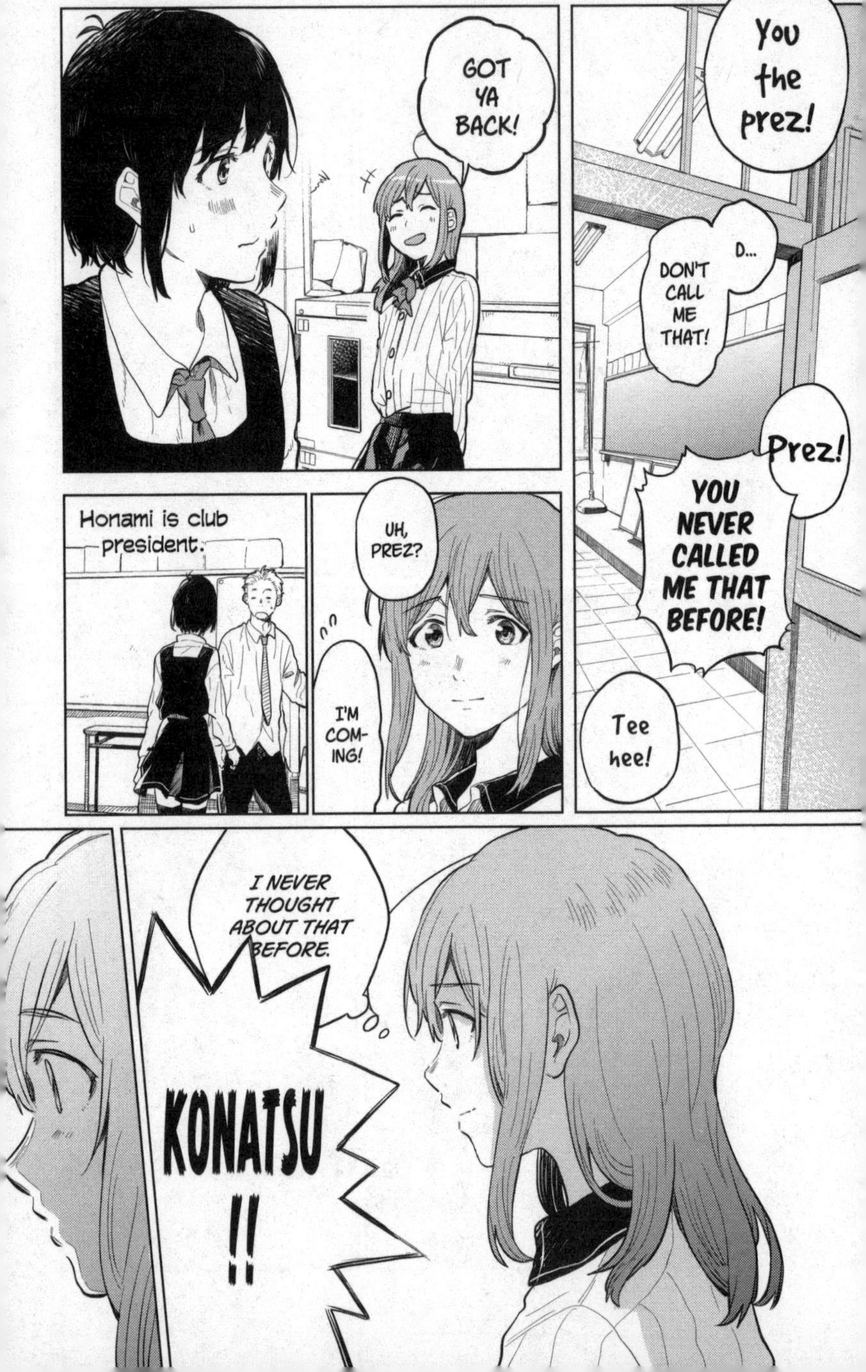
You the prez!
D... DON'T CALL ME THAT!
Prez!
YOU NEVER CALLED ME THAT BEFORE!
Tee hee!
GOT YA BACK!
UH, PREZ?
I'M COM-ING!
Honami is club president.
I NEVER THOUGHT ABOUT THAT BEFORE.
KONATSU !!

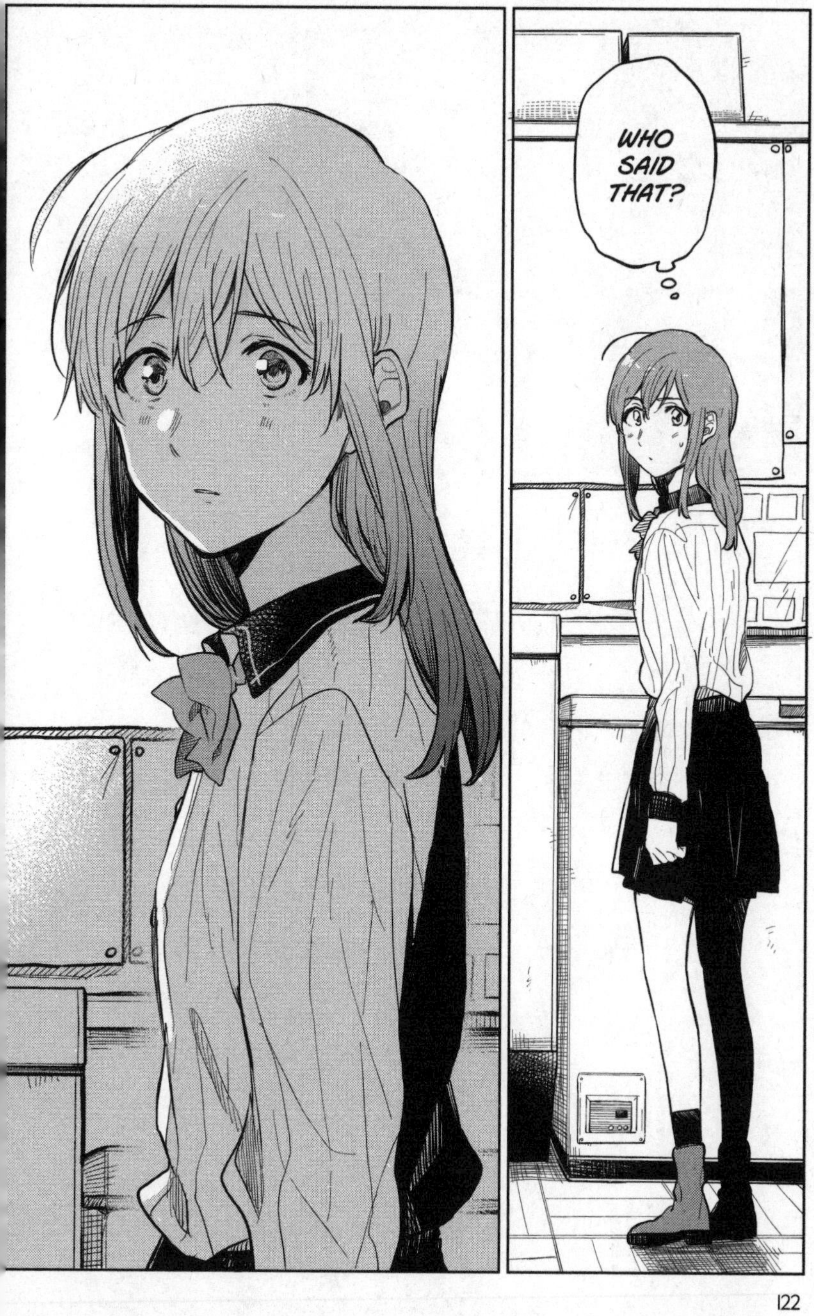
WHO SAID THAT?

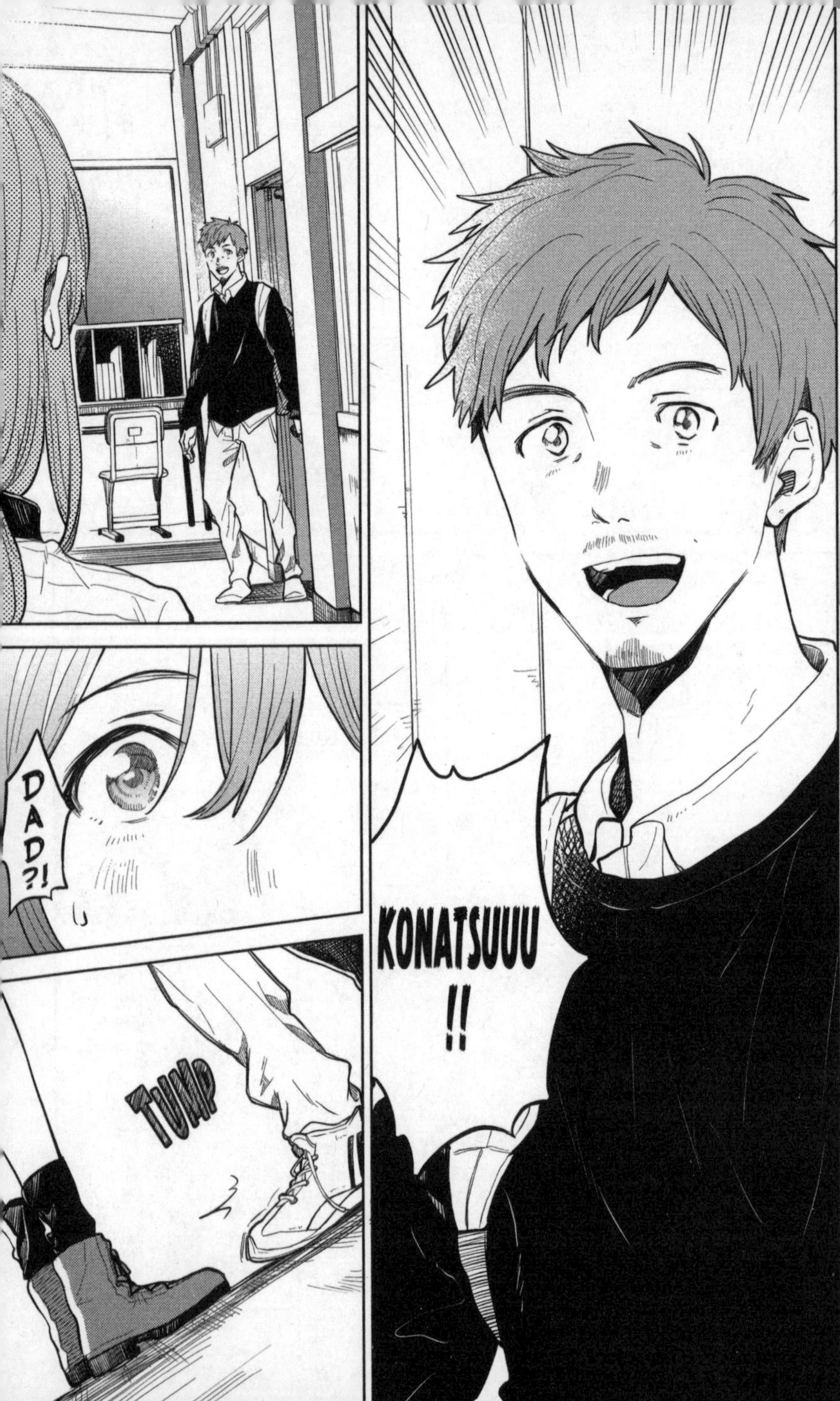
KONATSUUU !!
DAD?!
TUMP

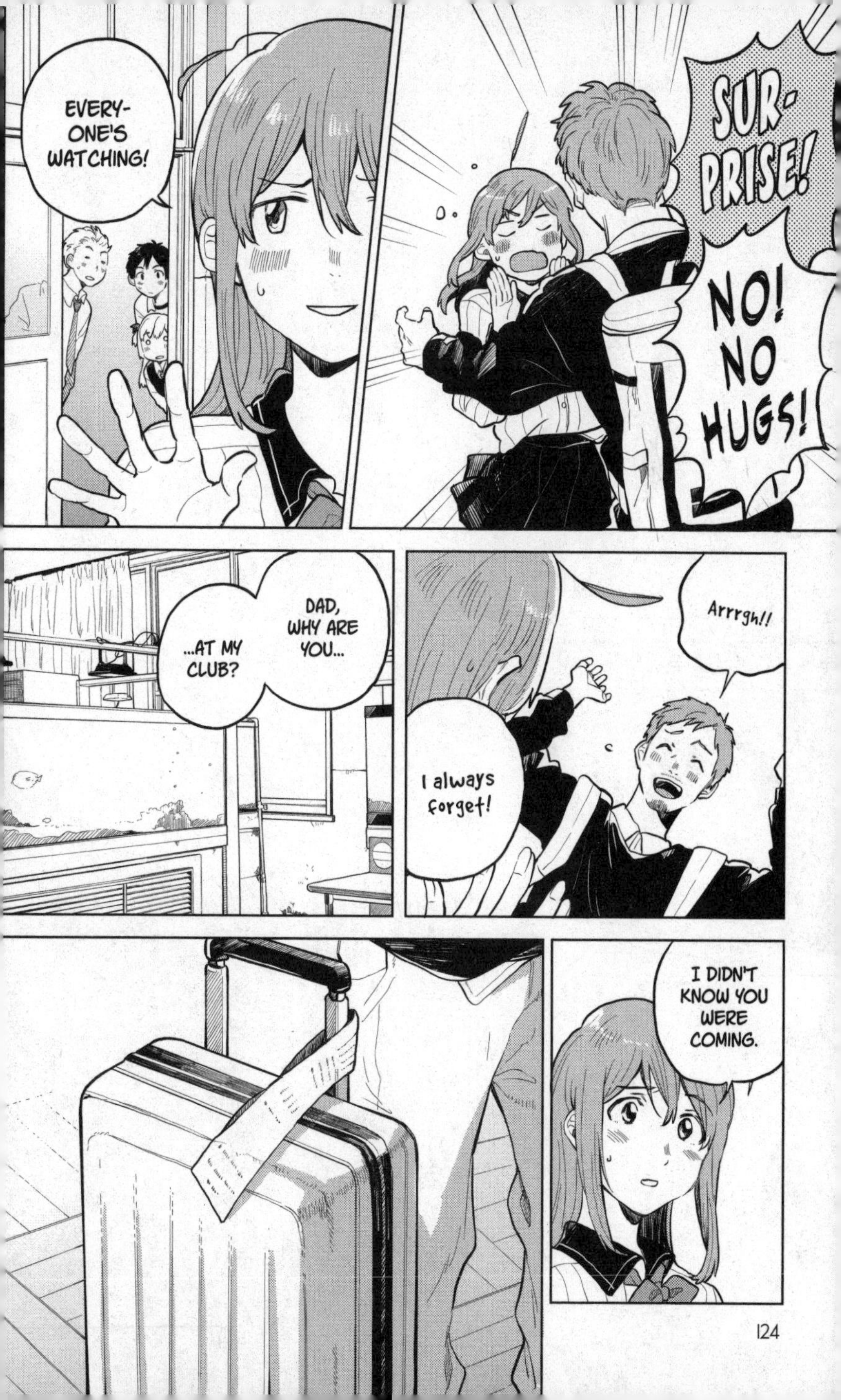
SUR-PRISE!
NO! NO HUGS!
EVERY-ONE'S WATCHING!
Arrrgh!!
I always forget!
DAD, WHY ARE YOU...
...AT MY CLUB?
I DIDN'T KNOW YOU WERE COMING.

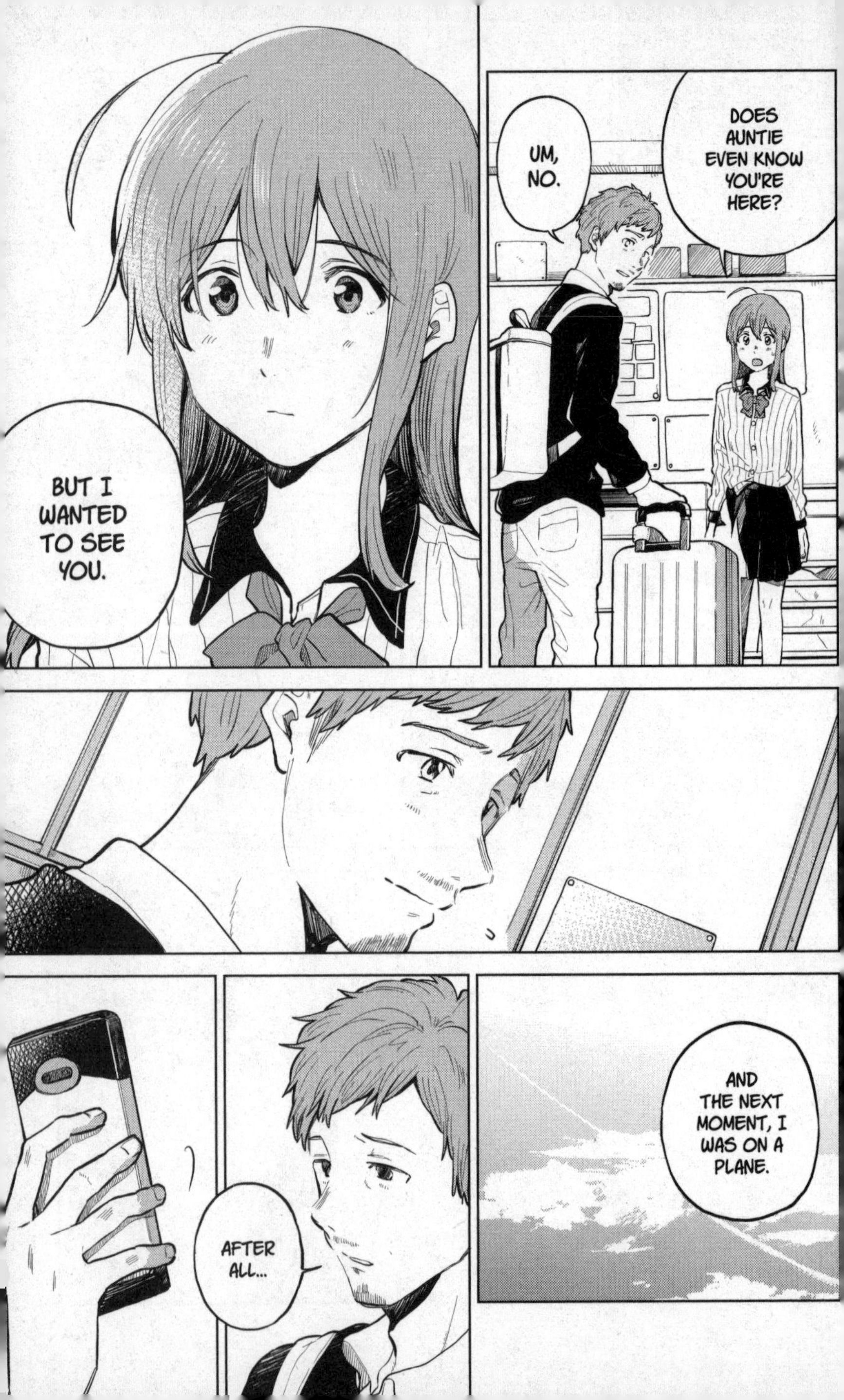
DOES AUNTIE EVEN KNOW YOU'RE HERE?
UM, NO.
BUT I WANTED TO SEE YOU.
AND THE NEXT MOMENT, I WAS ON A PLANE.
AFTER ALL...

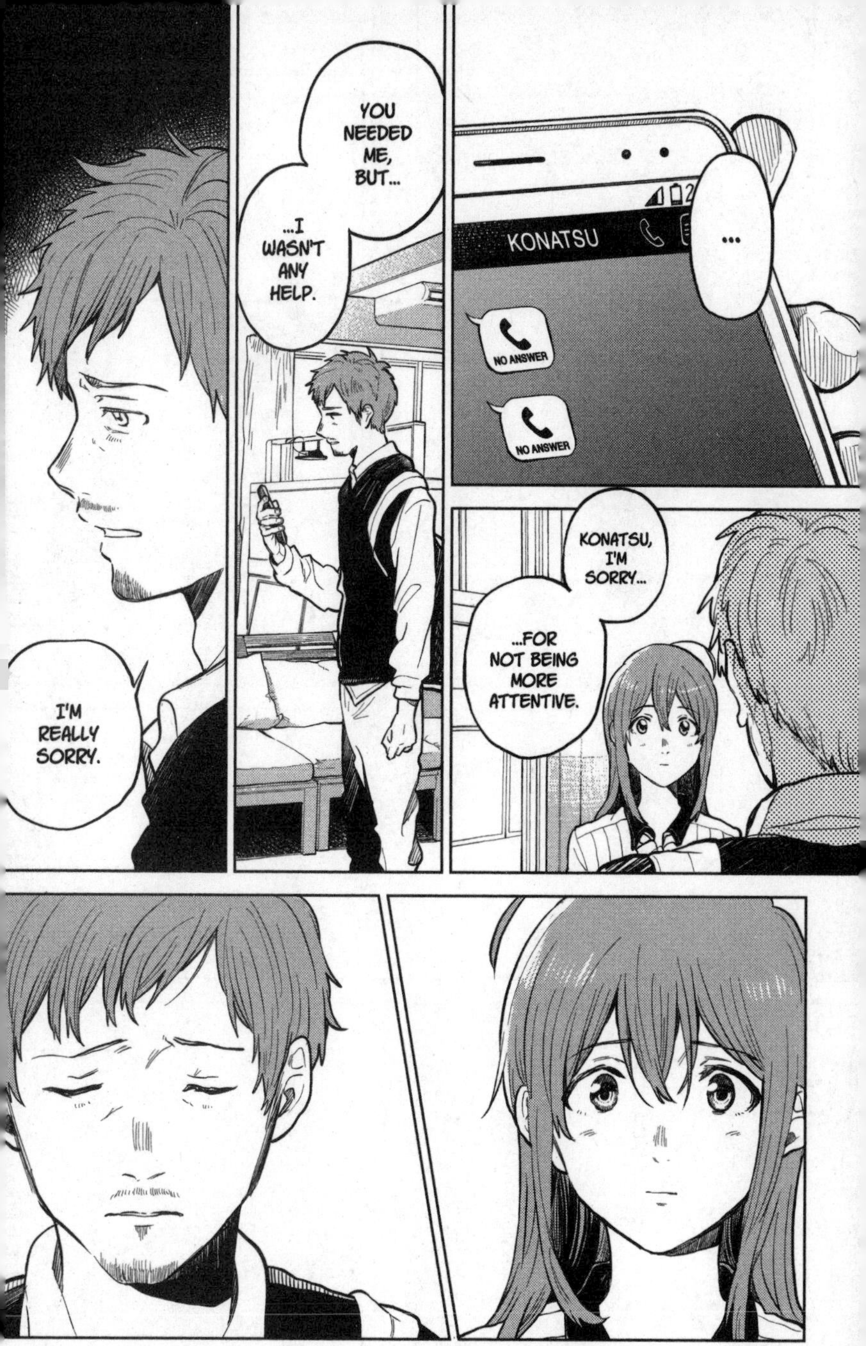
...
KONATSU
NO ANSWER
NO ANSWER
KONATSU, I'M SORRY...
...FOR NOT BEING MORE ATTENTIVE.
YOU NEEDED ME, BUT...
...I WASN'T ANY HELP.
I'M REALLY SORRY.

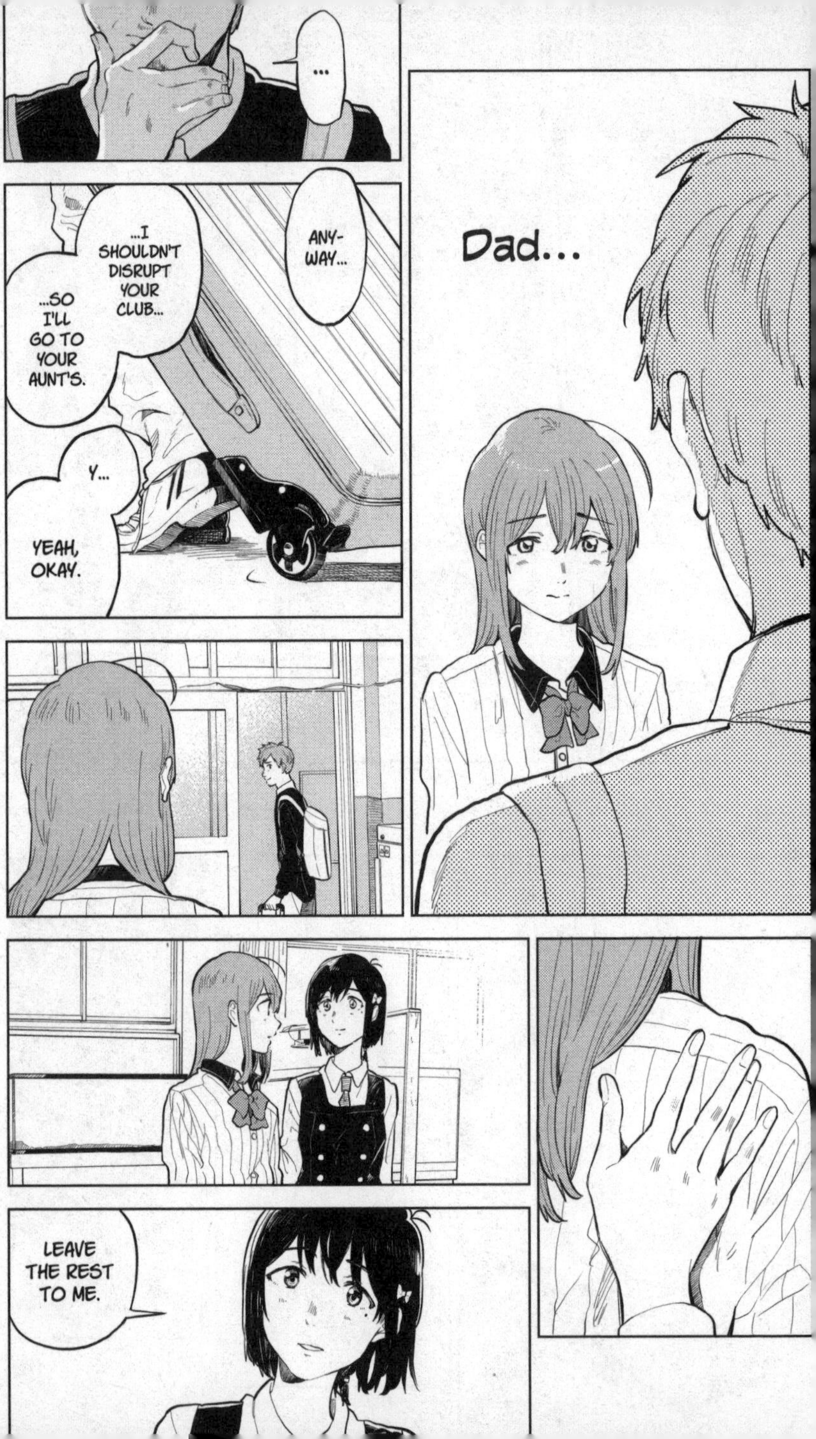
Dad...
...
ANY-WAY...
...I SHOULDN'T DISRUPT YOUR CLUB...
...SO I'LL GO TO YOUR AUNT'S.
Y... YEAH, OKAY.
LEAVE THE REST TO ME.

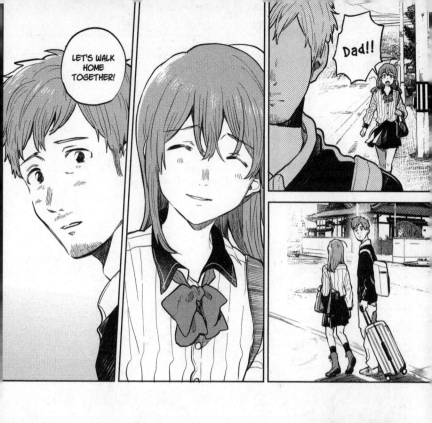

LET'S WALK HOME TOGETHER!

Dad!!

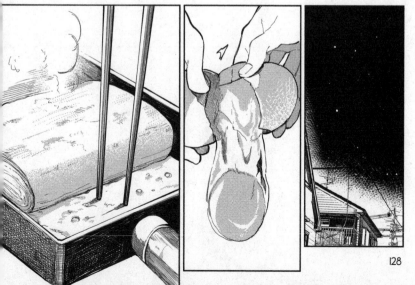

128

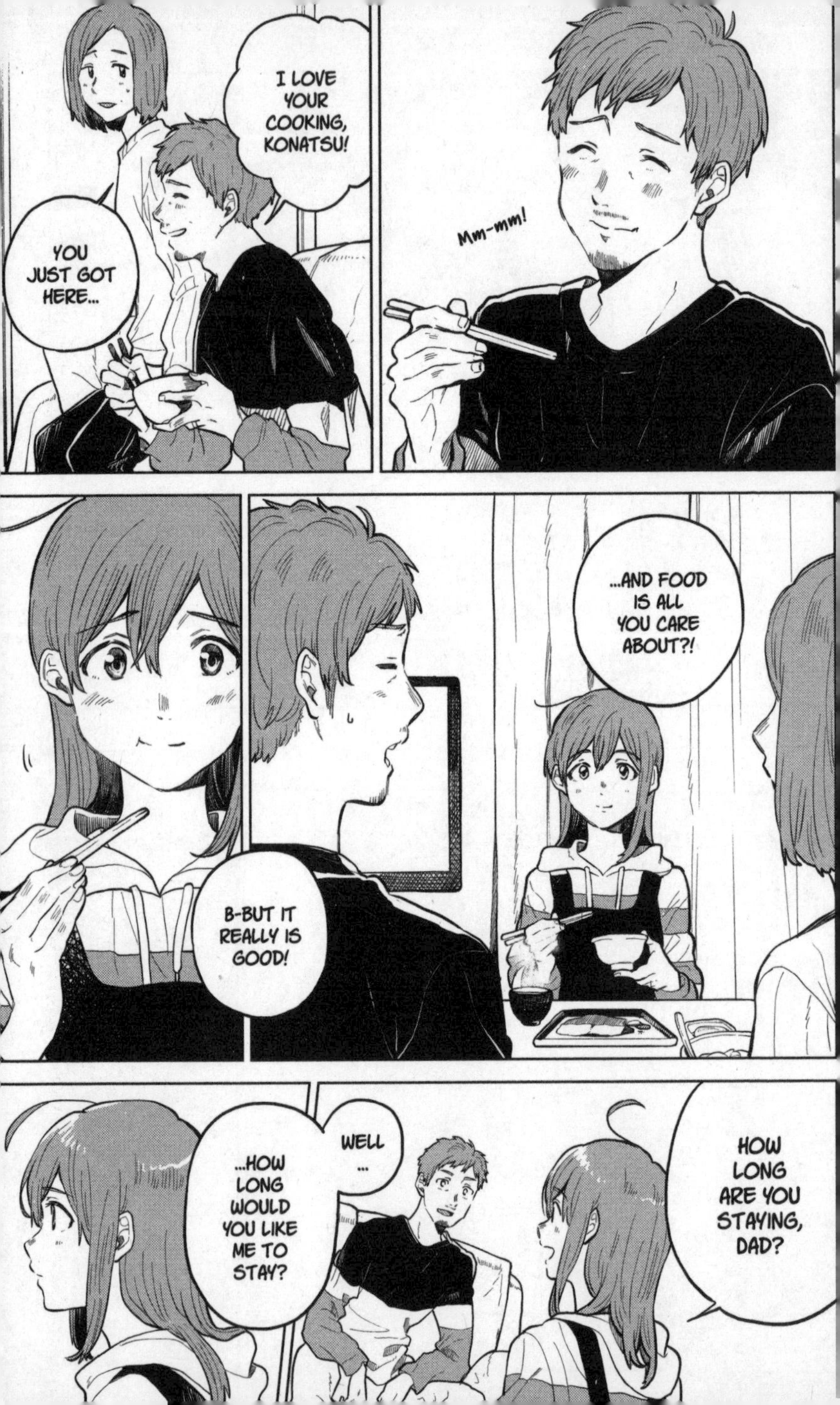
Mm-mm!
I LOVE YOUR COOKING, KONATSU!
YOU JUST GOT HERE...
...AND FOOD IS ALL YOU CARE ABOUT?!
B-BUT IT REALLY IS GOOD!
HOW LONG ARE YOU STAYING, DAD?
WELL ...
...HOW LONG WOULD YOU LIKE ME TO STAY?

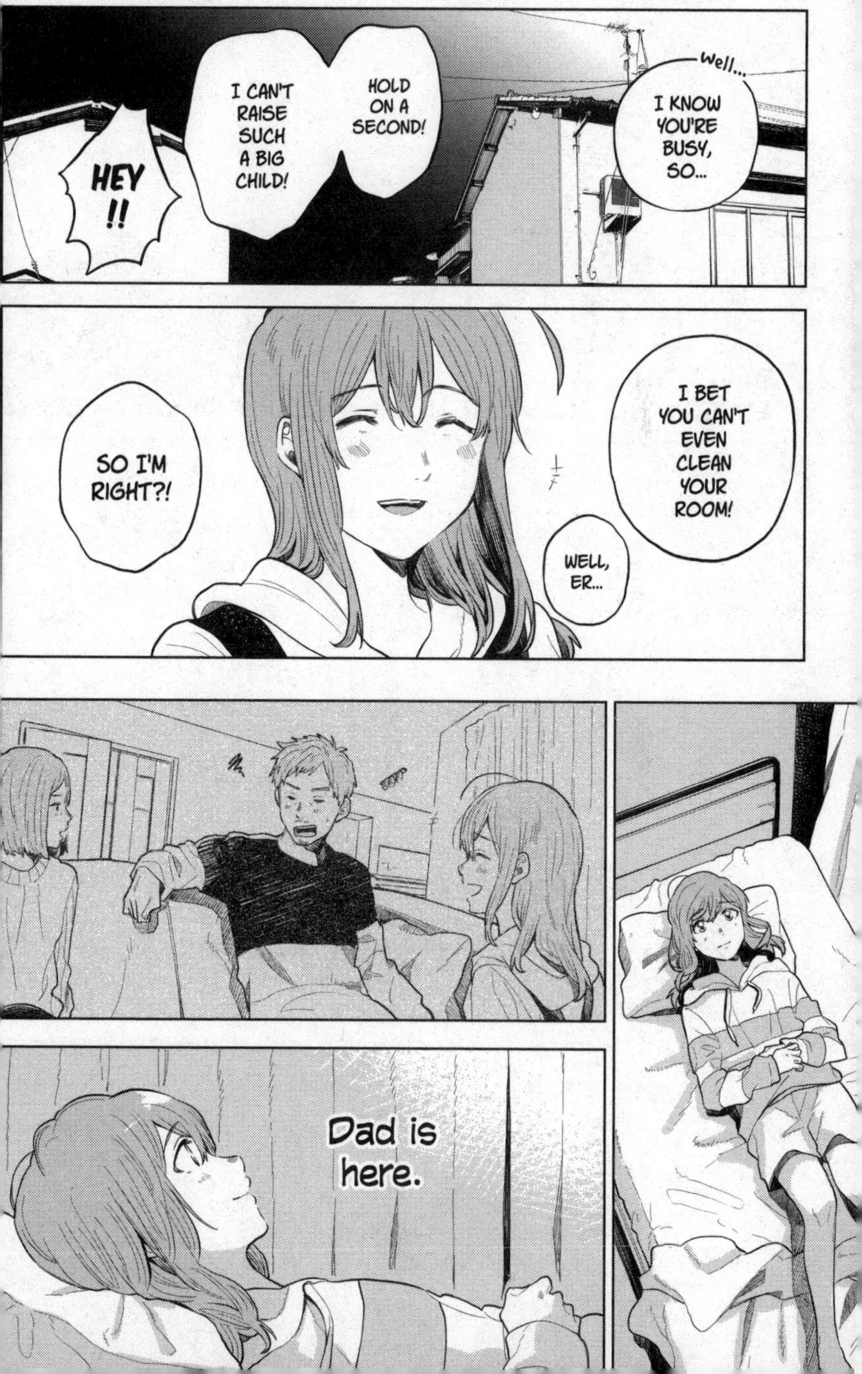
Well...
I KNOW YOU'RE BUSY, SO...
HOLD ON A SECOND!
I CAN'T RAISE SUCH A BIG CHILD!
HEY !!
I BET YOU CAN'T EVEN CLEAN YOUR ROOM!
WELL, ER...
SO I'M RIGHT?!
Dad is here.

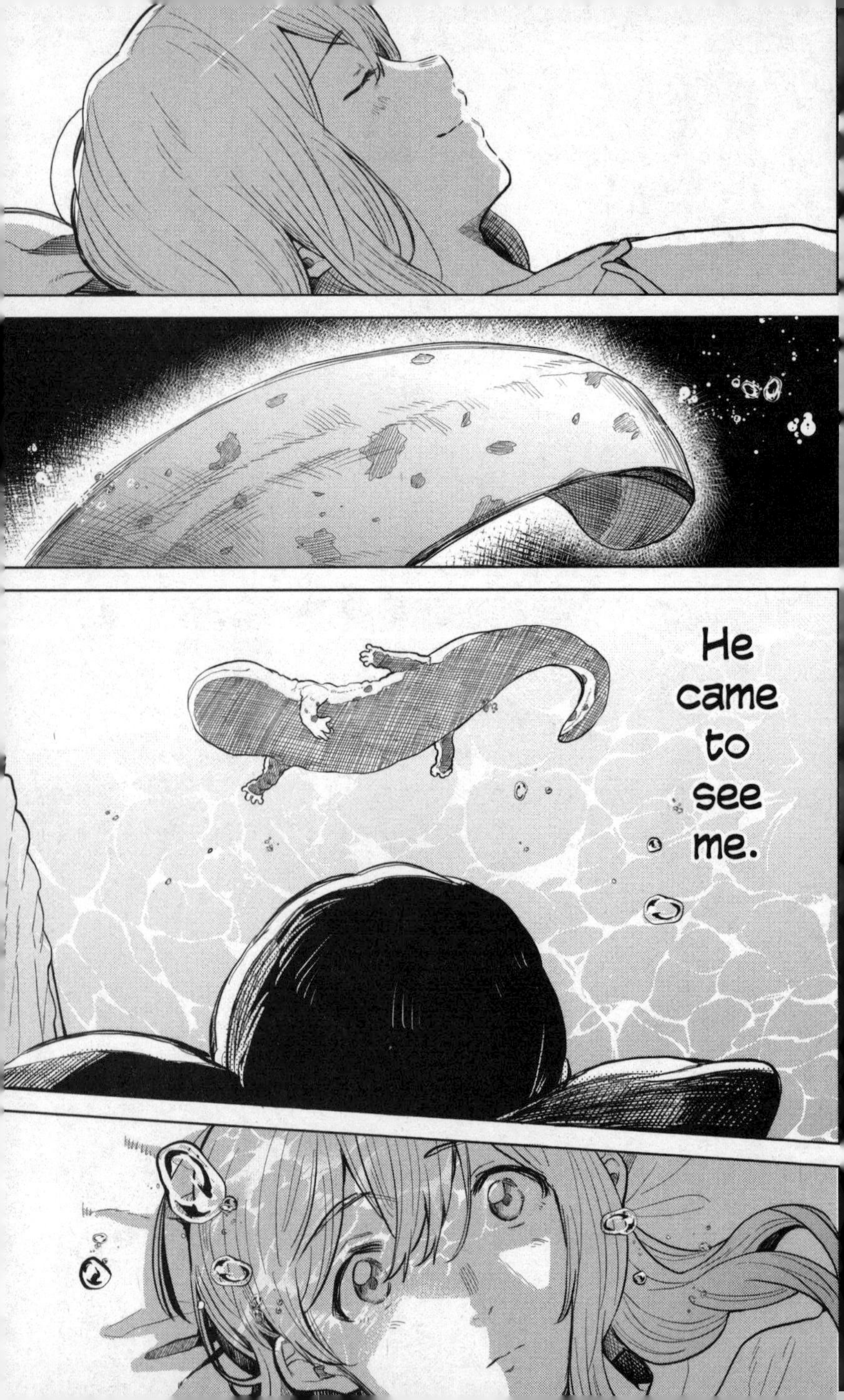
He came to see me.

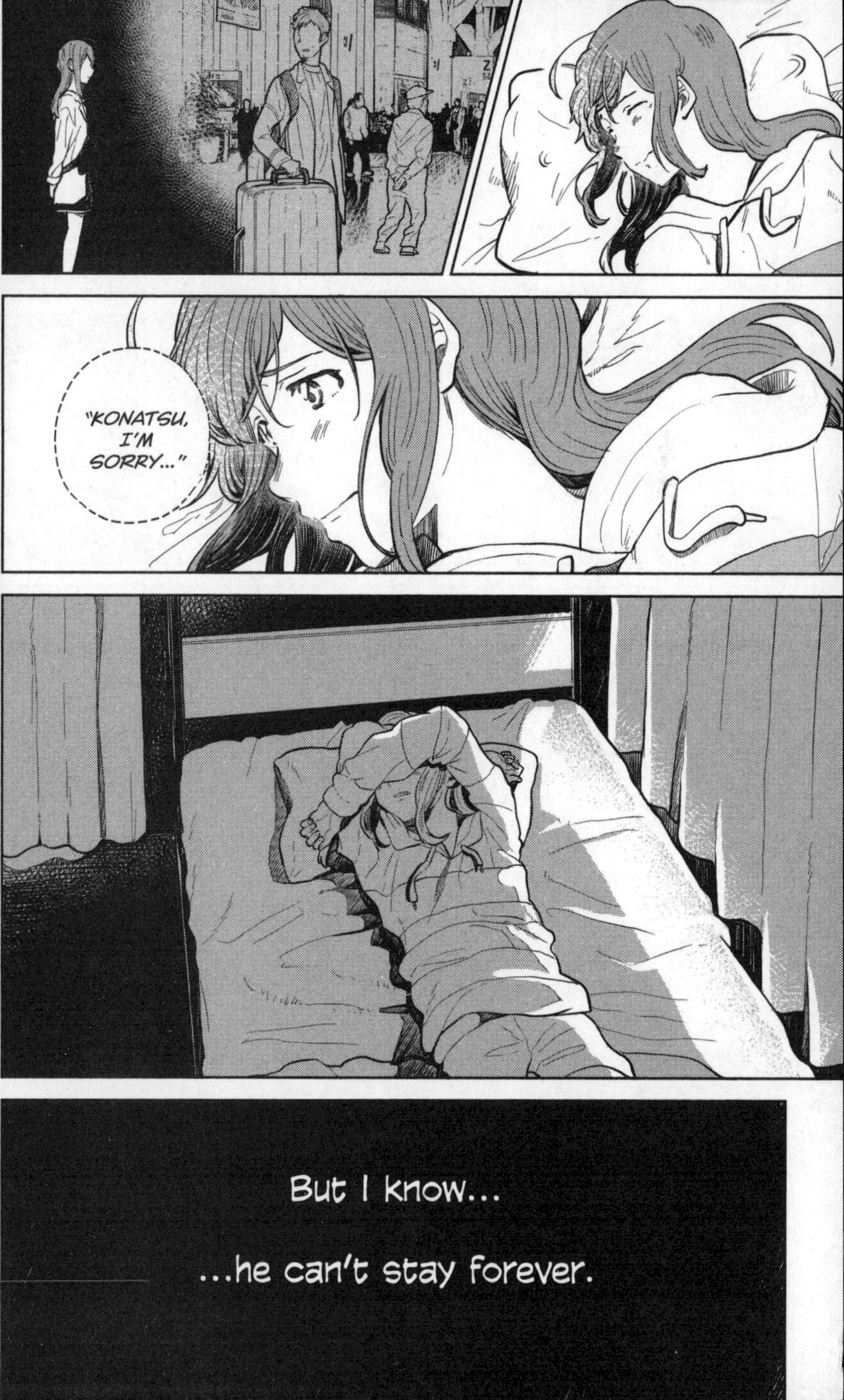
"KONATSU, I'M SORRY..."
But I know...
...he can't stay forever.

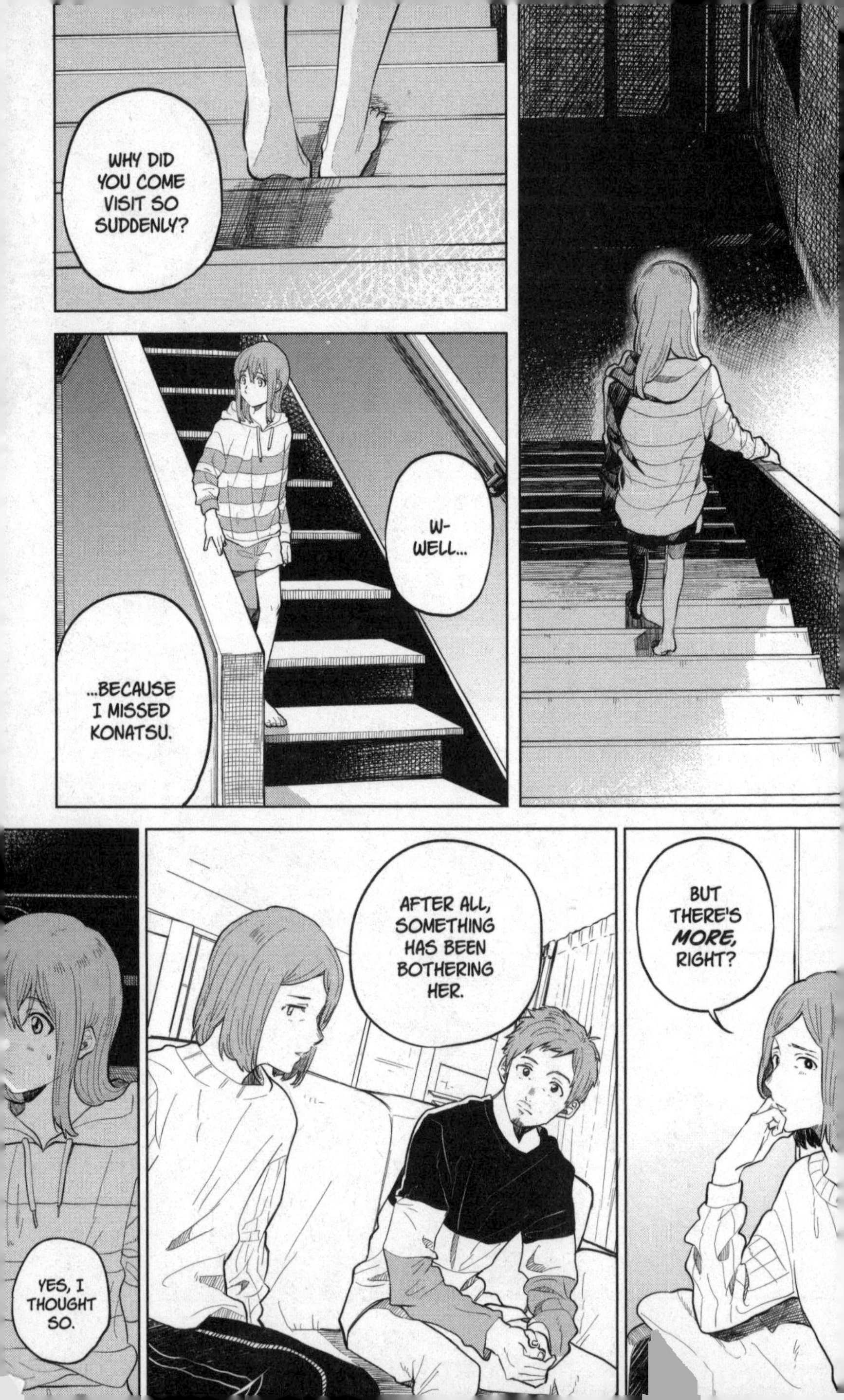
WHY DID YOU COME VISIT SO SUDDENLY?
W-WELL...
...BECAUSE I MISSED KONATSU.
BUT THERE'S *MORE*, RIGHT?
AFTER ALL, SOMETHING HAS BEEN BOTHERING HER.
YES, I THOUGHT SO.

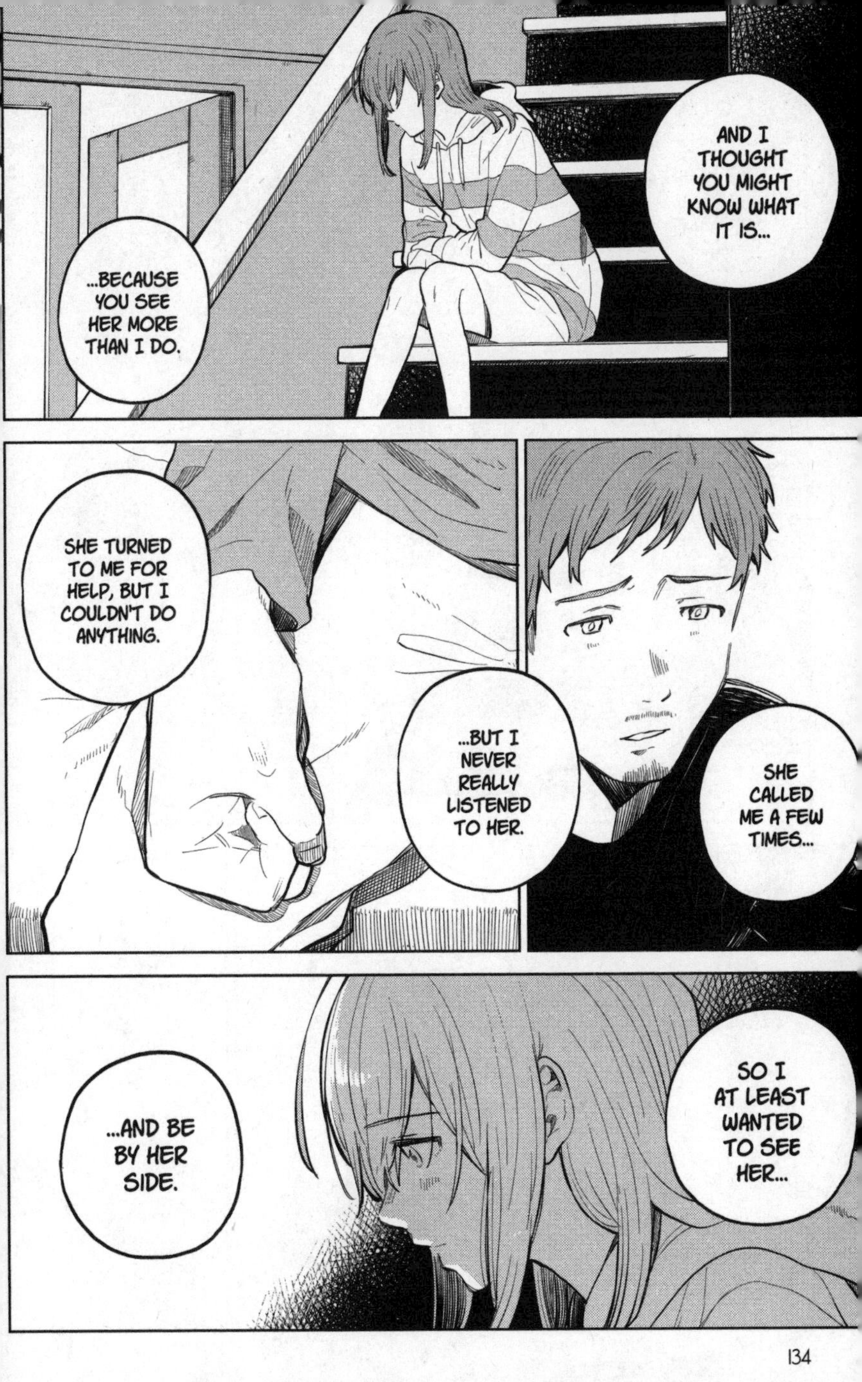
AND I THOUGHT YOU MIGHT KNOW WHAT IT IS...
...BECAUSE YOU SEE HER MORE THAN I DO.
SHE CALLED ME A FEW TIMES...
...BUT I NEVER REALLY LISTENED TO HER.
SHE TURNED TO ME FOR HELP, BUT I COULDN'T DO ANYTHING.
SO I AT LEAST WANTED TO SEE HER...
...AND BE BY HER SIDE.

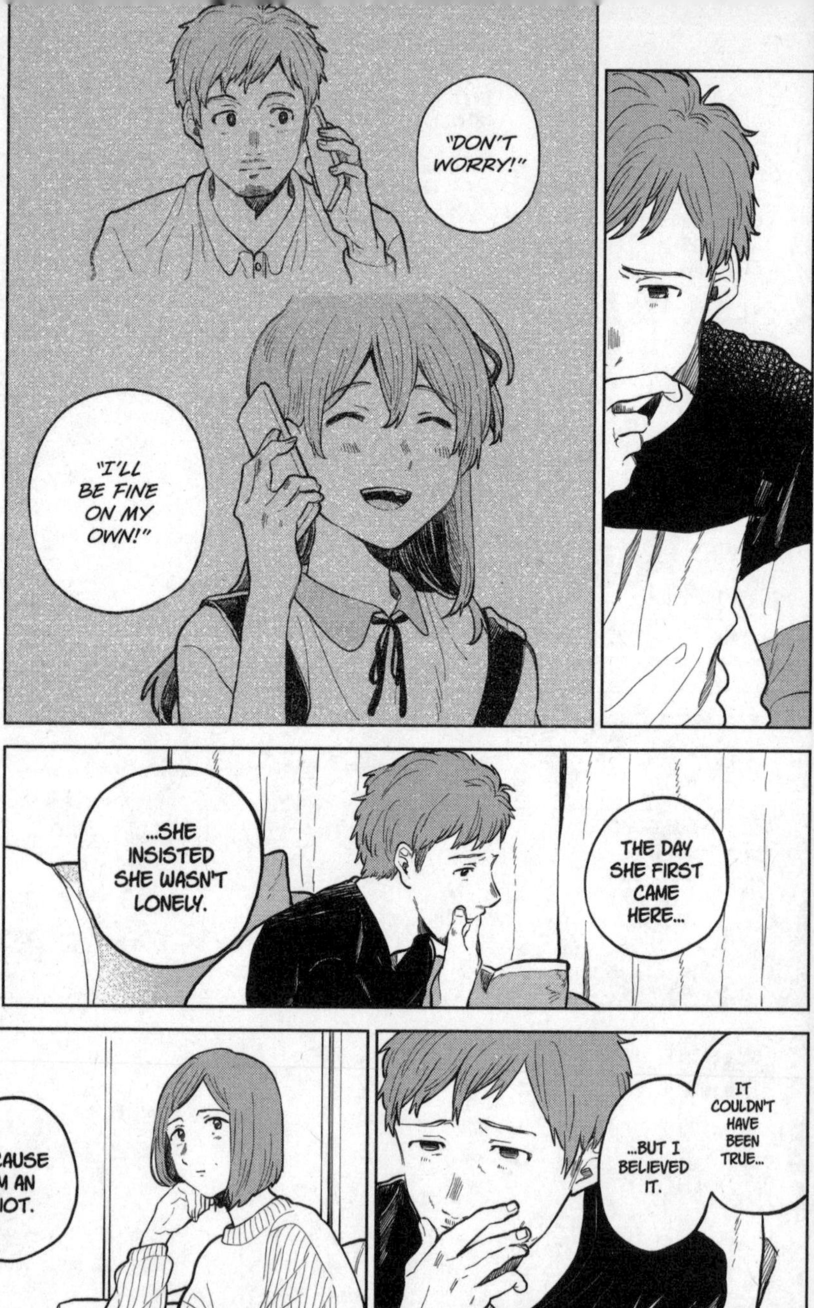
"DON'T WORRY!"
"I'LL BE FINE ON MY OWN!"
THE DAY SHE FIRST CAME HERE...
...SHE INSISTED SHE WASN'T LONELY.
IT COULDN'T HAVE BEEN TRUE...
...BUT I BELIEVED IT.
BECAUSE I'M AN IDIOT.

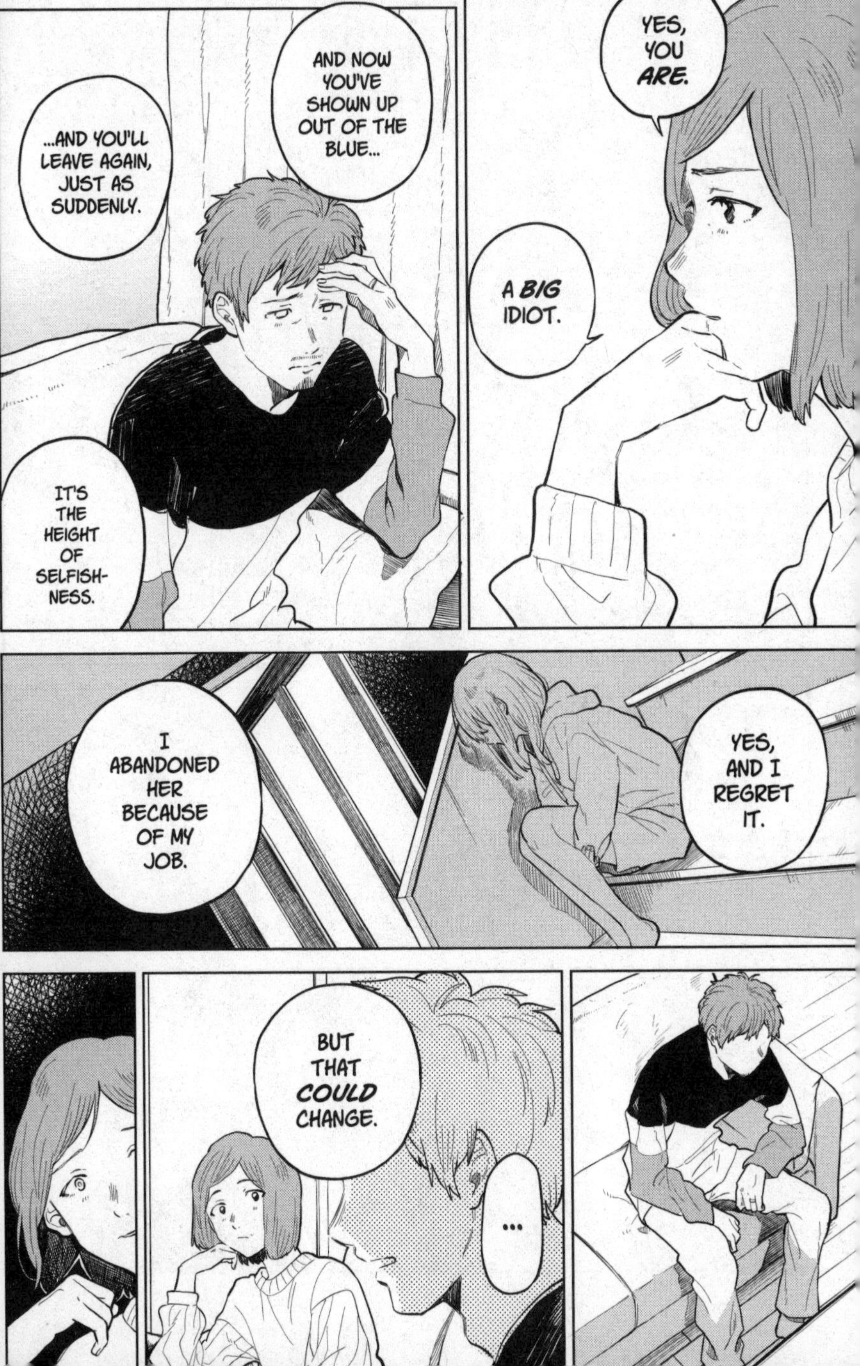
YES, YOU ARE.
A BIG IDIOT.
AND NOW YOU'VE SHOWN UP OUT OF THE BLUE...
...AND YOU'LL LEAVE AGAIN, JUST AS SUDDENLY.
IT'S THE HEIGHT OF SELFISH-NESS.
YES, AND I REGRET IT.
I ABANDONED HER BECAUSE OF MY JOB.
BUT THAT COULD CHANGE.
...

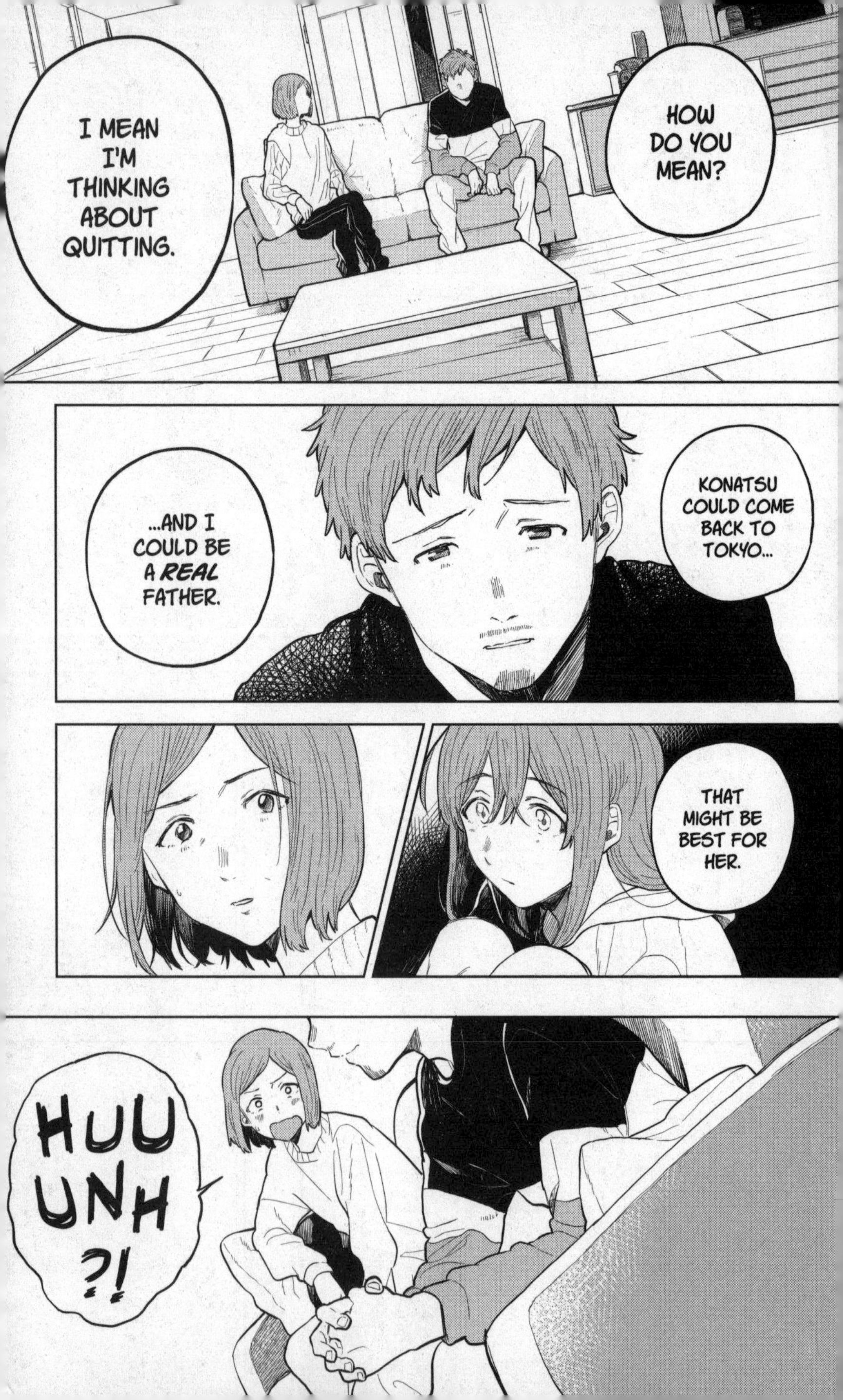
HOW DO YOU MEAN?
I MEAN I'M THINKING ABOUT QUITTING.
KONATSU COULD COME BACK TO TOKYO...
...AND I COULD BE A *REAL* FATHER.
THAT MIGHT BE BEST FOR HER.
HUUUNH?!

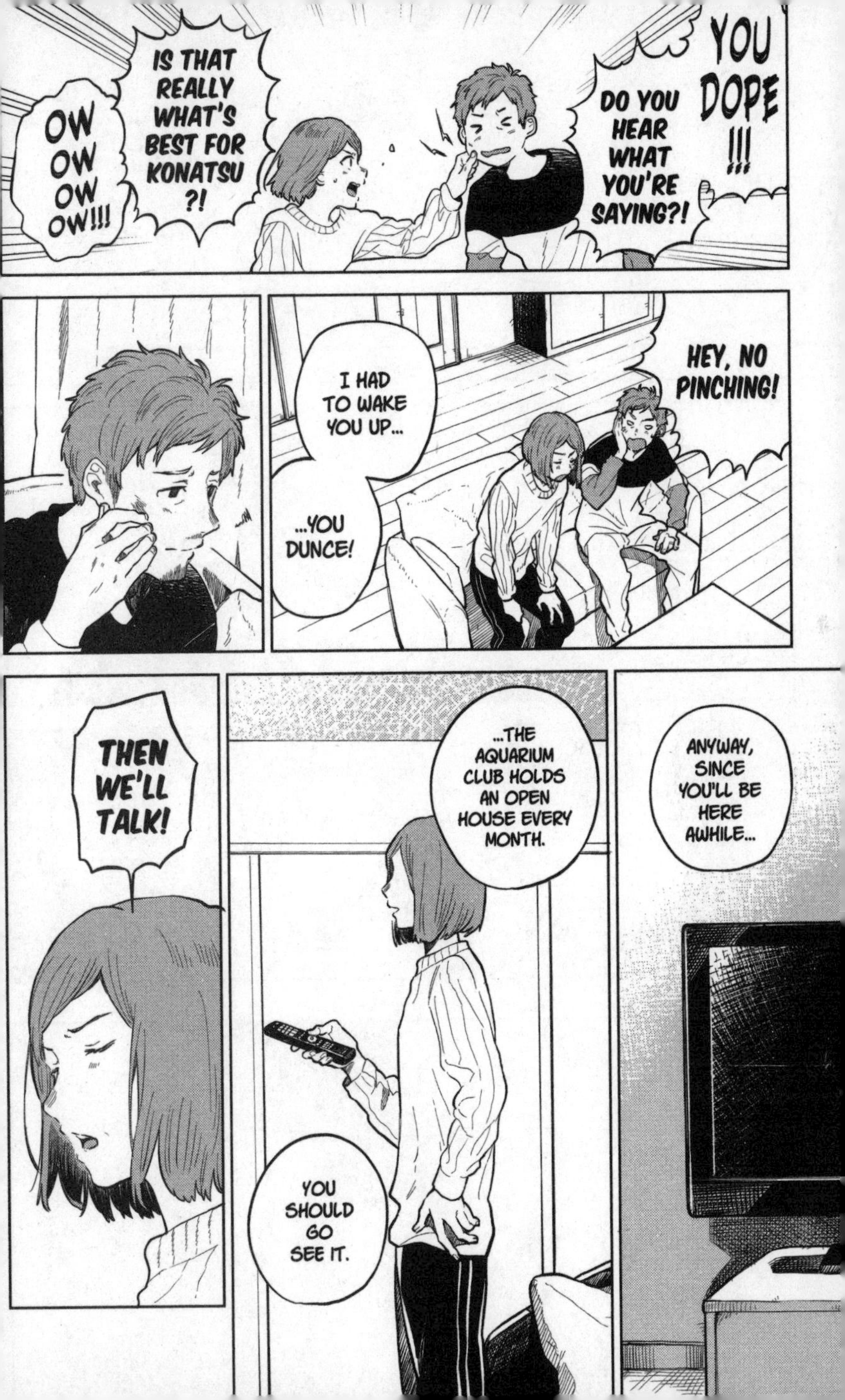
YOU DOPE!!!
DO YOU HEAR WHAT YOU'RE SAYING?!
IS THAT REALLY WHAT'S BEST FOR KONATSU?!
OW OW OW OW!!!
HEY, NO PINCHING!
I HAD TO WAKE YOU UP...
...YOU DUNCE!
ANYWAY, SINCE YOU'LL BE HERE AWHILE...
...THE AQUARIUM CLUB HOLDS AN OPEN HOUSE EVERY MONTH.
YOU SHOULD GO SEE IT.
THEN WE'LL TALK!

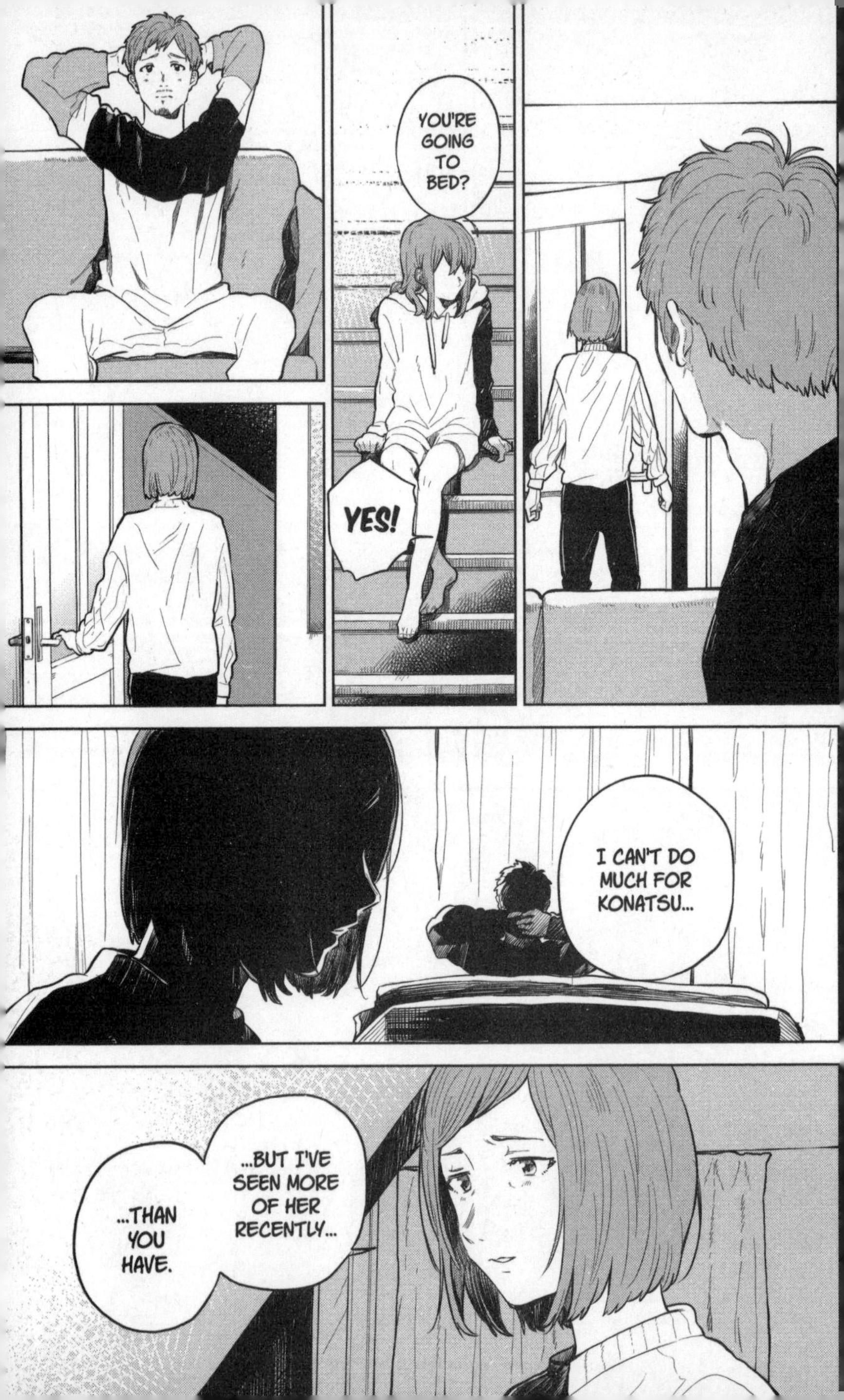
YOU'RE GOING TO BED?
YES!
I CAN'T DO MUCH FOR KONATSU...
...BUT I'VE SEEN MORE OF HER RECENTLY...
...THAN YOU HAVE.

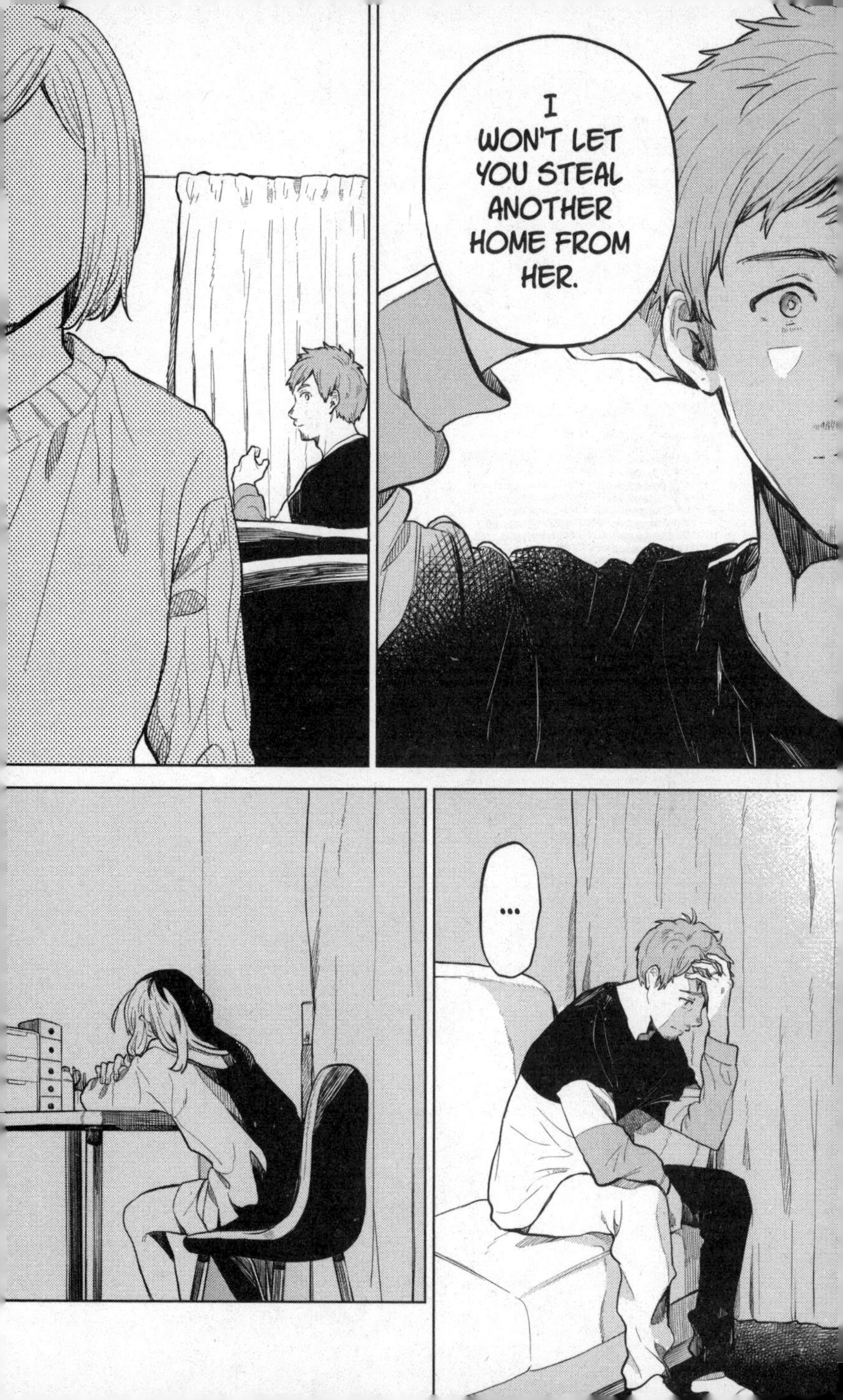
I WON'T LET YOU STEAL ANOTHER HOME FROM HER.
...

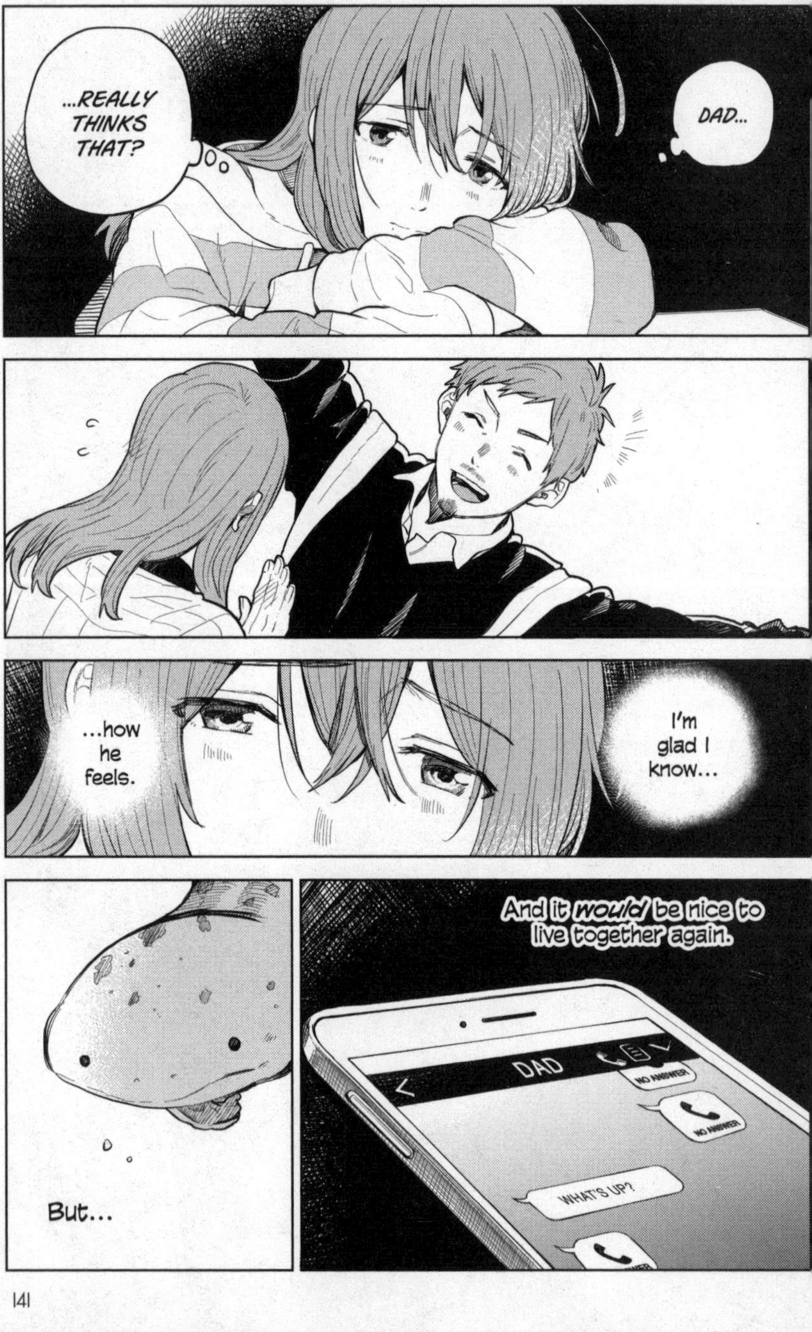
DAD...
...REALLY THINKS THAT?
I'm glad I know...
...how he feels.
And it *would* be nice to live together again.
DAD
NO ANSWER
NO ANSWER
WHAT'S UP?
But...

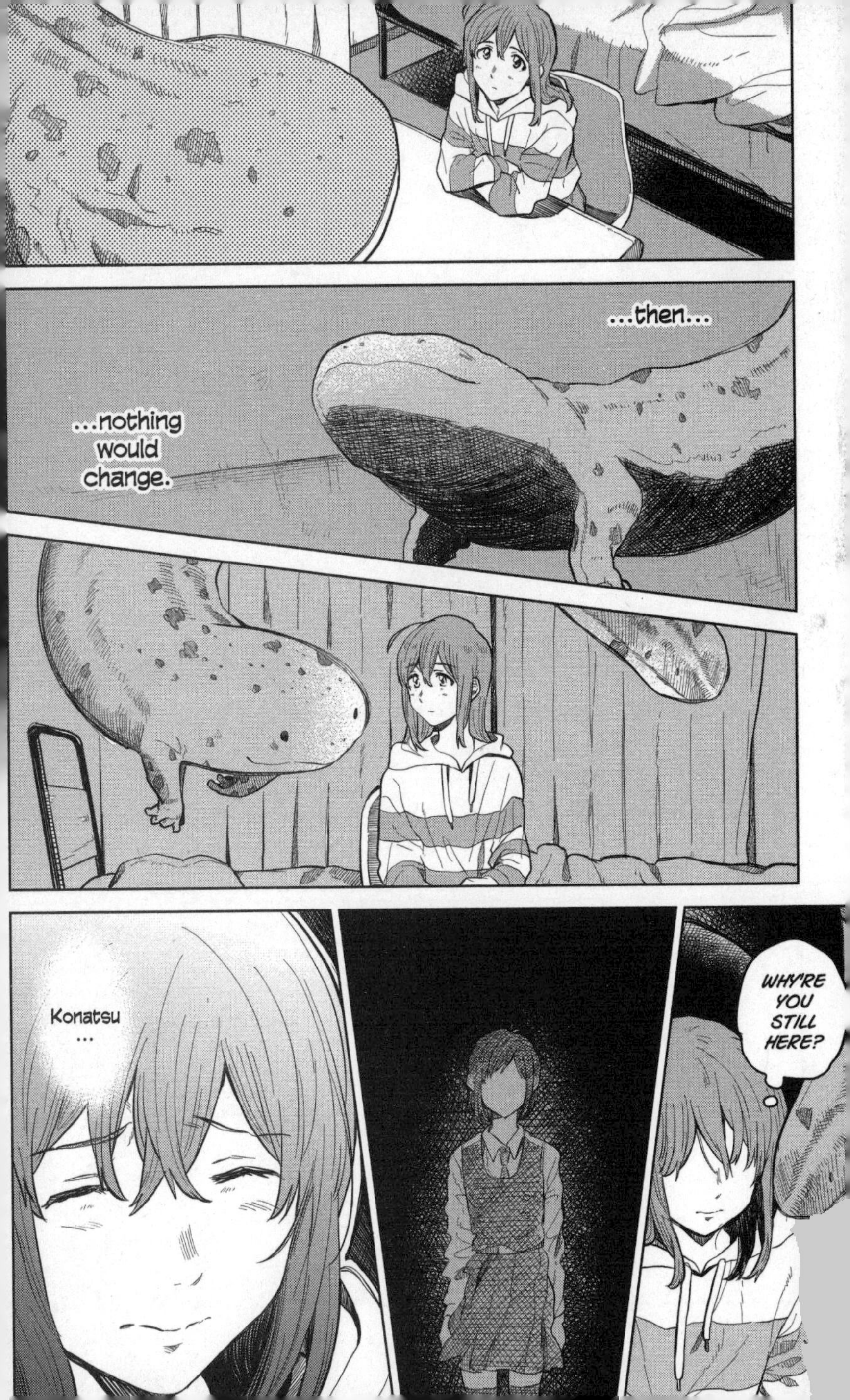
...then...
...nothing would change.
WHY'RE YOU STILL HERE?
Konatsu ...

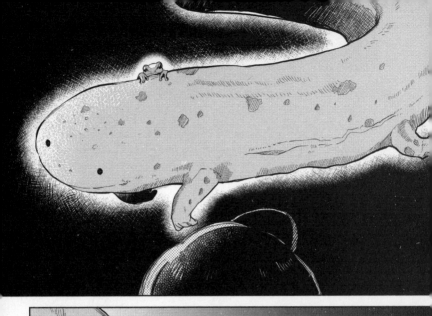

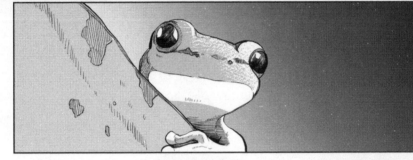

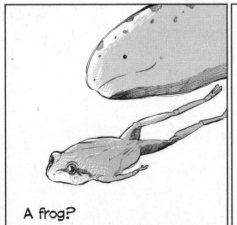

A frog?

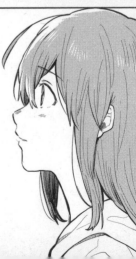

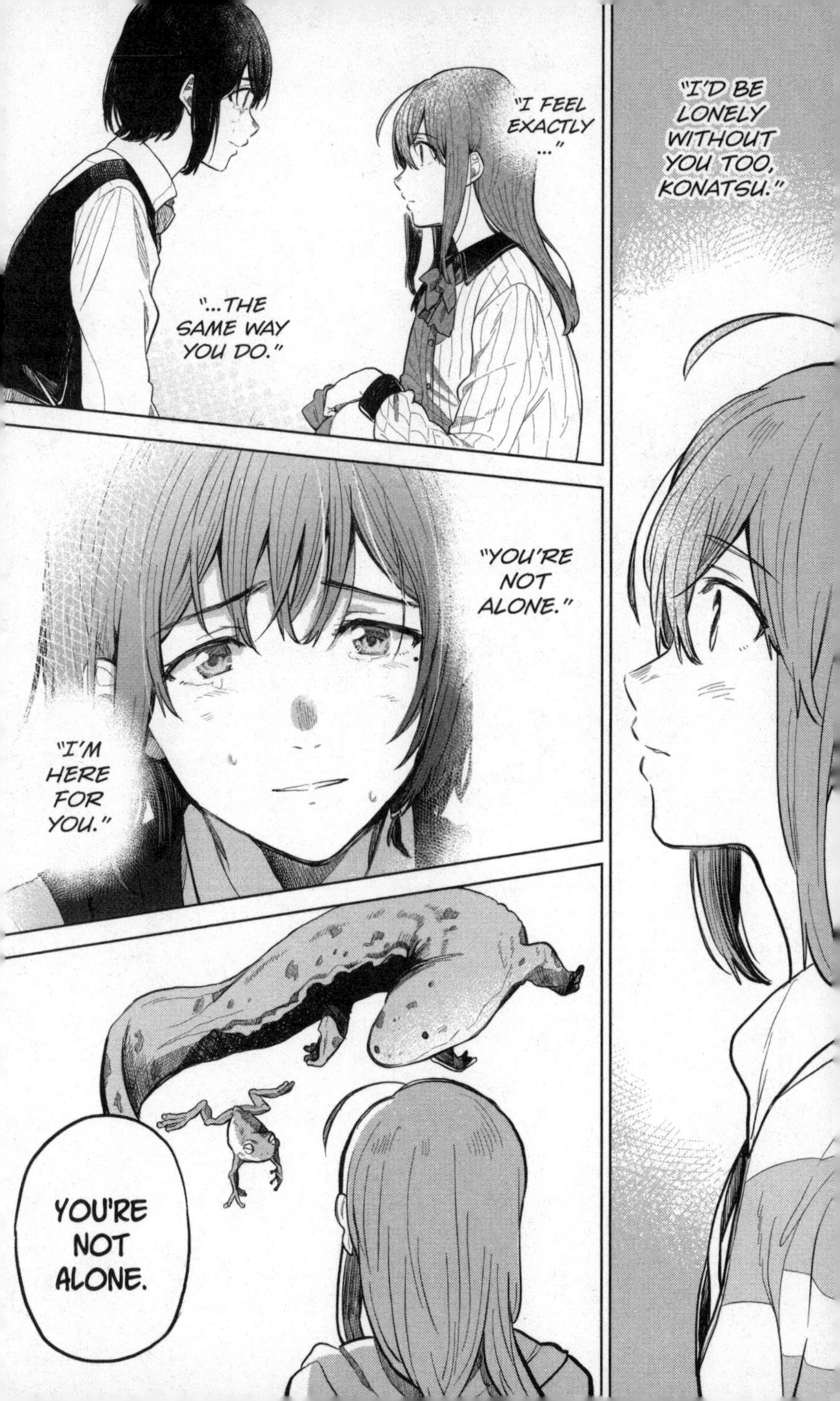
"I'D BE LONELY WITHOUT YOU TOO, KONATSU."
"I FEEL EXACTLY ..."
"...THE SAME WAY YOU DO."
"YOU'RE NOT ALONE."
"I'M HERE FOR YOU."
YOU'RE NOT ALONE.

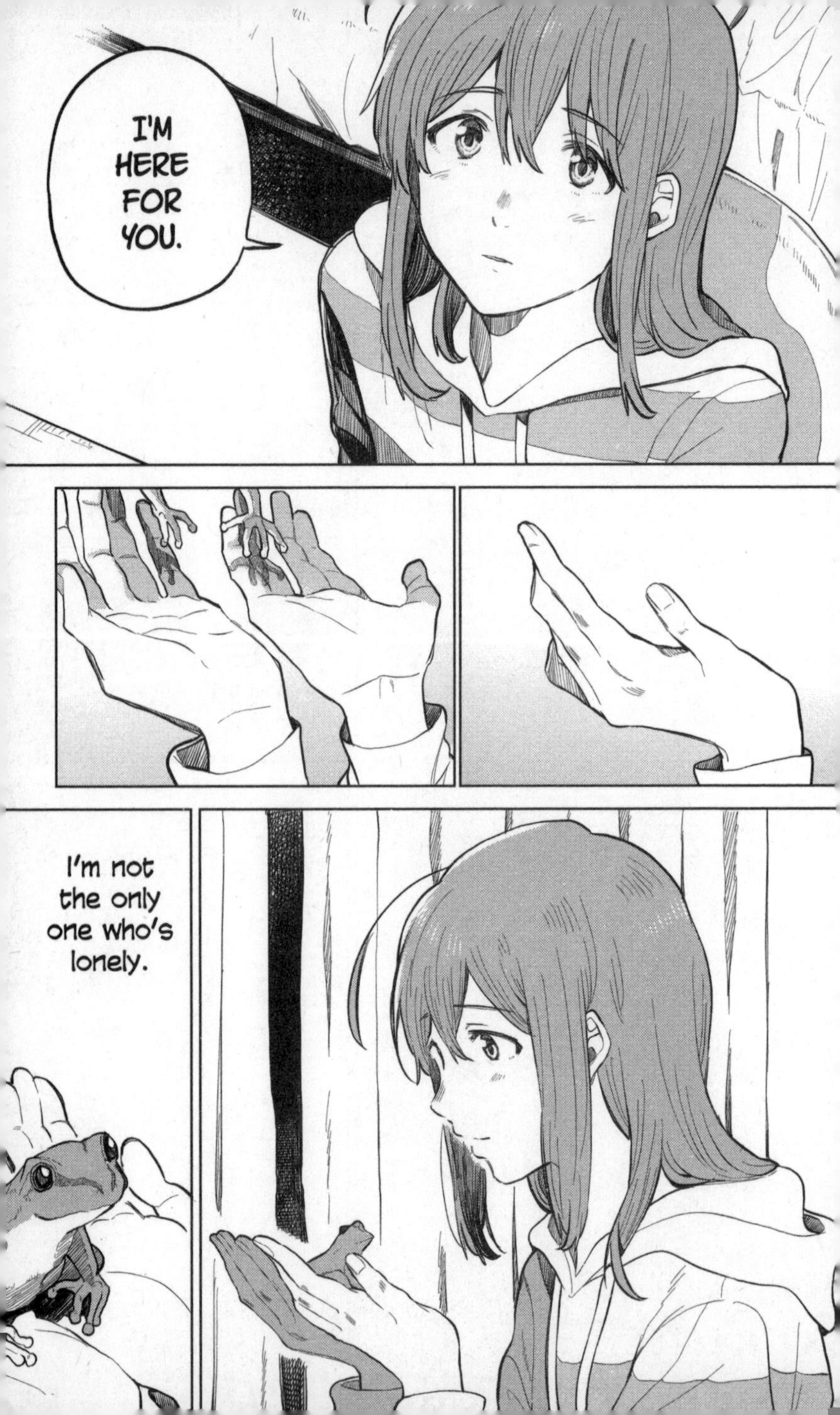
I'M HERE FOR YOU.
I'm not the only one who's lonely.

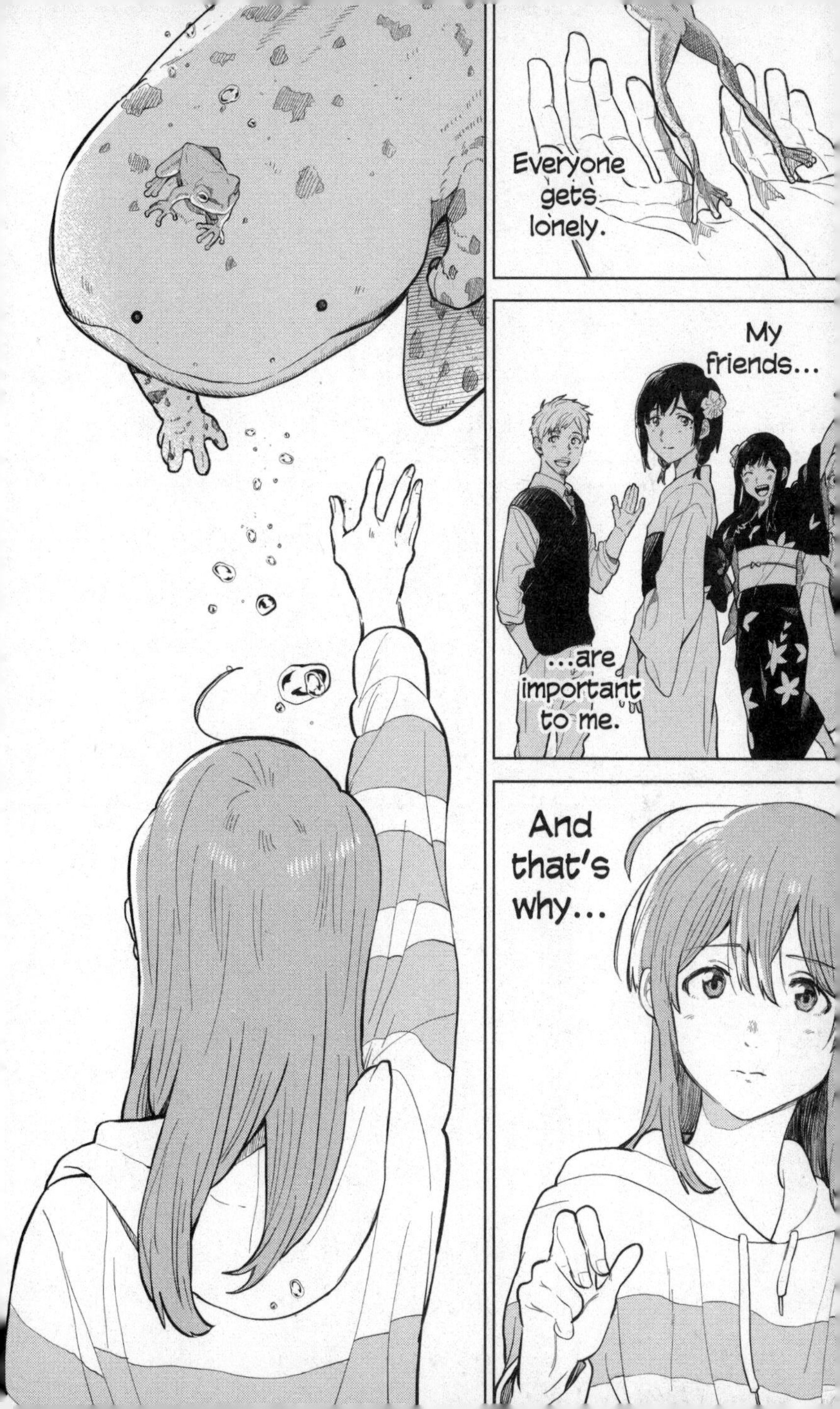
Everyone gets lonely.
My friends...
...are important to me.
And that's why...

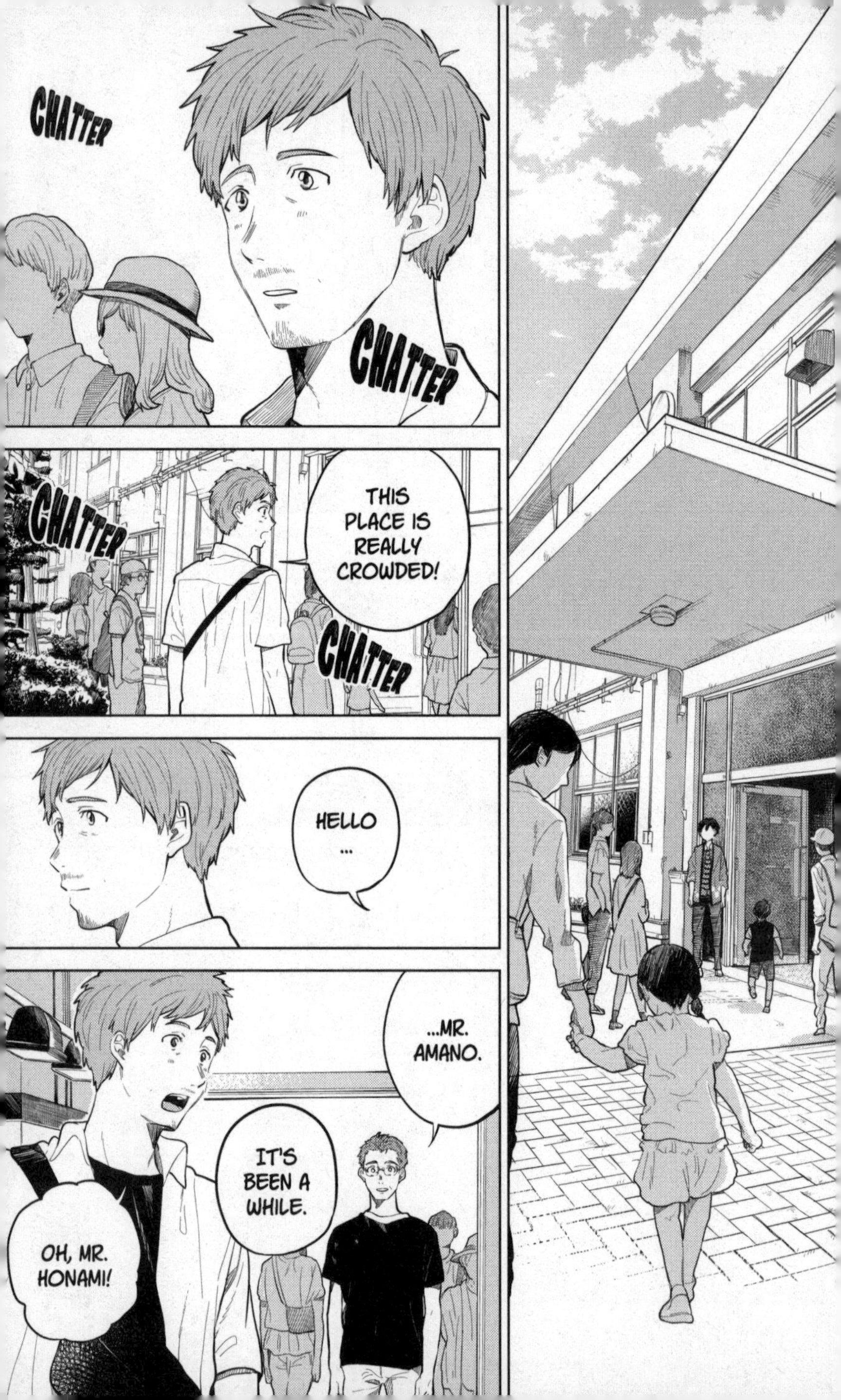
CHATTER
CHATTER
THIS PLACE IS REALLY CROWDED!
CHATTER
CHATTER
HELLO ...
...MR. AMANO.
IT'S BEEN A WHILE.
OH, MR. HONAMI!

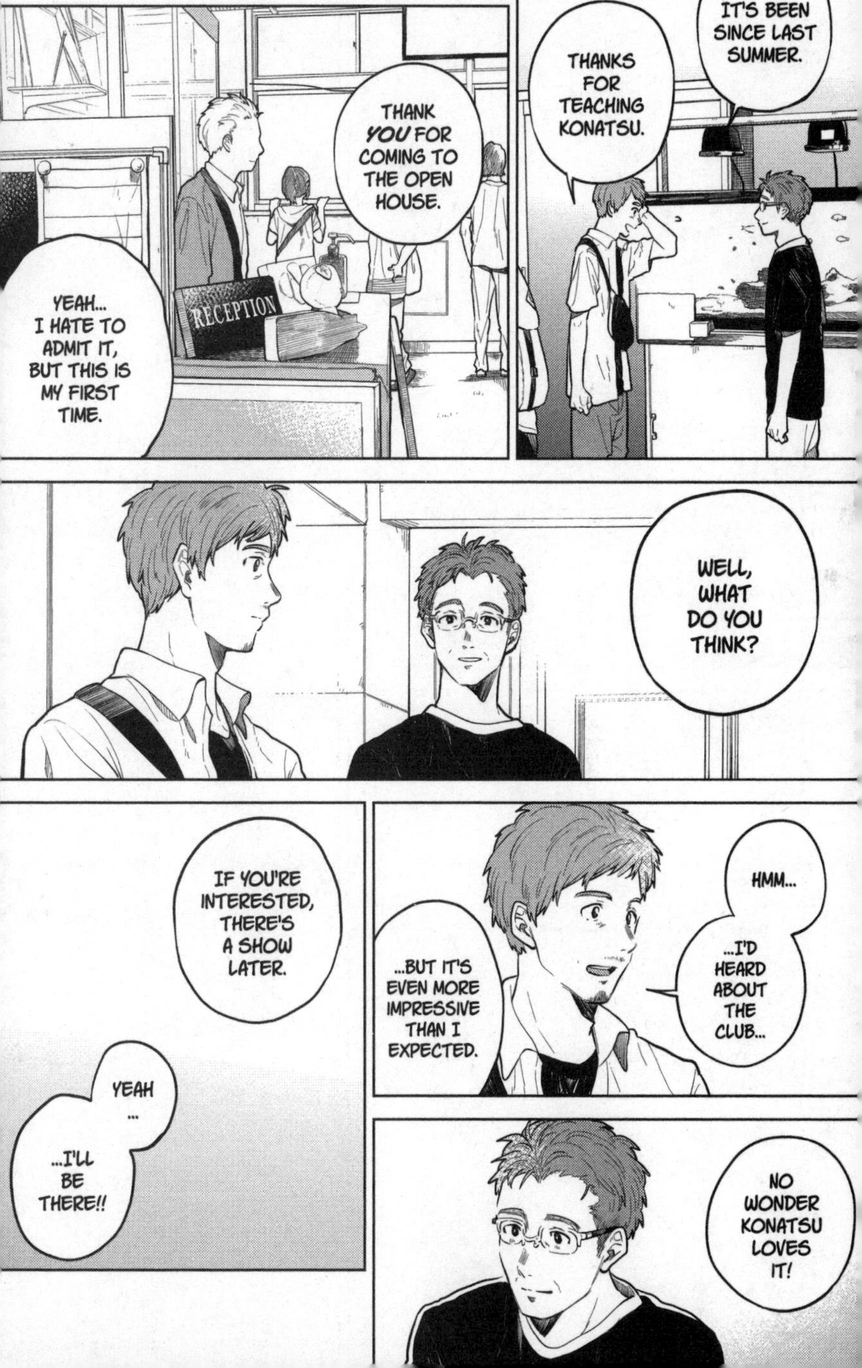
IT'S BEEN SINCE LAST SUMMER.
THANKS FOR TEACHING KONATSU.
THANK *YOU* FOR COMING TO THE OPEN HOUSE.
RECEPTION
YEAH... I HATE TO ADMIT IT, BUT THIS IS MY FIRST TIME.
WELL, WHAT DO YOU THINK?
HMM...
...I'D HEARD ABOUT THE CLUB...
...BUT IT'S EVEN MORE IMPRESSIVE THAN I EXPECTED.
NO WONDER KONATSU LOVES IT!
IF YOU'RE INTERESTED, THERE'S A SHOW LATER.
YEAH...
...I'LL BE THERE!!

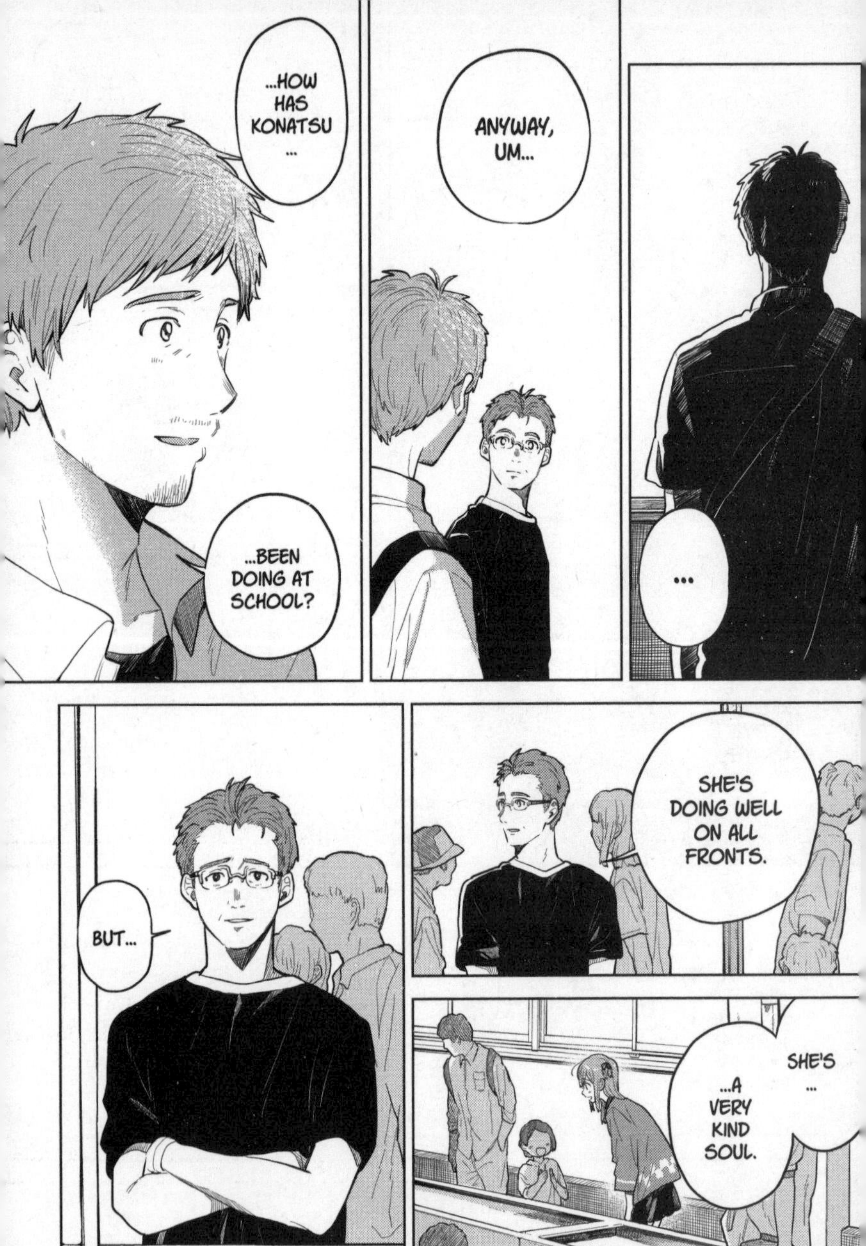
...
ANYWAY, UM...
...HOW HAS KONATSU ...
...BEEN DOING AT SCHOOL?
SHE'S DOING WELL ON ALL FRONTS.
SHE'S ...
...A VERY KIND SOUL.
BUT...

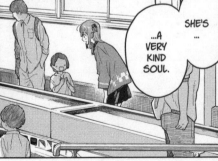

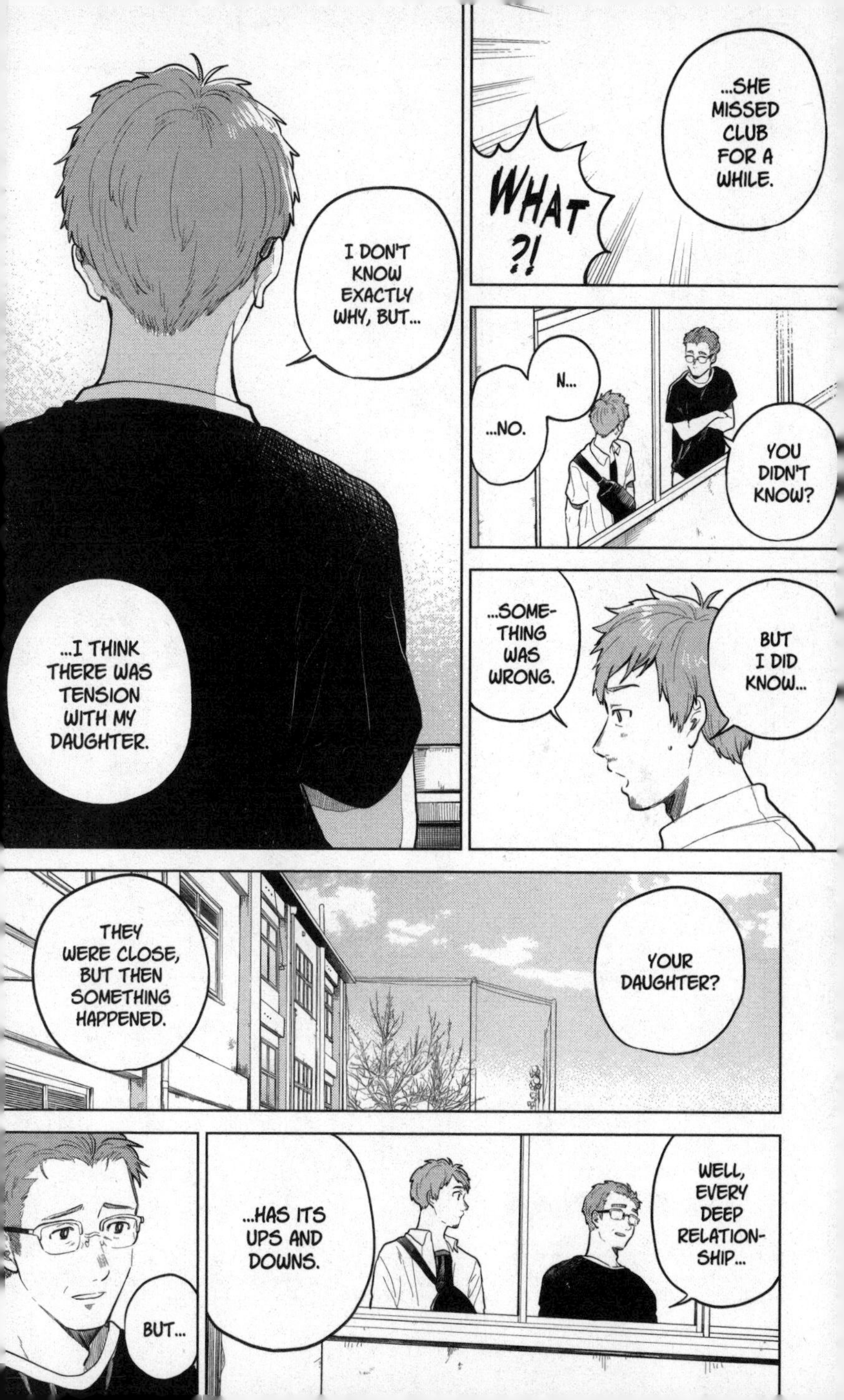
...SHE MISSED CLUB FOR A WHILE.
WHAT?!
YOU DIDN'T KNOW?
N... ...NO.
BUT I DID KNOW...
...SOMETHING WAS WRONG.
I DON'T KNOW EXACTLY WHY, BUT...
...I THINK THERE WAS TENSION WITH MY DAUGHTER.
YOUR DAUGHTER?
THEY WERE CLOSE, BUT THEN SOMETHING HAPPENED.
WELL, EVERY DEEP RELATIONSHIP...
...HAS ITS UPS AND DOWNS.
BUT...

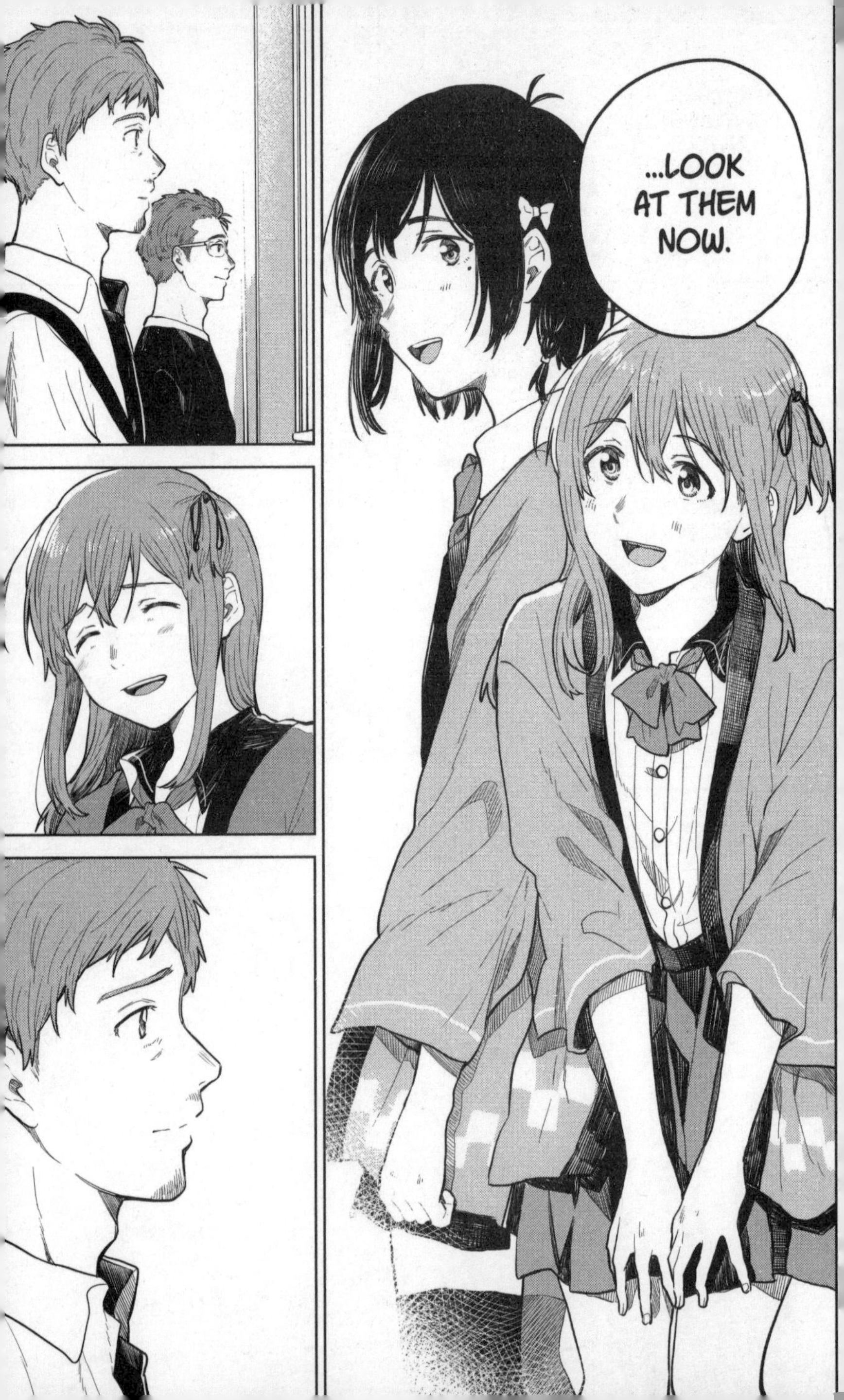
...LOOK AT THEM NOW.

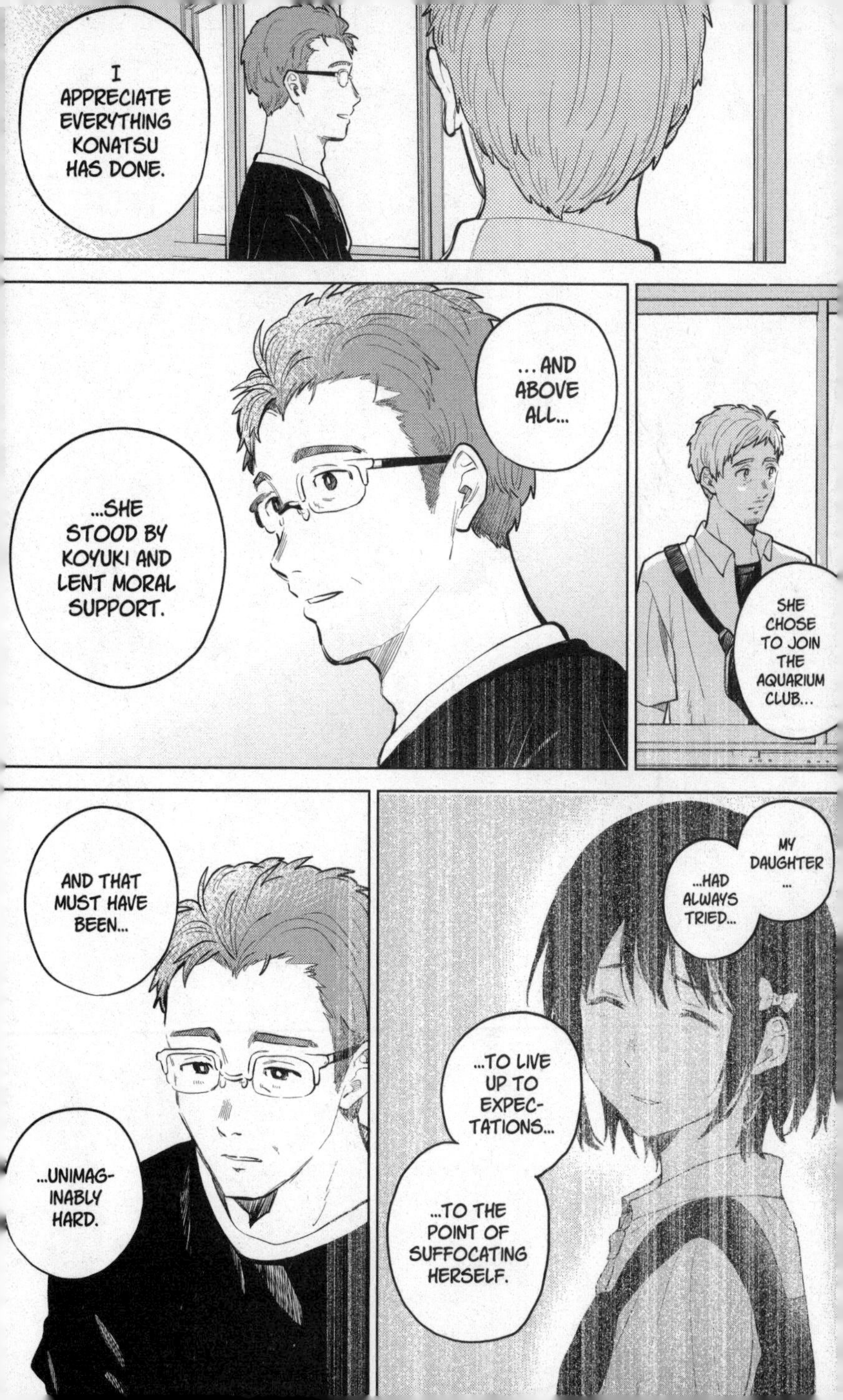
I APPRECIATE EVERYTHING KONATSU HAS DONE.
SHE CHOSE TO JOIN THE AQUARIUM CLUB...
...AND ABOVE ALL...
...SHE STOOD BY KOYUKI AND LENT MORAL SUPPORT.
MY DAUGHTER...
...HAD ALWAYS TRIED...
...TO LIVE UP TO EXPEC-TATIONS...
...TO THE POINT OF SUFFOCATING HERSELF.
AND THAT MUST HAVE BEEN...
...UNIMAG-INABLY HARD.

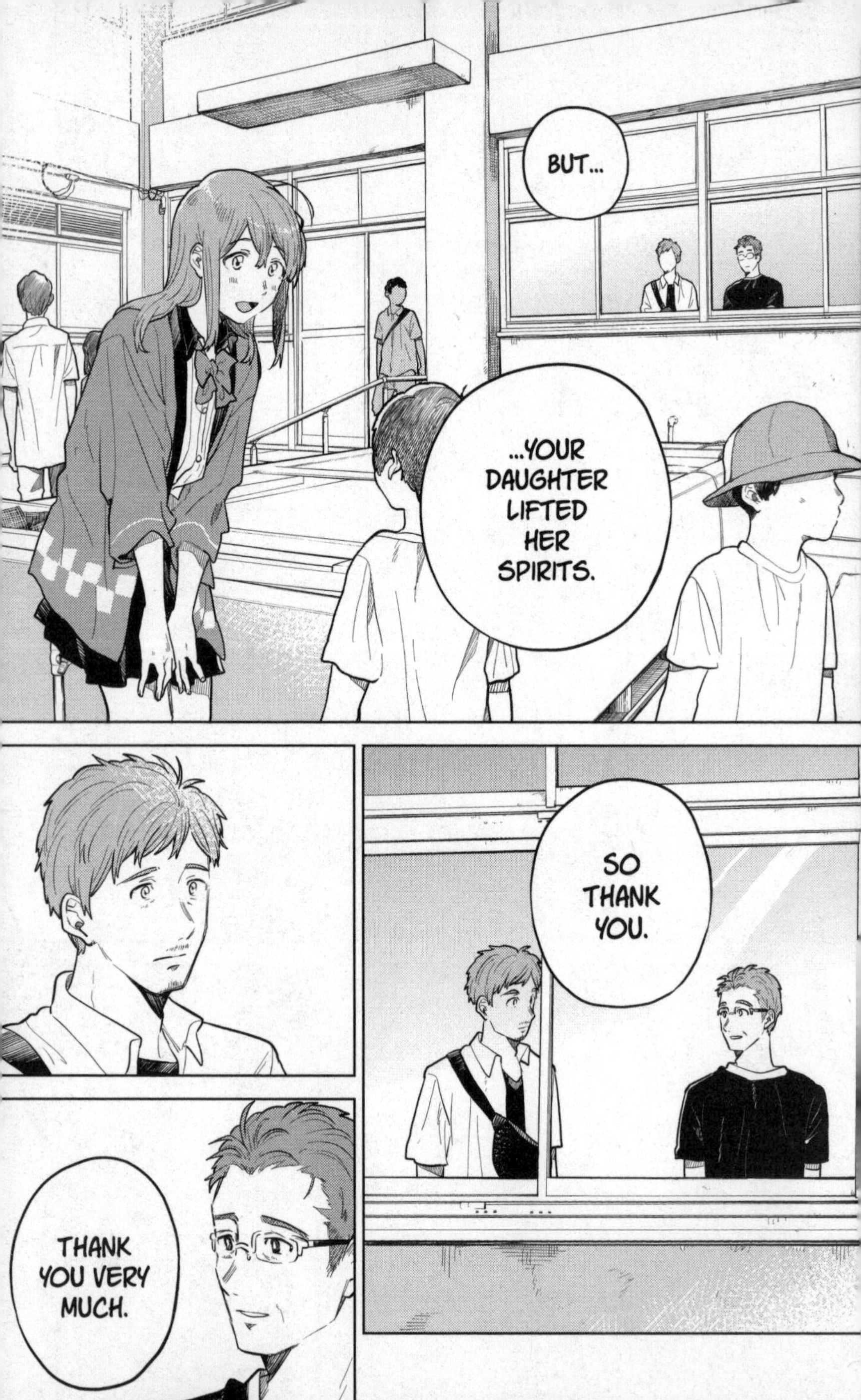
BUT...
...YOUR DAUGHTER LIFTED HER SPIRITS.
SO THANK YOU.
THANK YOU VERY MUCH.

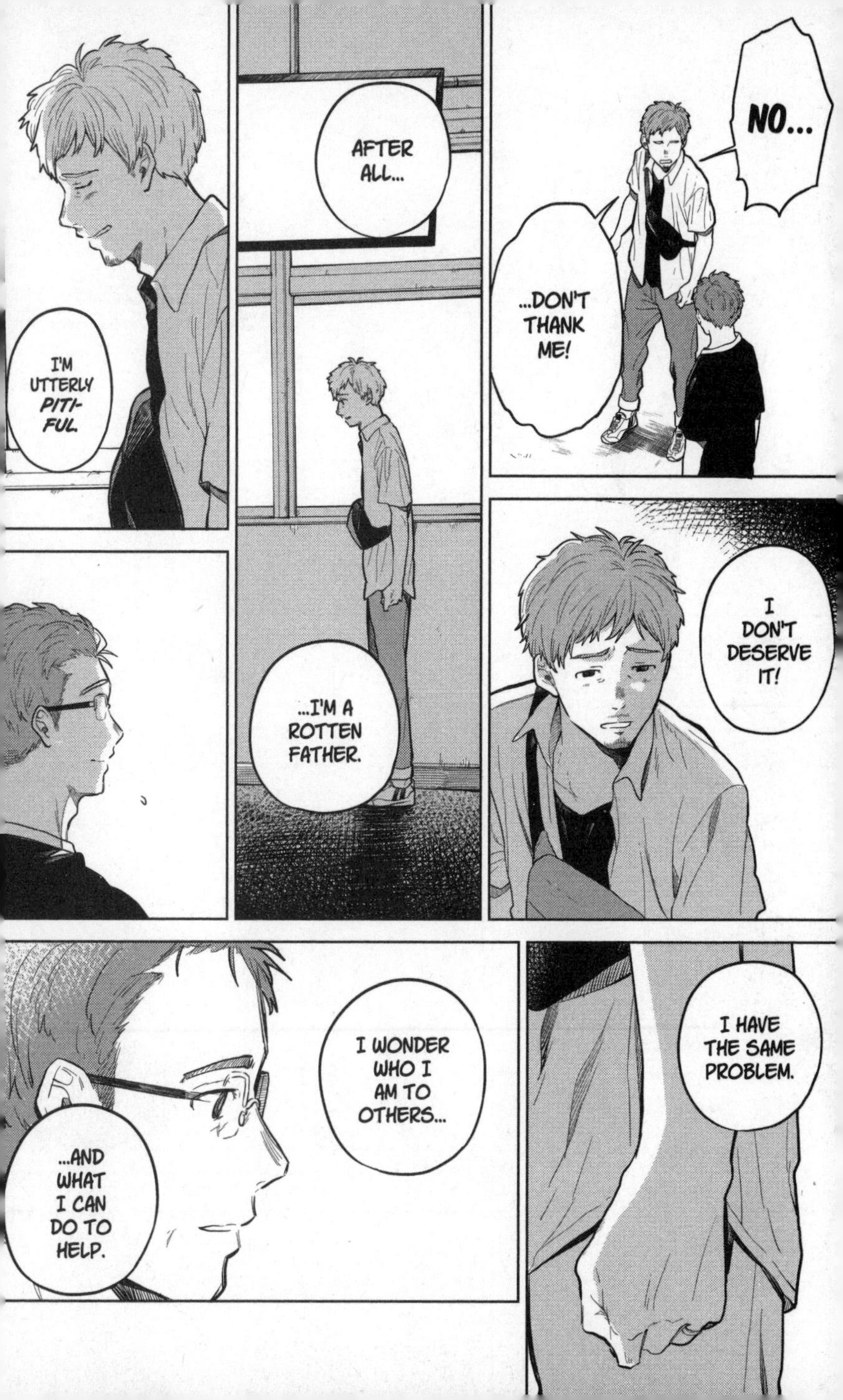
NO...
...DON'T THANK ME!
I DON'T DESERVE IT!
AFTER ALL...
...I'M A ROTTEN FATHER.
I'M UTTERLY PITIFUL.
I HAVE THE SAME PROBLEM.
I WONDER WHO I AM TO OTHERS...
...AND WHAT I CAN DO TO HELP.

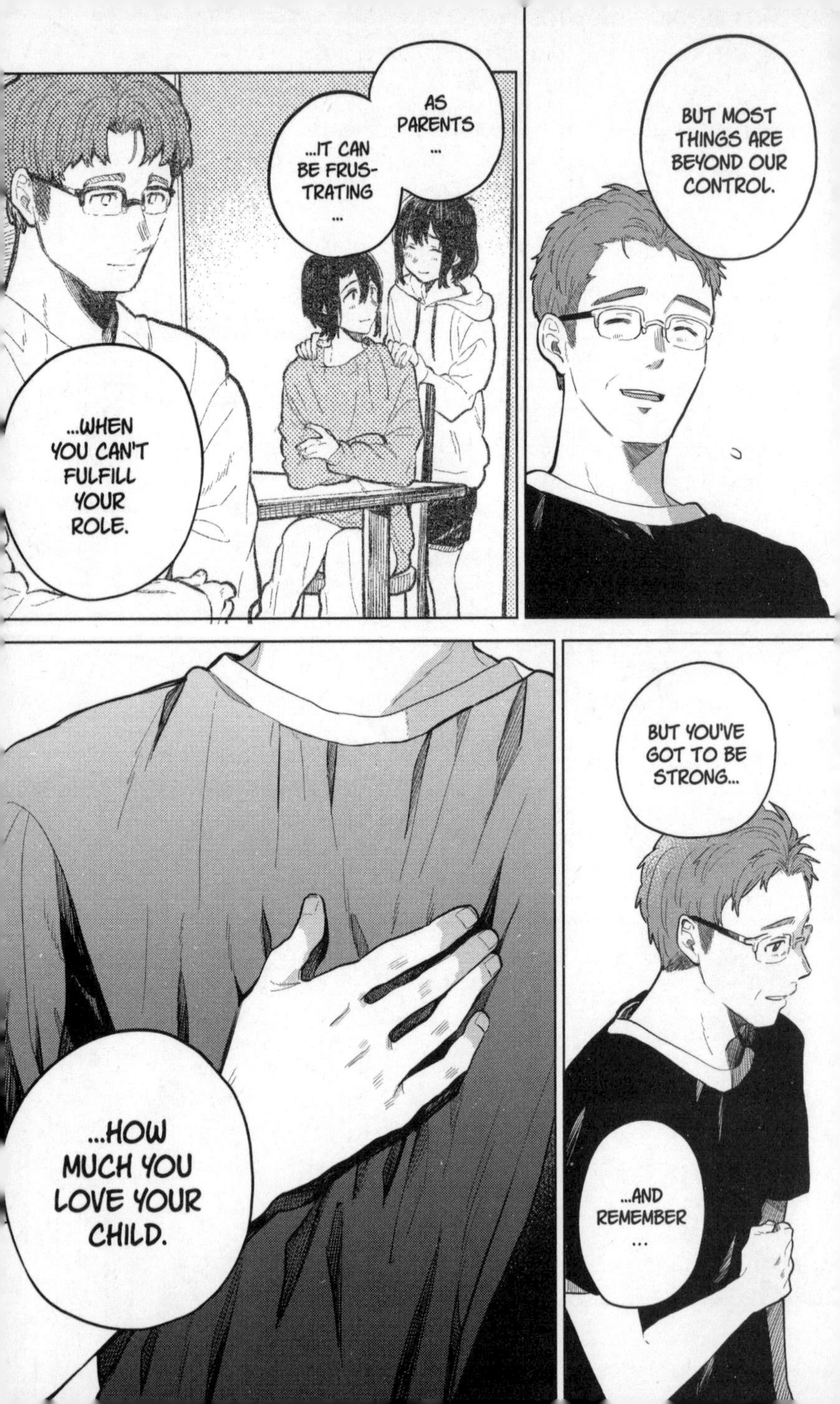
BUT MOST THINGS ARE BEYOND OUR CONTROL.
AS PARENTS ...
...IT CAN BE FRUS- TRATING ...
...WHEN YOU CAN'T FULFILL YOUR ROLE.
BUT YOU'VE GOT TO BE STRONG...
...AND REMEMBER ...
...HOW MUCH YOU LOVE YOUR CHILD.

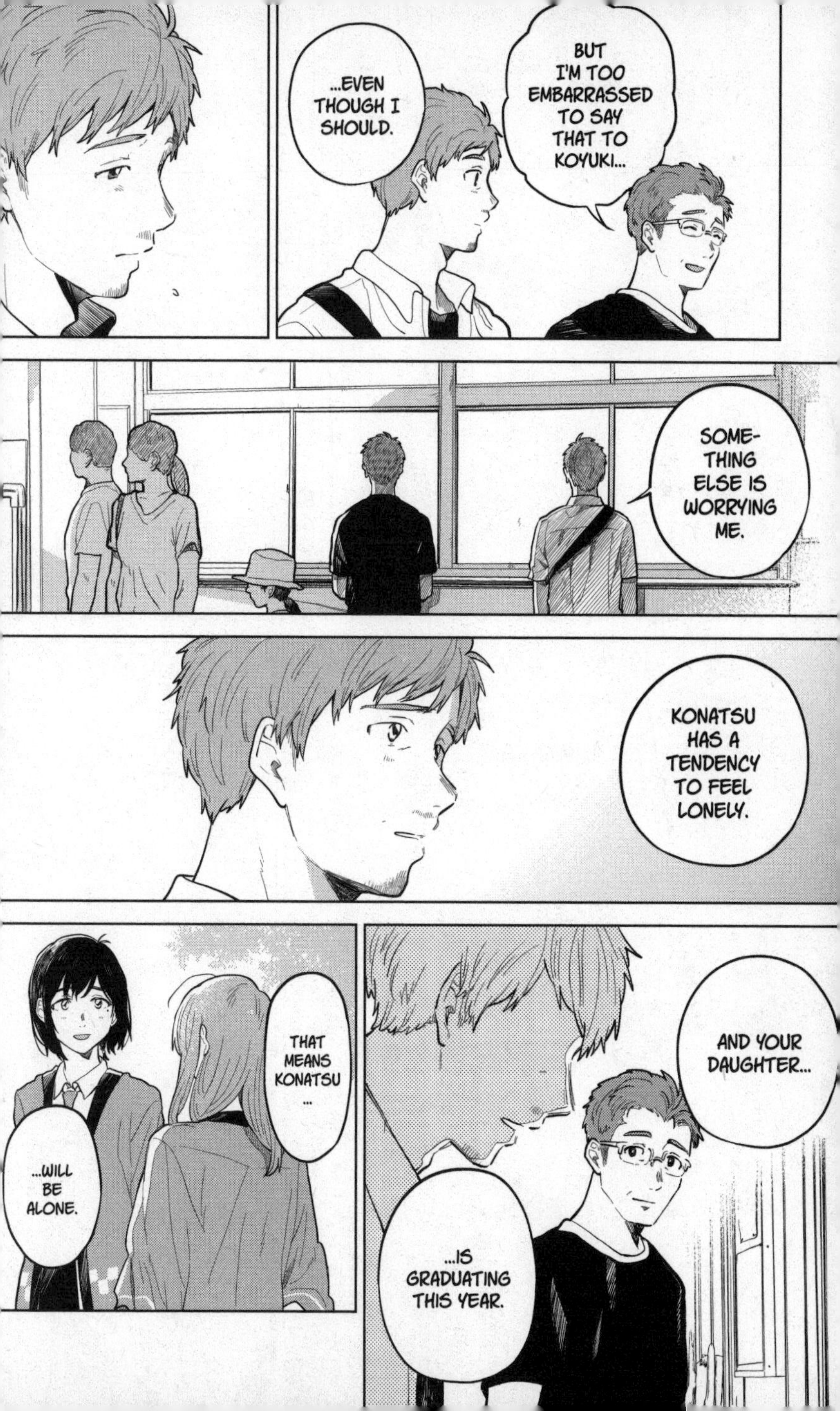
BUT I'M TOO EMBARRASSED TO SAY THAT TO KOYUKI...
...EVEN THOUGH I SHOULD.
SOME-THING ELSE IS WORRYING ME.
KONATSU HAS A TENDENCY TO FEEL LONELY.
AND YOUR DAUGHTER...
...IS GRADUATING THIS YEAR.
THAT MEANS KONATSU ...
...WILL BE ALONE.

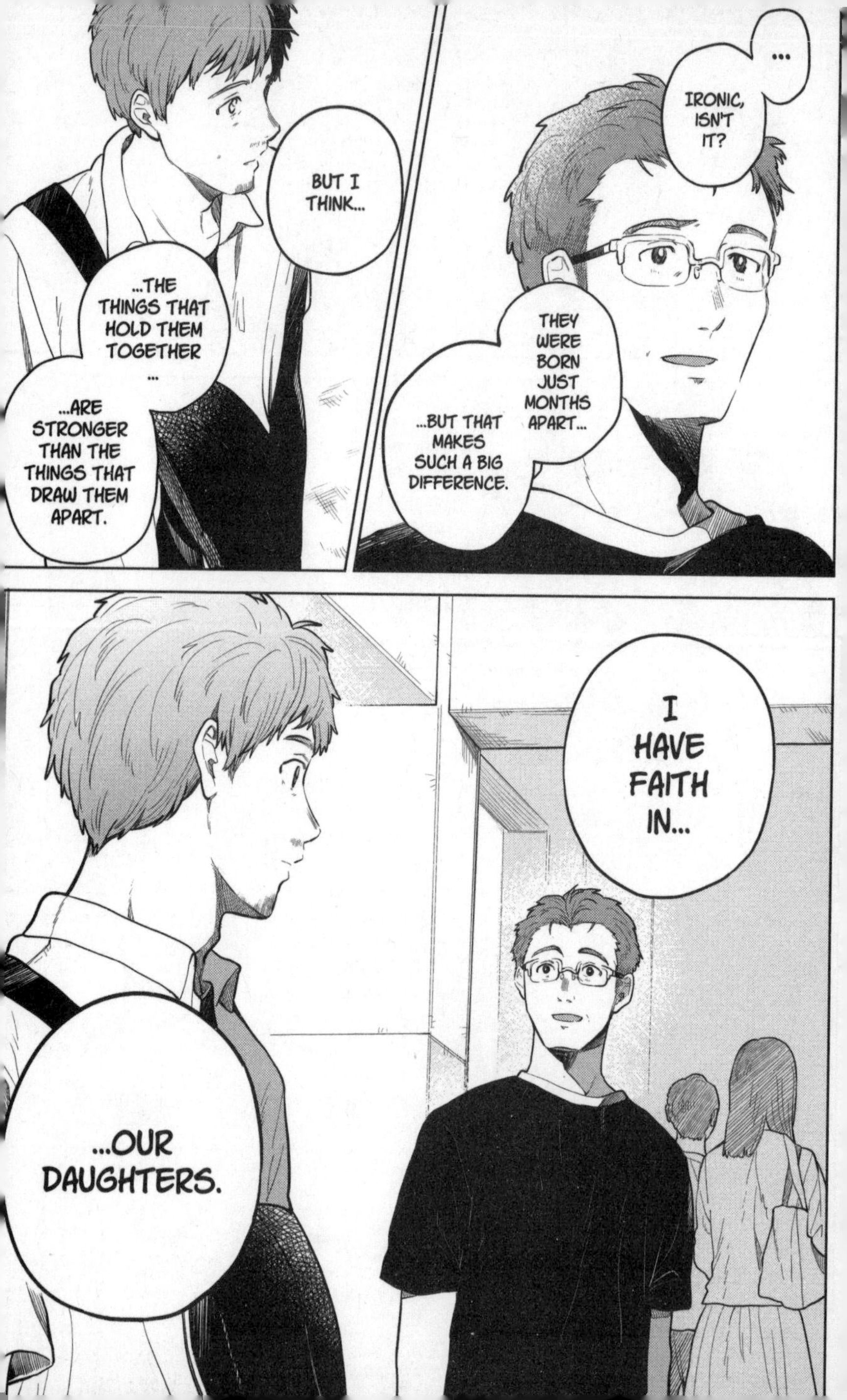
...
IRONIC, ISN'T IT?
THEY WERE BORN JUST MONTHS APART...
...BUT THAT MAKES SUCH A BIG DIFFERENCE.
BUT I THINK...
...THE THINGS THAT HOLD THEM TOGETHER ...
...ARE STRONGER THAN THE THINGS THAT DRAW THEM APART.
I HAVE FAITH IN...
...OUR DAUGHTERS.

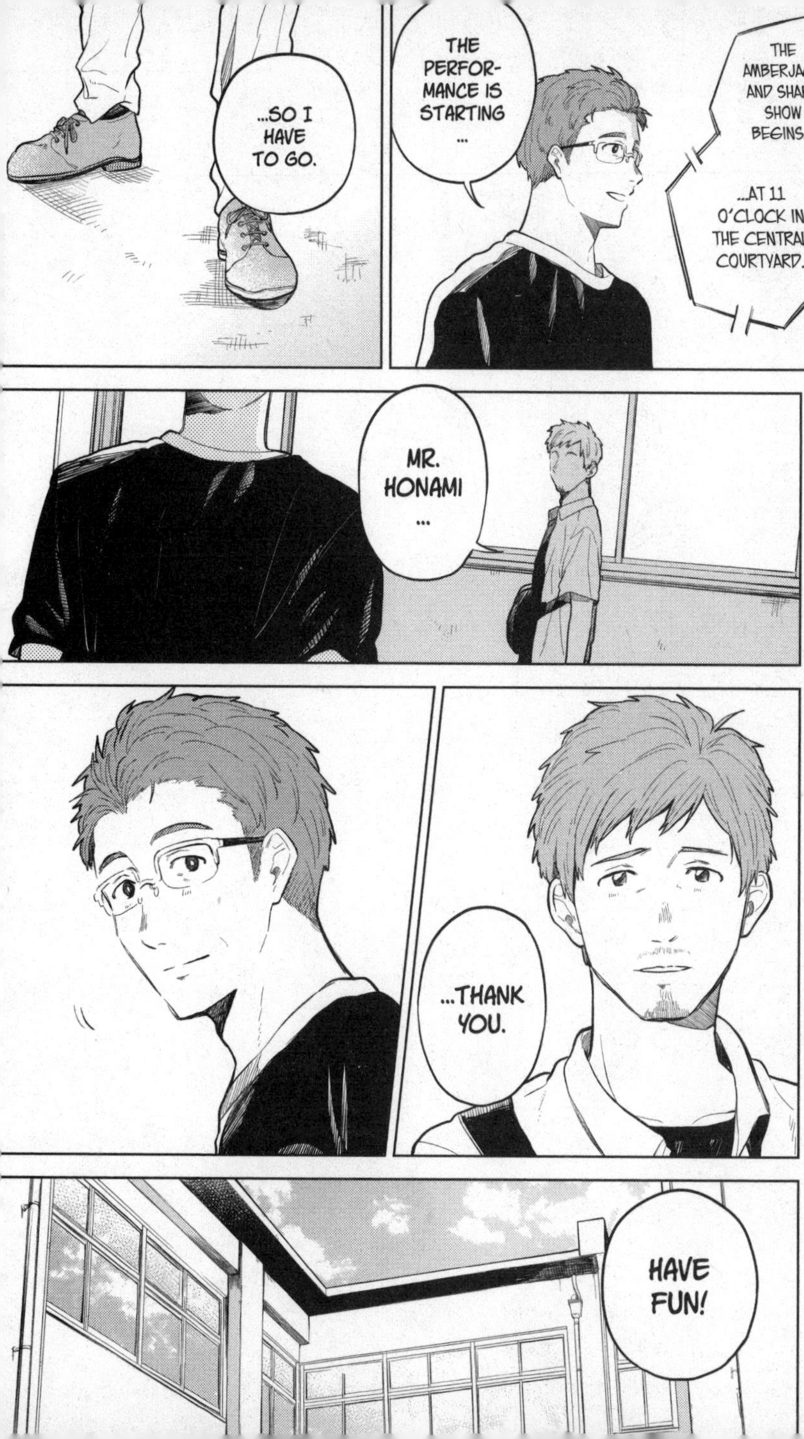
THE AMBERJACK AND SHARK SHOW BEGINS...
...AT 11 O'CLOCK IN THE CENTRAL COURTYARD.
THE PERFORMANCE IS STARTING...
...SO I HAVE TO GO.
MR. HONAMI...
...THANK YOU.
HAVE FUN!

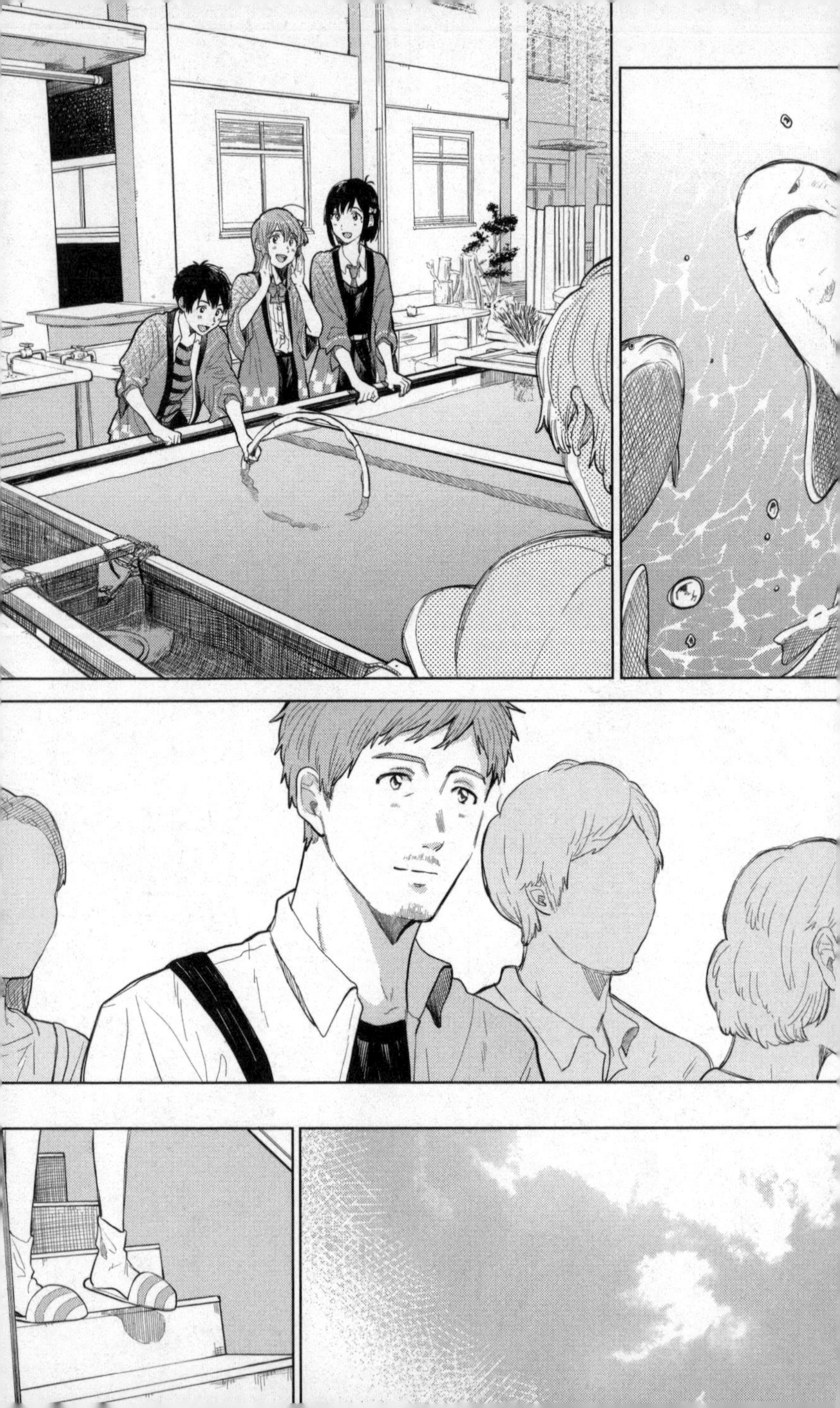

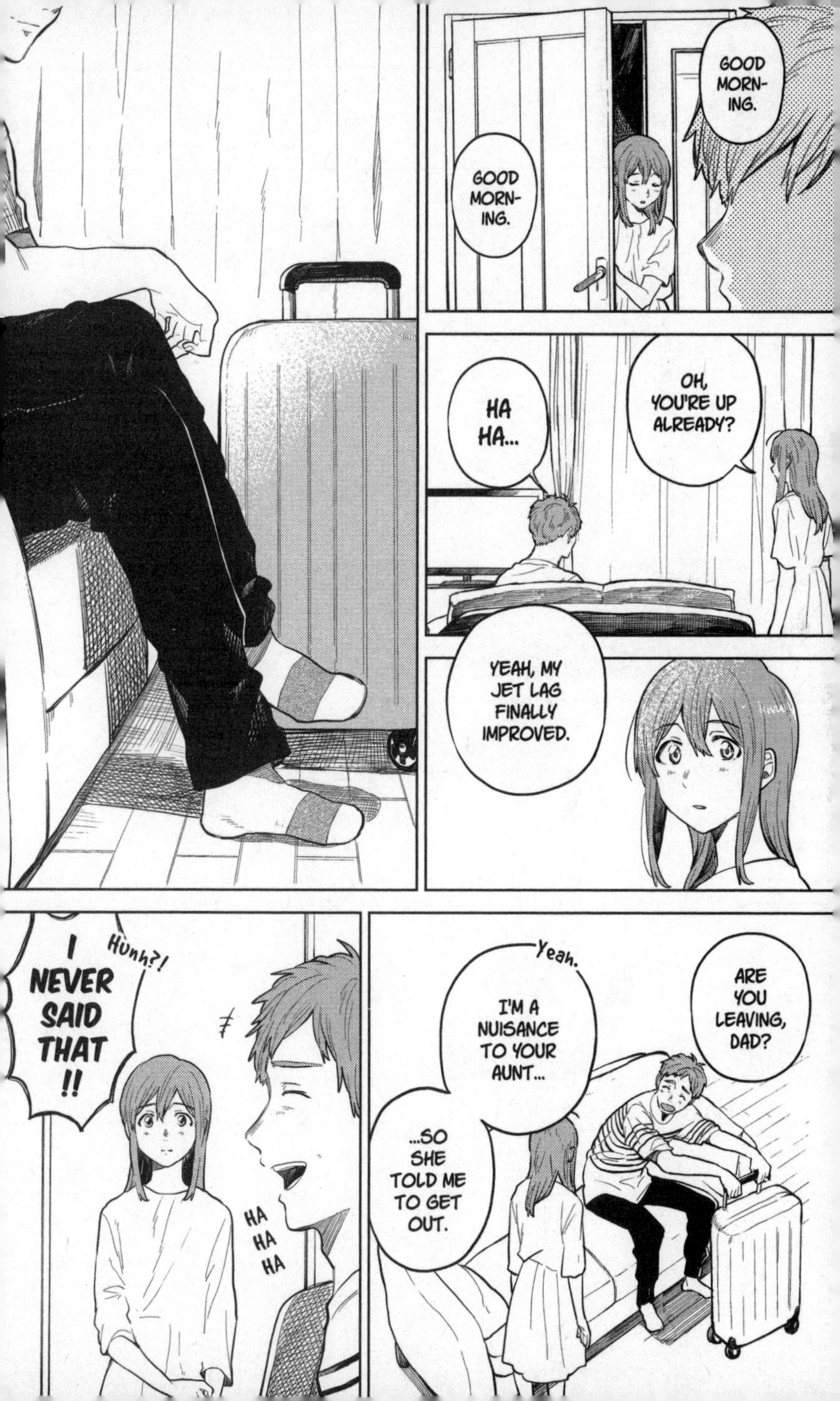
GOOD MORN-ING.
GOOD MORN-ING.
OH, YOU'RE UP ALREADY?
HA HA...
YEAH, MY JET LAG FINALLY IMPROVED.
ARE YOU LEAVING, DAD?
Yeah.
I'M A NUISANCE TO YOUR AUNT...
...SO SHE TOLD ME TO GET OUT.
Hunh?!
I NEVER SAID THAT!!
HA HA HA

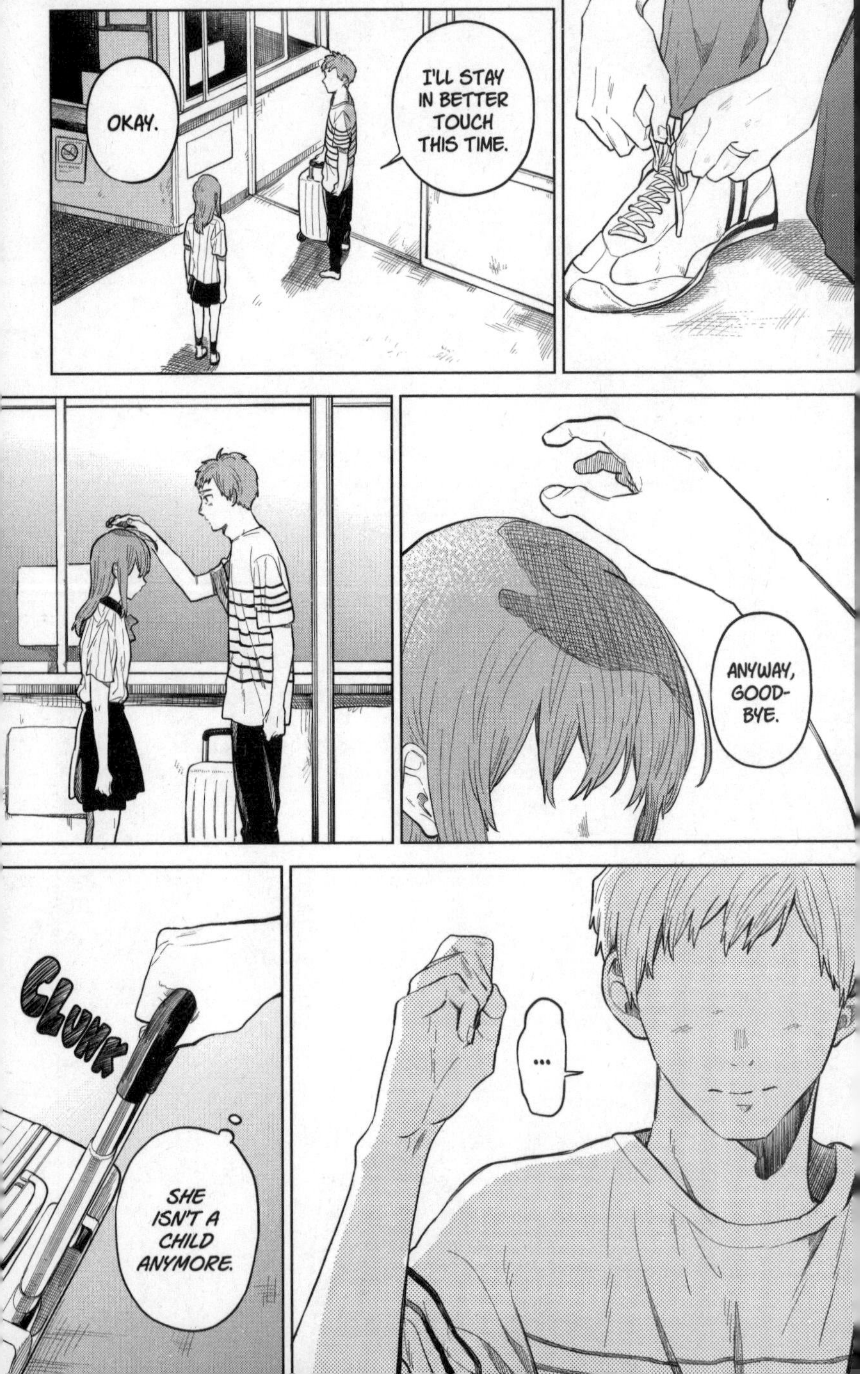

I'LL STAY IN BETTER TOUCH THIS TIME.
OKAY.
ANYWAY, GOOD-BYE.
...
CLUNK
SHE ISN'T A CHILD ANYMORE.

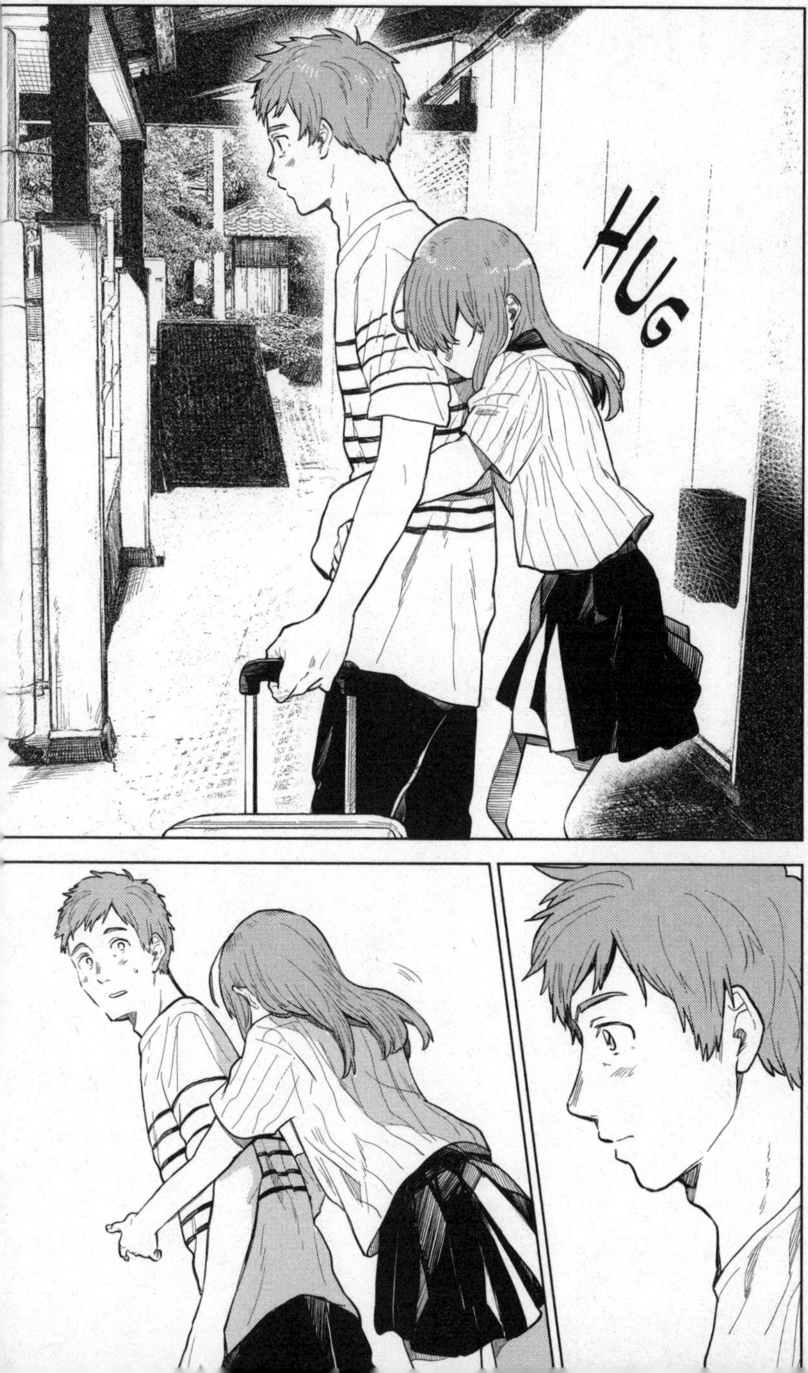
HUG

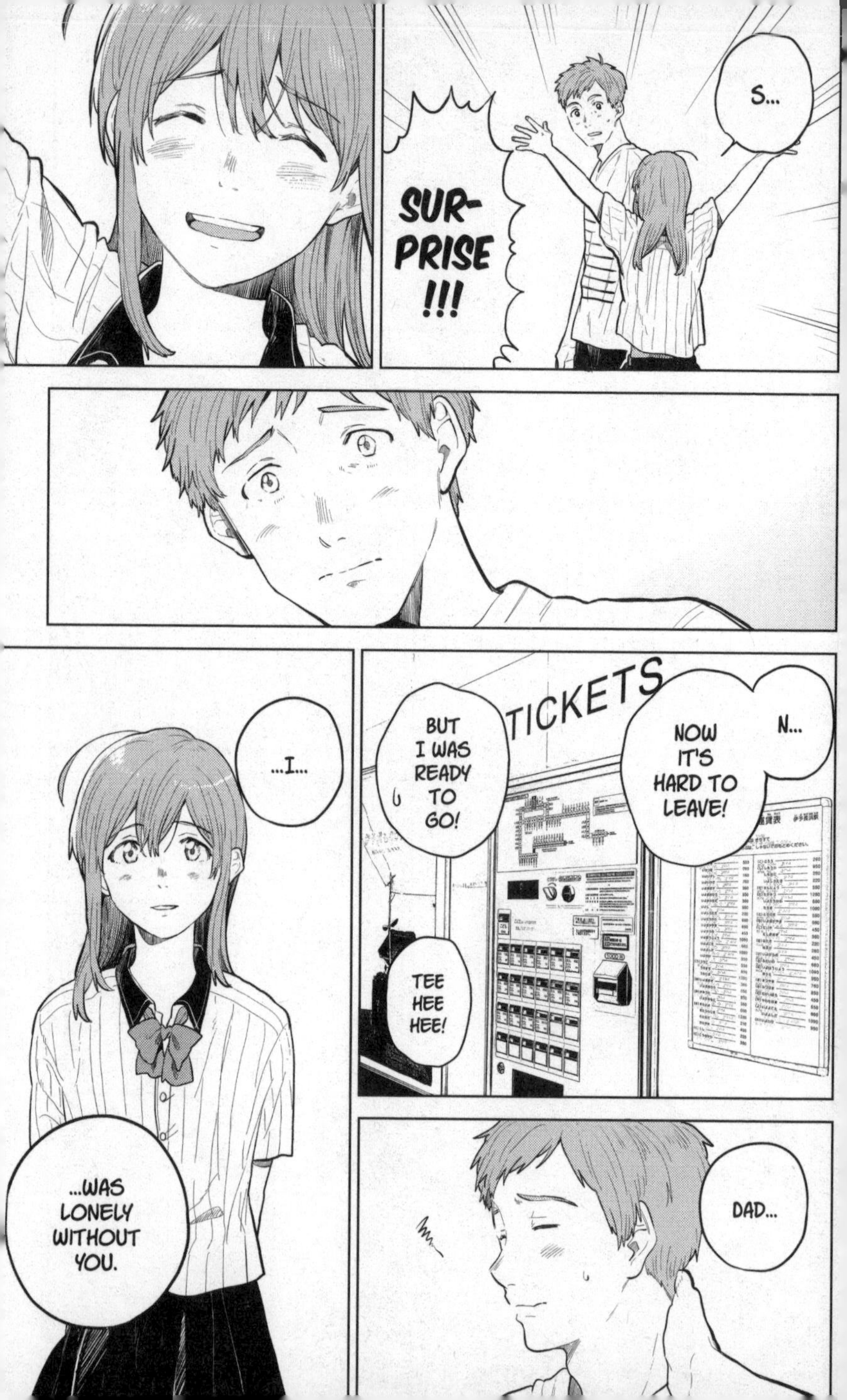
S...
SUR-PRISE!!!
N...
NOW IT'S HARD TO LEAVE!
TICKETS
BUT I WAS READY TO GO!
TEE HEE HEE!
DAD...
...I...
...WAS LONELY WITHOUT YOU.

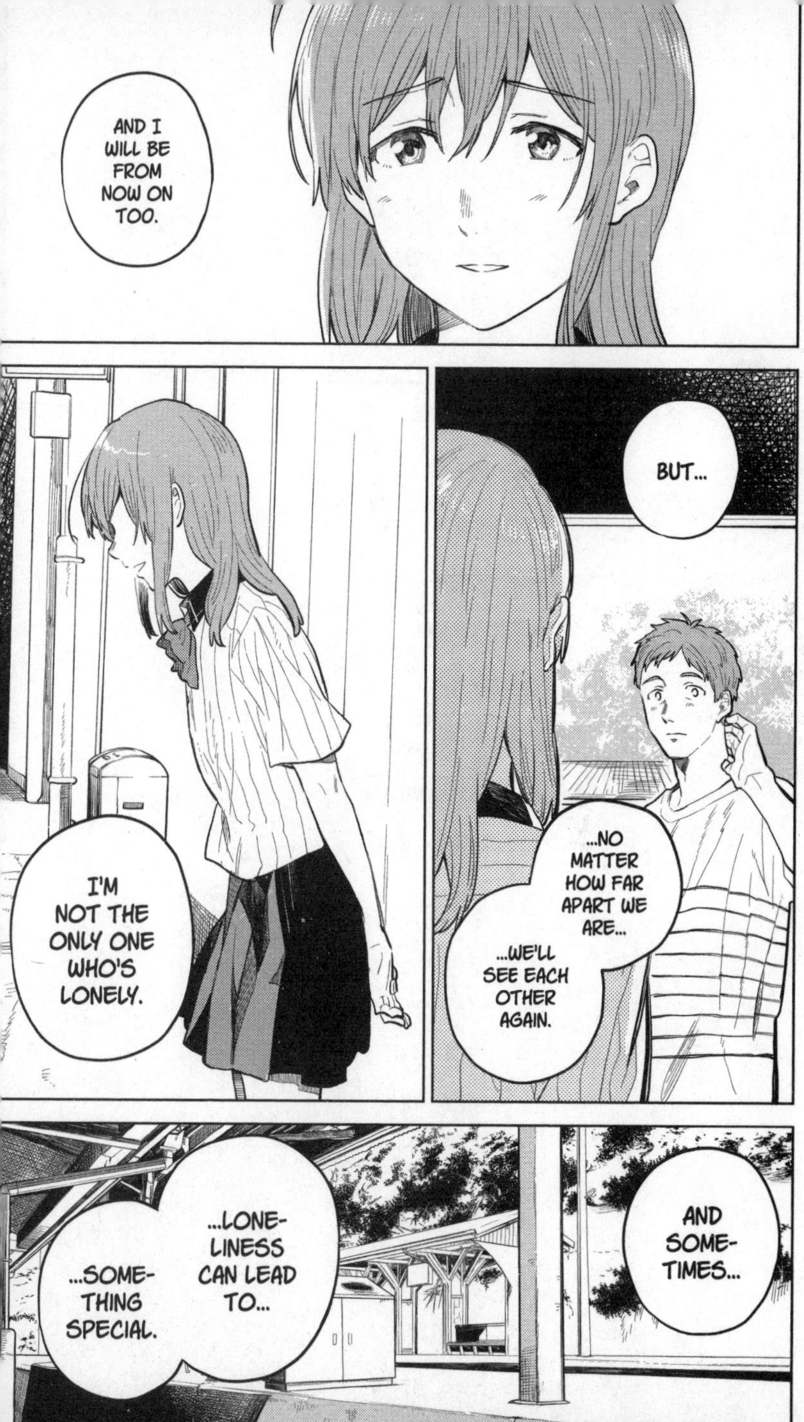
AND I WILL BE FROM NOW ON TOO.
BUT...
...NO MATTER HOW FAR APART WE ARE...
...WE'LL SEE EACH OTHER AGAIN.
I'M NOT THE ONLY ONE WHO'S LONELY.
AND SOME-TIMES...
...LONE-LINESS CAN LEAD TO...
...SOME-THING SPECIAL.

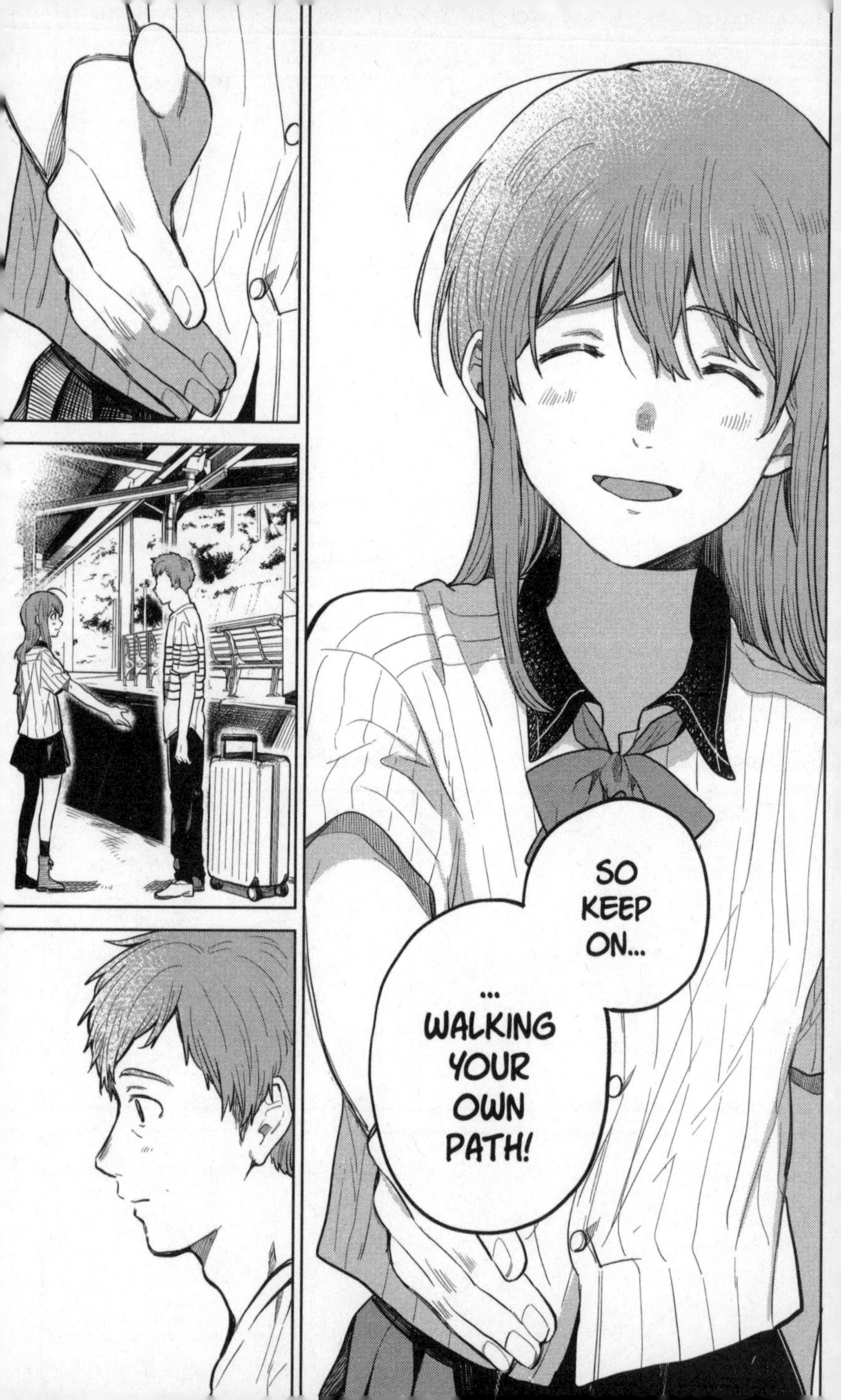
SO KEEP ON...
... WALKING YOUR OWN PATH!

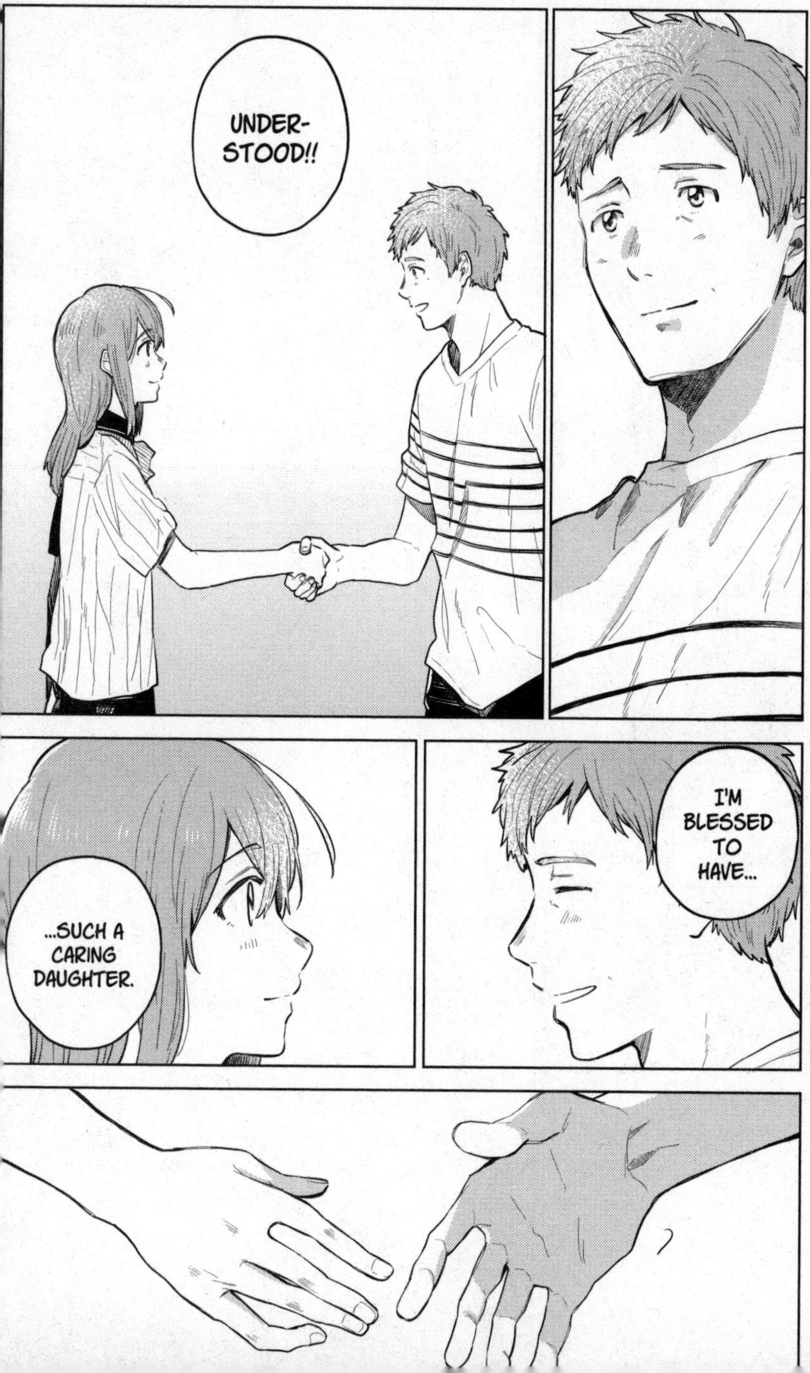
UNDER-STOOD!!
I'M BLESSED TO HAVE...
...SUCH A CARING DAUGHTER.

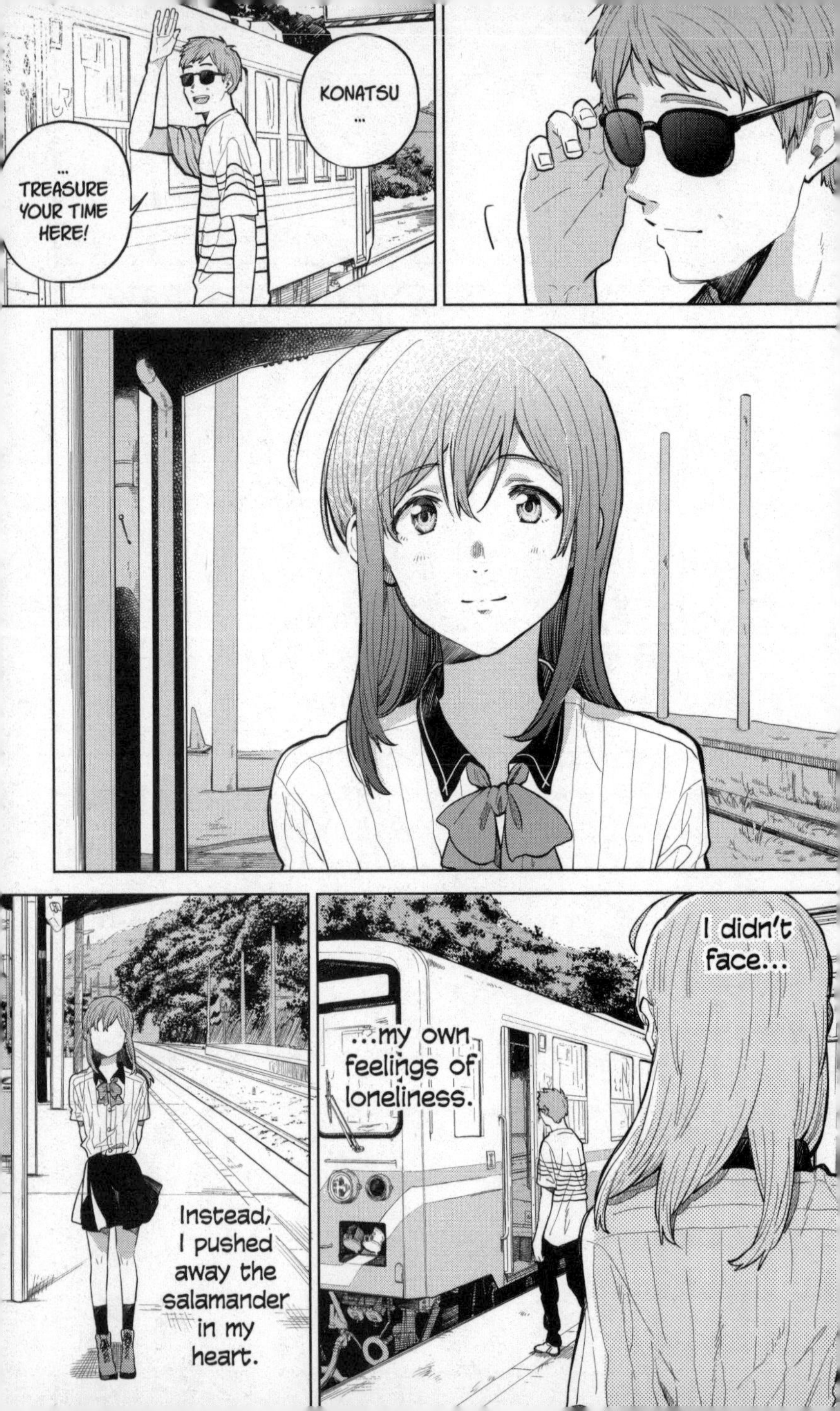
KONATSU ...
... TREASURE YOUR TIME HERE!
I didn't face...
...my own feelings of loneliness.
Instead, I pushed away the salamander in my heart.

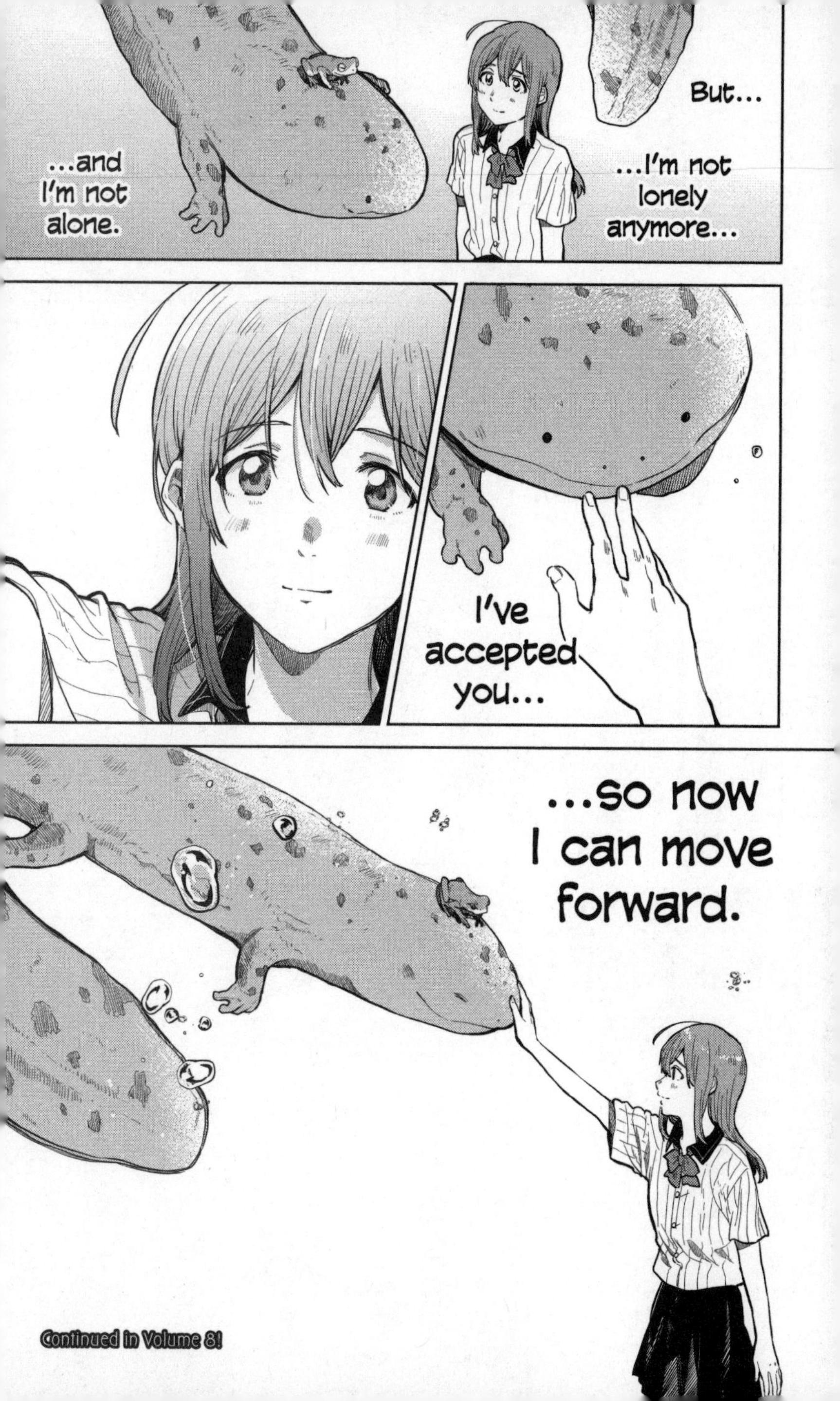
But...
...I'm not lonely anymore...
...and I'm not alone.
I've accepted you...
...so now I can move forward.
Continued in Volume 8!

A Tropical Fish
Yearns for Snow

Tank 27.5: Konatsu Amano is Unaware of It

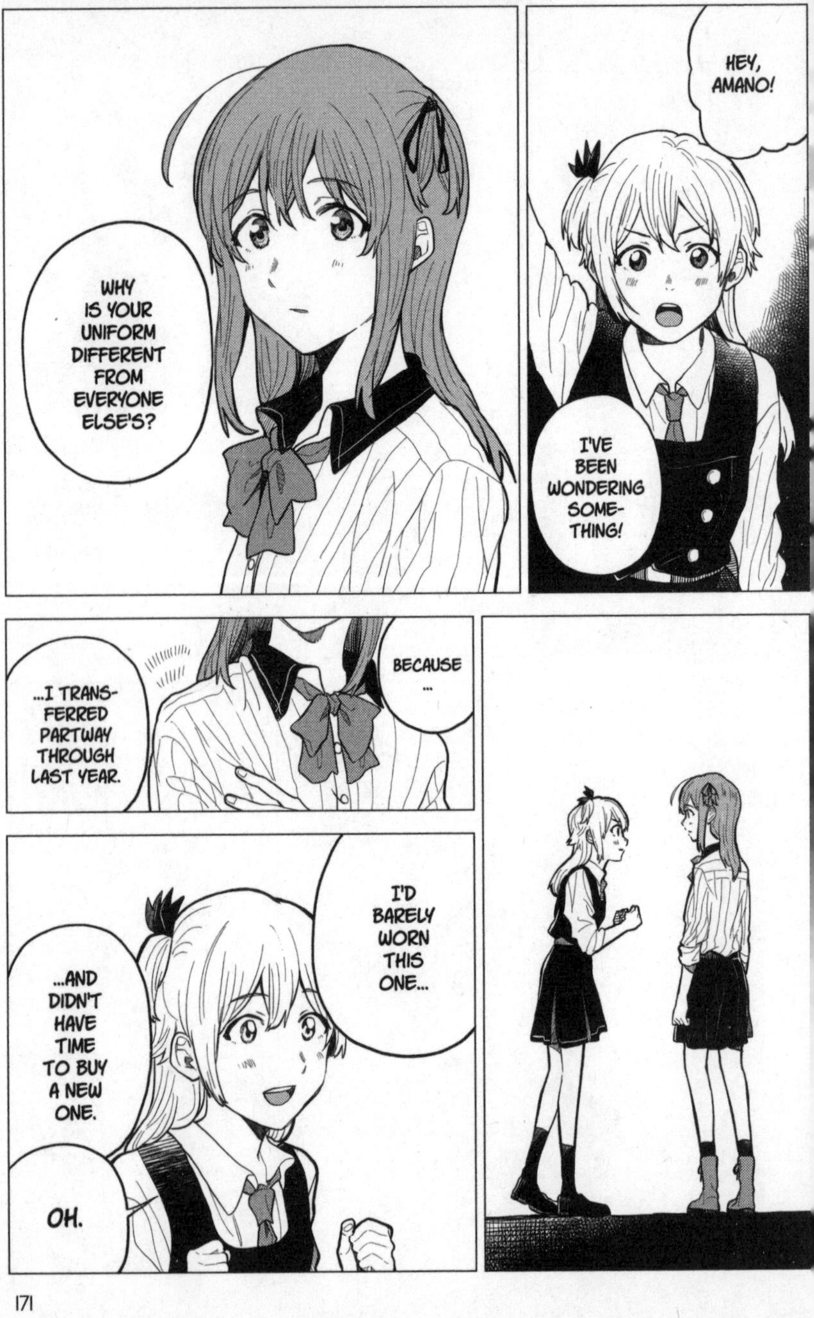
HEY, AMANO!
I'VE BEEN WONDERING SOME-THING!
WHY IS YOUR UNIFORM DIFFERENT FROM EVERYONE ELSE'S?
BECAUSE ...
...I TRANS-FERRED PARTWAY THROUGH LAST YEAR.
I'D BARELY WORN THIS ONE...
...AND DIDN'T HAVE TIME TO BUY A NEW ONE.
OH.

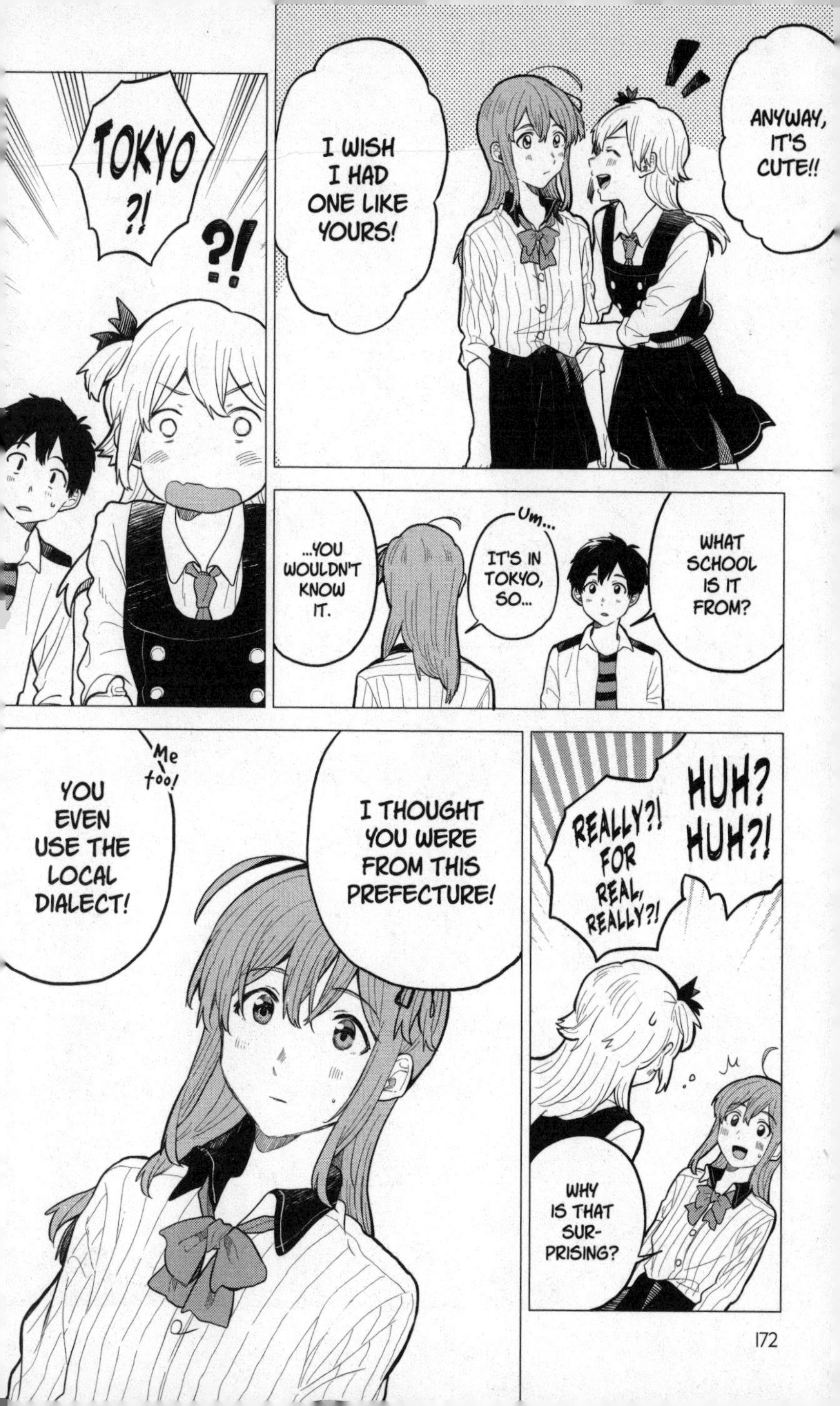
ANYWAY, IT'S CUTE!!
I WISH I HAD ONE LIKE YOURS!
WHAT SCHOOL IS IT FROM?
Um...
IT'S IN TOKYO, SO...
...YOU WOULDN'T KNOW IT.
TOKYO ?!
?!
HUH? HUH?!
REALLY?! FOR REAL, REALLY?!
WHY IS THAT SURPRISING?
I THOUGHT YOU WERE FROM THIS PREFECTURE!
Me too!
YOU EVEN USE THE LOCAL DIALECT!

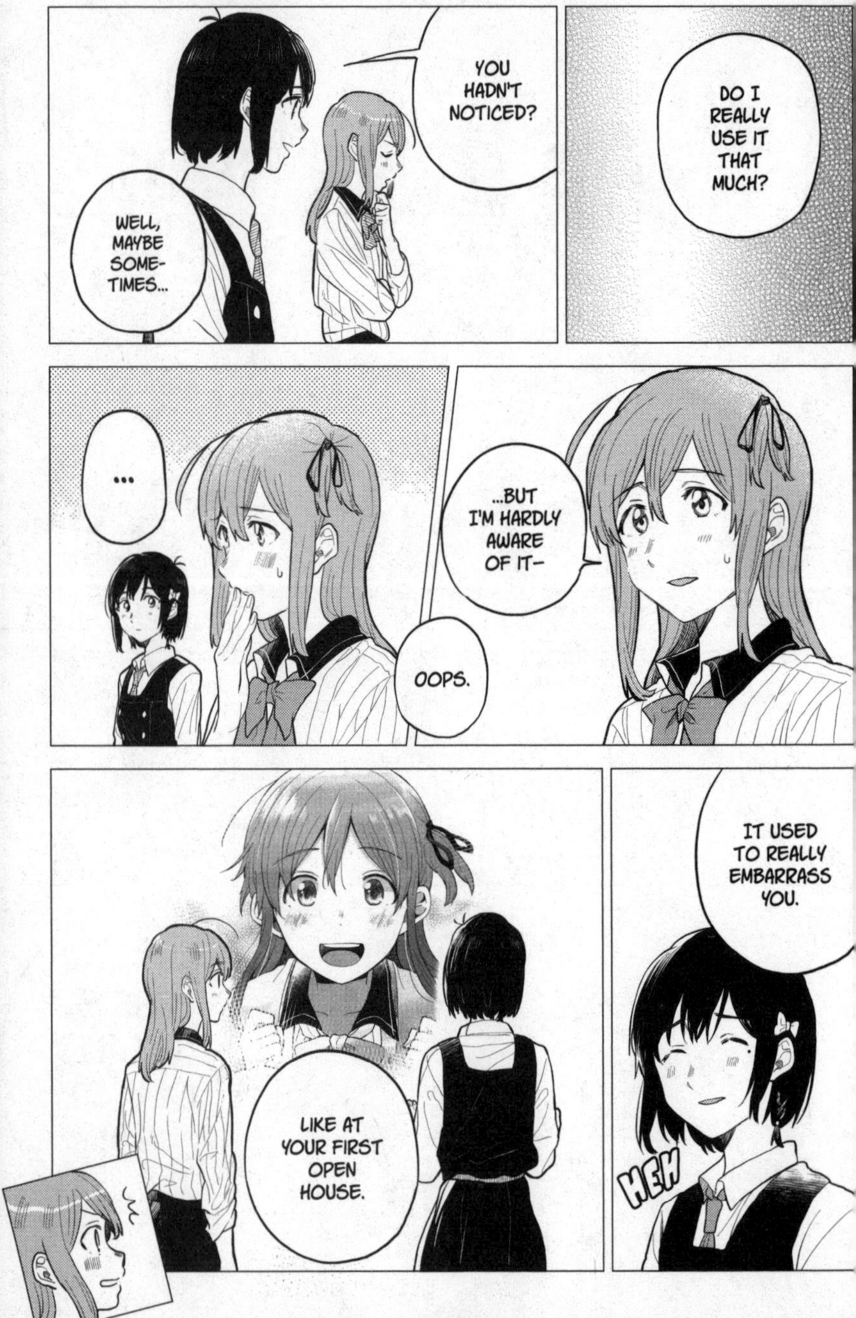
DO I REALLY USE IT THAT MUCH?
YOU HADN'T NOTICED?
WELL, MAYBE SOME-TIMES...
...BUT I'M HARDLY AWARE OF IT–
OOPS.
...
IT USED TO REALLY EMBARRASS YOU.
HEH
LIKE AT YOUR FIRST OPEN HOUSE.

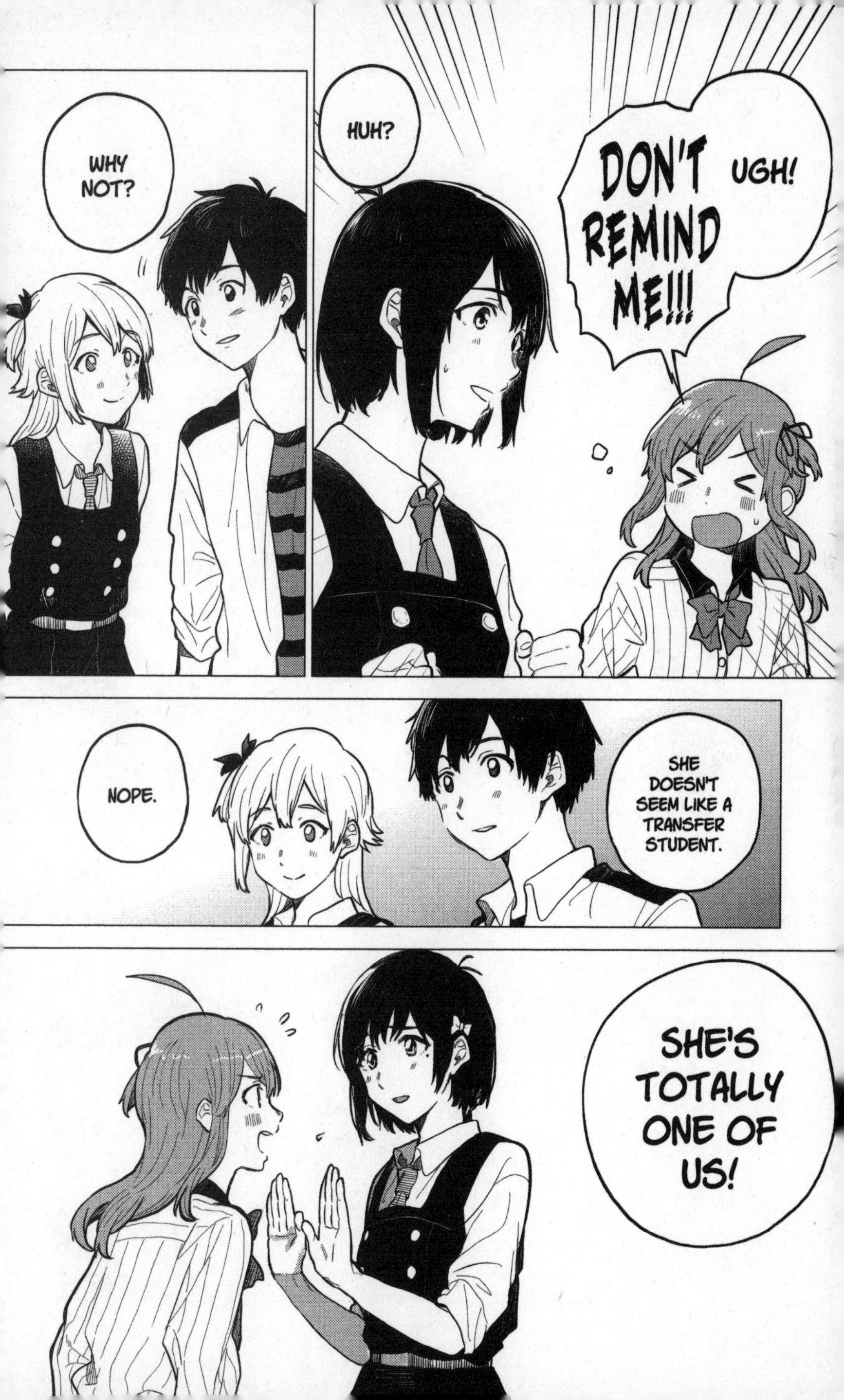
UGH!
DON'T REMIND ME!!!
HUH?
WHY NOT?
SHE DOESN'T SEEM LIKE A TRANSFER STUDENT.
NOPE.
SHE'S TOTALLY ONE OF US!

A Tropical Fish
Yearns for Snow

Afterword

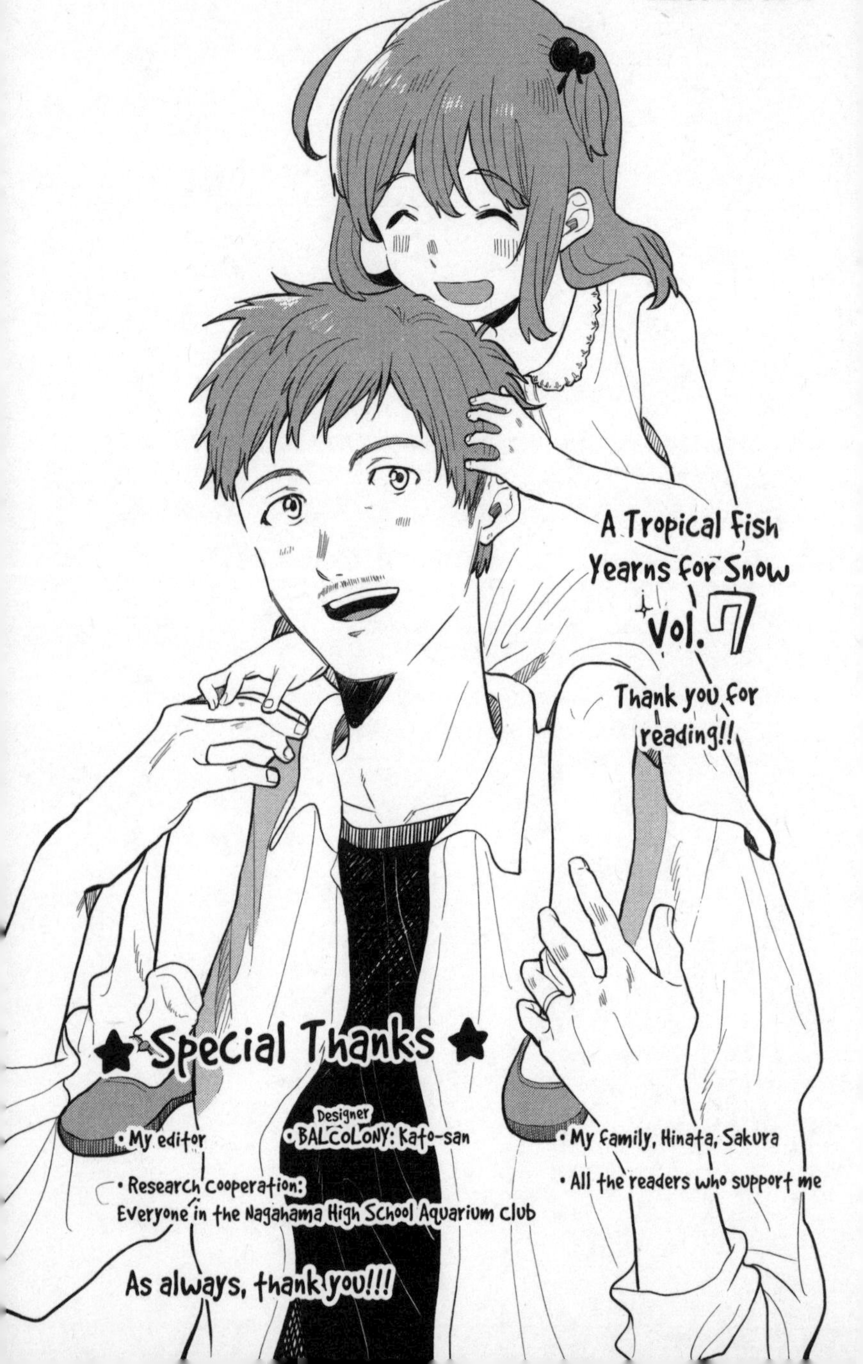
A Tropical Fish Yearns for Snow
Vol. 7
Thank you for reading!!
Special Thanks
Designer
• My editor
• BALCOLONY: Kato-san
• My family, Hinata, Sakura
• Research cooperation:
Everyone in the Nagahama High School Aquarium club
• All the readers who support me
As always, thank you!!!

A TROPICAL FISH YEARNS FOR SNOW
Vol. 7
VIZ Media Edition

STORY AND ART BY
MAKOTO HAGINO

English Translation & Adaptation/John Werry
Touch-Up Art & Lettering/Eve Grandt
Design/Yukiko Whitley
Editor/Pancha Diaz

NETTAIGYO WA YUKI NI KOGARERU Vol. 7
©Makoto Hagino 2020
First published in Japan in 2020 by KADOKAWA CORPORATION, Tokyo.
English translation rights arranged with KADOKAWA CORPORATION, Tokyo.

Printed in the U.S.A.

Published by VIZ Media, LLC
P.O. Box 77010
San Francisco, CA 94107

10 9 8 7 6 5 4 3 2 1
First printing, May 2021

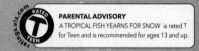

PARENTAL ADVISORY
A TROPICAL FISH YEARNS FOR SNOW is rated T
for Teen and is recommended for ages 13 and up.

viz.com

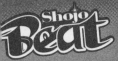 **Romances by IO SAKISAKA**

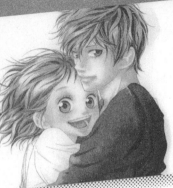

STROBE EDGE

When Ninako meets Ren, the handsome, enigmatic guy that all the girls worship, her life takes an unexpected turn. With just a few words and a smile, he changes her world...

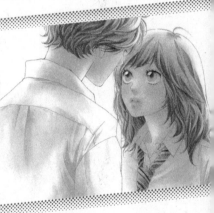

Ao Haru Ride

As soon as Futaba realized she really liked Kou in junior high, he had already moved away. Now, in high school, Kou has reappeared, but is he still the same boy she fell in love with?

Love Me, Love Me Not

Fast friends Yuna and Akari are complete opposites—Yuna is an idealist, while Akari is a realist. When lady-killer Rio and the oblivious Kazuomi join their ranks, love and friendship become quite complicated!

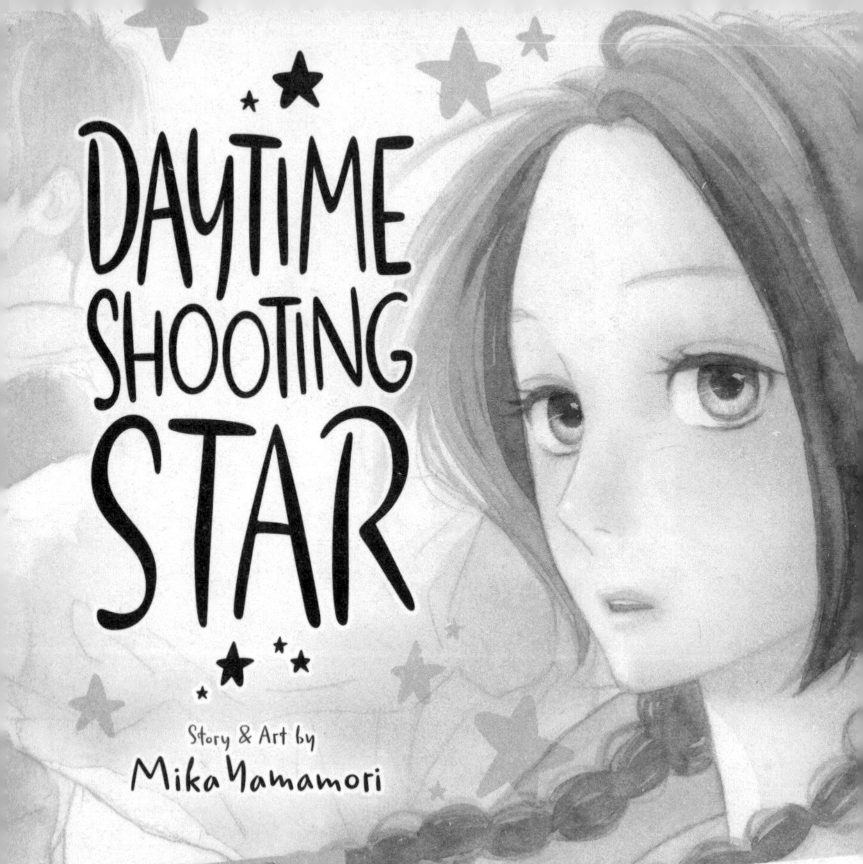

DAYTIME SHOOTING STAR

Story & Art by
Mika Yamamori

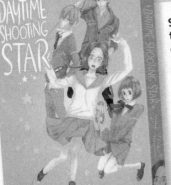

Small town girl Suzume moves to Tokyo and finds her heart caught between two men!

After arriving in Tokyo to live with her uncle, Suzume collapses in a nearby park when she remembers once seeing a shooting star during the day. A handsome stranger brings her to her new home and tells her they'll meet again. Suzume starts her first day at her new high school sitting next to a boy who blushes furiously at her touch. And her homeroom teacher is none other than the handsome stranger!

HIRUNAKA NO RYUSEI © 2011 by Mika Yamamori/SHUEISHA Inc.

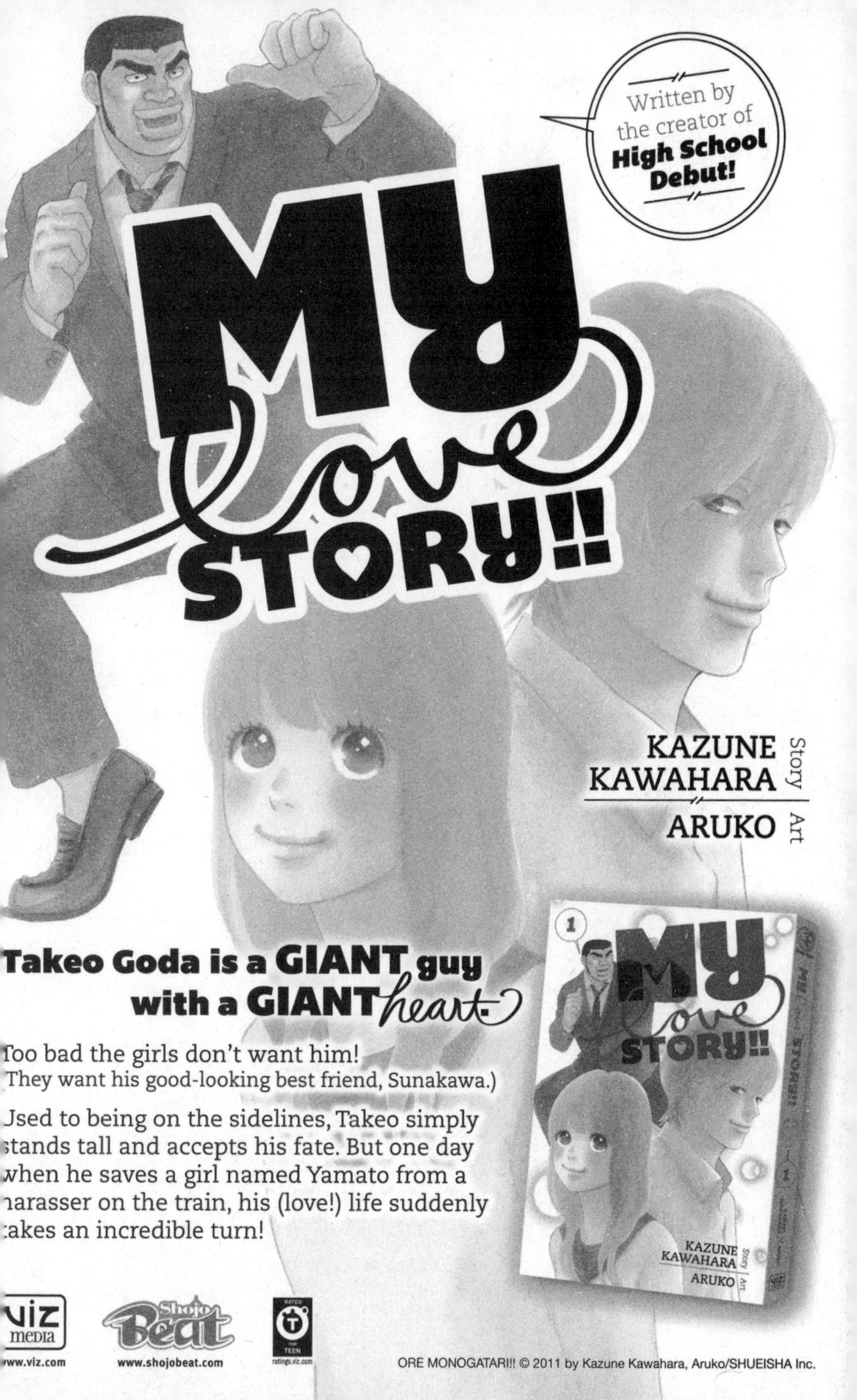
Written by the creator of High School Debut!
MY love STORY!!
KAZUNE KAWAHARA Story
ARUKO Art
Takeo Goda is a GIANT guy with a GIANT heart
Too bad the girls don't want him! (They want his good-looking best friend, Sunakawa.)
Used to being on the sidelines, Takeo simply stands tall and accepts his fate. But one day when he saves a girl named Yamato from a harasser on the train, his (love!) life suddenly takes an incredible turn!
1
MY love STORY!!
KAZUNE KAWAHARA Story
ARUKO Art
viz media
www.viz.com
Shojo Beat
www.shojobeat.com
RATED T FOR TEEN
ratings.viz.com
ORE MONOGATARI!! © 2011 by Kazune Kawahara, Aruko/SHUEISHA Inc.

SHORTCAKE CAKE

STORY AND ART BY suu Morishita

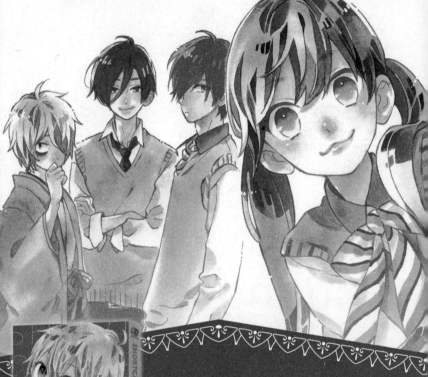

An unflappable girl and a cast of lovable roommates at a boardinghouse create bonds of friendship and romance!

When Ten moves out of her parents' home in the mountains to live in a boardinghouse, she finds herself becoming fast friends with her male roommates. But can love and romance be far behind?

VIZ

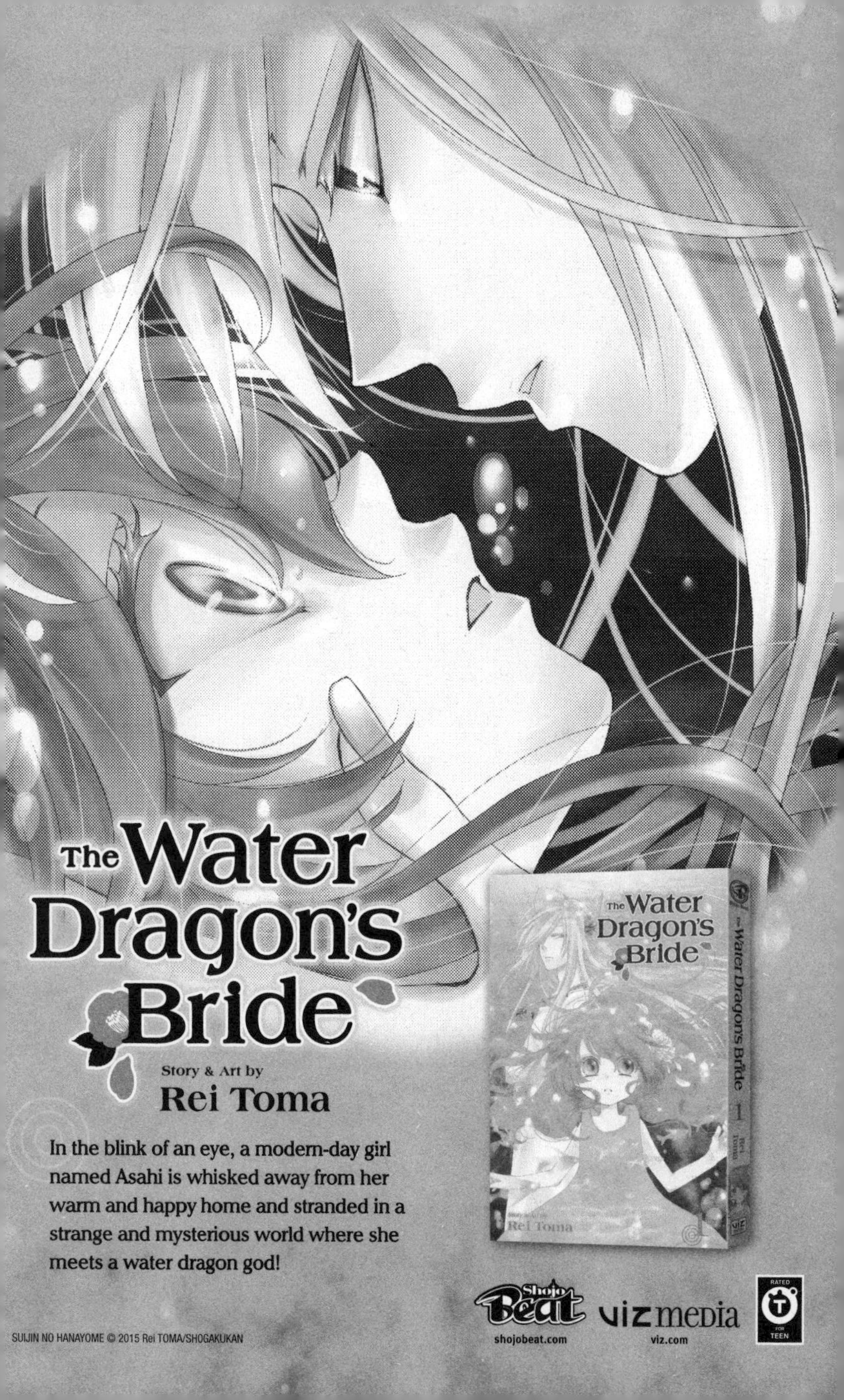
The Water Dragon's Bride
Story & Art by
Rei Toma
In the blink of an eye, a modern-day girl named Asahi is whisked away from her warm and happy home and stranded in a strange and mysterious world where she meets a water dragon god!
Shojo Beat
shojobeat.com
viz media
viz.com
RATED T FOR TEEN
SUIJIN NO HANAYOME © 2015 Rei TOMA/SHOGAKUKAN

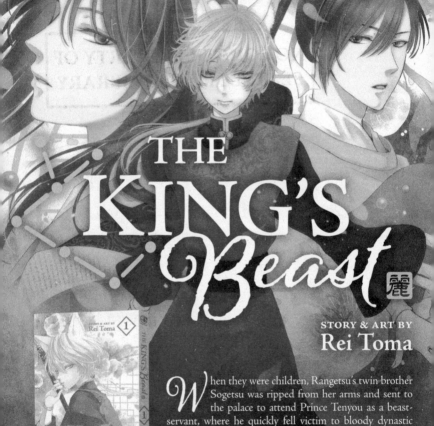

This is the last page.

A Tropical Fish Yearns for Snow **has been printed in the original Japanese format to preserve the orientation of the artwork.**

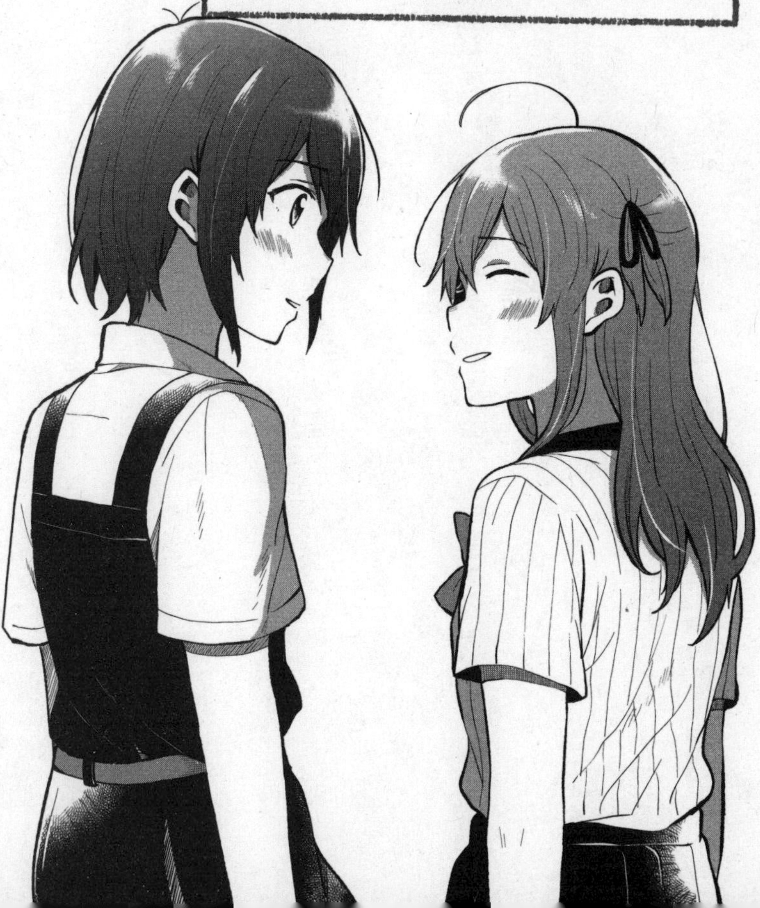